FROM WALT TO WOODSTOCK

FROM WALT
TO WOODSTOCK

Douglas Brode

How Disney Created
the Counterculture

 UNIVERSITY OF TEXAS PRESS, AUSTIN

Requests for permission to reproduce material from this
work should be sent to Permissions, University of Texas
Press, P.O. Box 7819, Austin, TX 78713-7819.

⊗ The paper used in this book meets the minimum re-
quirements of ANSI/NISO z39.48-1992 (R1997) (Permanence of Paper).

Library of Congress Cataloging-in-Publication Data

Brode, Douglas, 1943–
From Walt to Woodstock : how Disney created the
counterculture / Douglas Brode.—1st ed.
        p.   cm.
ISBN 0-292-70924-2 (cloth : alk. paper)—
ISBN 0-292-70273-6 (pbk. : alk. paper)
1. Walt Disney Company.   2. Counterculture—United
States—History—20th century.   I. Title.
PN1999.W27B76   2004
741.5′8′0973—dc22

                                        2003025801

For Walt Shepperd

Another Walt who helped conjure the counterculture

Contents

Acknowledgments

All photographs/stills included in this volume were either mailed or hand-delivered over the years to the author, in his longtime capacity as a professional commentator on movies, television, and the media, by publicity people representing Walt Disney Productions, Buena Vista Releasing, and/or RKO Motion Pictures. This was done with the understanding that, under the existing rules of fair usage, the author would then employ all such unsolicited visual properties in order to positively publicize the films of Walt Disney in various print forms. It is with such an understanding firmly in mind, and to that purpose alone, that they are included in this current academic analysis of Walt Disney and his life's work.

A RECURRING IMAGE. Numerous Disney films—including *Song of the South* (1946), *Pollyanna* (1960), *Follow Me, Boys* (1966), and (seen here) *So Dear to My Heart* (1948)—open with the image of a vehicle that transports denizens of progressive big cities into traditionalist small towns; the ensuing give-and-take between those elements allows for a portrait of America in transition.

Introduction

Disney's Version/Disney's Vision
The World According to Walt

DEEPER MEANING RESIDES IN THE FAIRY TALES TOLD ME IN MY
CHILDHOOD THAN IN THE TRUTH THAT IS TAUGHT BY LIFE.
—Schiller, *The Piccolomini*, 111.4

THANK YOU FOR INDIVIDUAL PERCEPTION.
—Mort Sahl, 1968

Woodstock; Summer 1969. What follows is a modern urban legend that, if only apocryphal, remains true in spirit. One longhair, passing a toke to a companion, studiously observes the sex, drugs, and rock 'n' roll around him. Smiling wryly, he sarcastically comments: "Can you believe these kids were raised on *Disney* films?" His friend, while attempting to inhale, chokes on his own laughter.

End of story; beginning of book . . .

My purpose with *From Walt to Woodstock: How Disney Created the Counterculture* is to remove any trace of humor from that statement. The argument here is that Disney was anything but what he is generally considered by most fans and foes alike: the most conventional of all major American moviemakers. This position will be advanced through three strategies, presented simultaneously: a close textual analysis of individual films, a concurrent relating of the movies to one another as an oeuvre that expresses the singular imagination of an auteur, and a sociopolitical analysis of Walt's work within its historical context. Disney was not, I hope to prove by book's end, a person who, had he lived to see Woodstock (Walt died in 1966),[1] would have been horrified at what occurred. More likely, if the movies express the man as I believe they do, he would have been thrilled.

My aim is to show that Disney's output—as experienced at the movies, on television, and in person at theme parks—played a major role in transforming mid-1950s white-bread toddlers into the rebellious teenage youth of the late sixties. No one, of course, can achieve such a lofty task alone; countless other artists, as well as people from other walks of life, played their roles in the metamorphosis of our world from Eisenhower-era mendacity to post-Woodstock iconoclasm. Still, no other single figure of the past century has had such a wide, deep, and pervasive influence on the public imagination as Walt Disney. He did, after all, reach us first (and, therefore, foremost), at that very point in our youthful development when either an individual or a generation is most receptive (and vulnerable) to such forces and ideas. The title of this tome, if admittedly exaggerated, holds true. More than any other influence in American popular discourse, Disney ought to be considered the primary creator of the counterculture, which the public imagination views as embracing values that are the antithesis of those that the body of his work supposedly communicated to children.

Even daring to suggest such a reversal of long-held opinion is risky, some might say foolhardy. The term "Disneyfication" long ago entered into our idiomatic American English as a stigma. Whenever anything is said to have been Disney*ized* or Disney*fied*, a harsh criticism is implied. Substance in the source has been eliminated, the original's impact diluted. This renders the work's materials more easily accessible to modern mainstream families while removing all the dark edges and thematic depth, or so goes the claim. Disney's films, according to such assumptions, are awash in the worst sort of sentimentality. As a result, they prove garishly appealing to the lowest common denominator of audience intelligence. Also, it is presupposed that the films contain and convey a set of values that is, politically speaking, simplistically rightist—moderately conservative to those who barely tolerate Disney, cryptofascist for others who perceive his work as insidious, even dangerous.

This notion has been accepted for so long, particularly among academics and intellectuals, that it no longer is considered a subjective opinion but has taken on the weight of irrefutable fact. The point is, none of this has any basis in the work itself. The demeaning reputation of Disney as superficial—compounded by the commercial success of his work more than thirty-five years after the man's passing, which in some corners only adds to the reprehensibility of his image—fails to hold up under close scrutiny of his output. That no one has seriously challenged that perception of Disney merely attests that such a negative assessment is considered not a perception but reality.

The myth (for this is the best word to describe such an ingrained false vision) of Disney as provider of pro-Establishment entertainment is remarkably widespread. When reviewers in the popular press noted any *anti*-Establishment values in a film, they felt a need to reconcile this supposedly "unique" movie with longstanding misconceptions. Such confusion can be detected in the opening sentence of Bosley Crowther's positive critique of *Moon Pilot* (1962): "*Of all people*, Mr. Disney is making good-natured *fun* of the high-minded scientific project of firing a man around the moon"[2] (emphasis added). *Time*, also in a laudatory piece, revealed its critic's prejudice:

Sacred cows, if skillfully milked, produce tons of fun; but Hollywood usually avoids them because they often kick back. The more reason to be pleasantly *surprised* that Walt Disney, *not* particularly *known for sociopolitical daring*, should have herded three of these pampered critters—the FBI, the Air Force, and the astronaut-program—into the same plot.[3] (emphasis added)

Disney's films actually contain more "sociopolitical daring" than those of any other commercial filmmaker from Hollywood's golden era. This element proves so consistent—from the earliest cartoon experiments to the most elaborate live-action projects—that no one who observes them closely (and without invisible blinders) can, like *Time*'s reviewer, claim to be "surprised" to find such stuff in any film. For it is there— should we finally choose to see it—in *every* film. This holds true not only for the animated classics—lauded for their technical proficiency even by those who don't approve of Disney—but for the live-action programmers, too.

An exemplary case in point: the all-but-forgotten 1959 film *Third Man on the Mountain*, based on James Ramsey Ullman's novel *Banner in the Sky*. Like most of Walt's work, this film fuses aspects of Disney's own life with a characteristic synergy. Disney's then-recent vacation in Switzerland inspired him to do a film about the area,[4] which in turn led to the creation of a Matterhorn ride at Disneyland park. The focal character, Rudi Matt (James MacArthur), is a young man who vows to climb the awe-inspiring Citadel; his father died trying years earlier. Rudi's well-intentioned mother forbids him to make an attempt, fearing she may lose him, too. But backed by a notably independent young woman (Janet Munro), whom he loves, Rudi sets out anyway. Mentored by an experienced climber, Captain Winter (Michael Rennie), Rudi learns that the key to successful mountain climbing is putting one's own personal glory aside for the greater good of a team. By blind luck or a true miracle, Rudi finds a fabled passageway that allows him to reach the top before his competitors. In this place, Rudi rediscovers a radical inner innocence. For the first time since childhood, he perceives a spiritual beauty in nature that does not exist in civilization. When another climber is accidentally hurt, the youth allows Winter to reach the peak first, while Rudi saves the unconscious man's life.

At first glance, *Third Man on the Mountain* seems an anomaly. Disney never again expressed interest in mountain climbing. This was not for him a recurring interest, as, say, the bullfight is in the work of writer-director Budd Boetticher (*The Bullfighter and the Lady*, 1952; *The Magnificent Matador*, 1956; *Arruza*, 1972). Subject matter, however, is merely one (and not necessarily the most effective) means of determining a filmmaker's personal concerns. In many respects, modern film criticism was born when Robin Wood discerned recurring themes and a consistent style in the films of Howard Hawks, who dabbled in every possible genre and historical period. Yet even in a movie as crassly and unapologetically commercial as *Rio Bravo* (1959), in which rock 'n' roller Rick Nelson was allowed to be-bop in a frontier setting, "every character, every situation, every sequence expresses [Hawks] as surely as every detail in an Antonioni film expresses Antonioni."[5] An art film like *L'Avventura* (1960) conveys the strong and unique personality of its maker no less yet no more than a rowdy western, as each key element that appears onscreen in the latter "emanate[s] from Hawks's personality which per-

THE HERO OF A THOUSAND FACES. As was the case with the ancient heroes of myth, at least as related in the writings of Joseph Campbell, each Disney protagonist must undergo a personal quest, during which he makes the transition from boy to adult, in *Third Man on the Mountain* (1959), a young orphan (James MacArthur) achieves the dream his late father failed to realize, scaling the Matterhorn.

vades the whole" film. This personality carries over from one work to the next, in Hawks's films to *El Dorado* (1966) and in Antonioni's to *La Notte* (1961).[6]

The discovery of a continuing, consistent vision in such varied genres (as opposed to, say, the westerns of John Ford or Alfred Hitchcock's suspense thrillers, which seem more likely to form an organic whole) has much to do with the subsequent deification of Hawks as a legendary producer-director among auteur critics. Likewise, *Third Man* shares much with other, seemingly unrelated Disney films—from nature documentaries to Donald Duck shorts. The hero is a rebellious teenager who will not follow parental orders, eventually proving himself right rather than merely arrogant. He is an orphan, haunted by a death in the past. He lives on the edge of an abyss—in this case, literally! His mother remains the most significant force in his life, though Rudi ultimately must leave her company and become romantically involved with his chosen mate. He comes to understand that the natural world is more pure than the social realm. Yet he learns that when dealing with society, community loyalty is far more valuable than rugged individualism. Rudi's initial hubris gives way to humility as he realizes that self-interest is the lowest form of human motivation, whereas achieving success in one's own mind, and on one's own terms, is truly important. Finally, Rudi redeems himself while discovering a basic set of truths that prove essential to every Disney hero, from the cartoon creation Bambi to the fanciful Merlin Jones, an obvious precursor to today's much-loved Harry Potter.

As to attacks by the religious right on contemporary author J. K. Rowling's literature for children, such complaints are effectively summed up by a letter to the editor appearing in a typical Middle American daily newspaper: "Should I let my child read about Harry's seemingly justified lying, breaking rules and disobeying authority figures (which, I might add, he actually gets rewarded for)?"[7] The outraged citizen's argument implies that, once upon a time, a storyteller did exist who could be trusted to lead children in the "right" direction. That, of course, was Walt Disney. But Harry physically resembles (and unconsciously may have been derived from) Merlin Jones, a live-action Disney hero. And Harry's situations—effectively summarized by the letter—are in line with all Disney protagonists', ranging from Davy Crockett to Pollyanna. The fact-based male adult and the fictional little girl lie, break rules, and disobey authority figures. Ultimately, they are rewarded for doing precisely that, within a dramatic or comedic context that clearly approves of such actions.

Vividly contained within a pleasant, if in truth forgettable, film like *Third Man on the Mountain* is a paradigm for personal behavior. This (to borrow from Noel Coward) design for living proves to be essentially *moral* in its implications, though just as clearly avoids being simplistically *moralistic*—that is, actualizing in its narrative the current code of a status quo. Rudi rebels against elders who are supposed to know best. As it turns out, here, as in the entire Disney canon, youth often does know best; the child, as the Romantic poet Wordsworth put it in 1804, serves as father of the man, not the other way around, as Classicists before and since insist. In all art of the latter persuasion, "the matter is given to [an artist] by his age."[8] Conversely, the Romantic reacts against the social conventions of his time, as do his heroic protagonists within any one story.

In this sense—and this sense alone—Disney *does* qualify as a reactionary. That is, after all, true of all Romantic artists, since they employ cautionary fables to argue against previously unassailed convictions, thereby blazing new trails of thought with hopes of opening the eyes of those around them. There can be no rebel without an existing order to rebel against. In this tradition, a phrase once employed by Tennyson to describe Victor Hugo fits Disney nicely: "a weird Titan." Titanic, surely, in terms of influence, and far more weird than the general notion of Disney as a genial if lightweight entertainer.

Disney's meanings and messages are deeply embedded in the films' iconography. This language without words is the essence of all cinematic form, in this case revealing an entirely other Disney than the commonly agreed-upon one. When all prejudice is removed from our vision, Disney movies clearly tell us that youth, not age, knows best and moreover is right in refusing to follow the dictates of those who are supposedly wiser simply because they happen to be older. Still, truly wise adults do exist and should be given full attention; children and adolescents can learn much from such mentors. The greatest problem with being young is the difficulty of discerning whom we ought to listen to and when we should reject the "knowledge" of an older generation.

All of which connects Walt to the Woodstock generation that came of age watching his films. In 1968, a striking number of young people rejected President Lyndon Johnson (owing to his continuation of the Vietnam War), while embracing peace candidate Senator Eugene J. McCarthy. The so-called "flower children" intuitively grasped the distinction between an adult who had lost an ability to connect with youth's unique needs and another who maintained what Wordsworth long ago termed the "primal sympathy"—a youthful spirit that does not necessarily diminish with age. Even Bob Dylan, leading troubadour to the Woodstock generation, agreed in song that the trick is not (as some radical youths of the sixties insisted) to mistrust anyone over the age of thirty, rather to remain "forever young."

Once the youth movement has been mentioned, a key question must be: where did hippies get such ideas? Who inspired them to carefully pick and choose between adults in power? Who, among adults, first told them it was "okay" to rebel, even if only (as Abbie Hoffman famously put it) for the hell of it? A countercultural zeitgeist that flourished, brightly if briefly, during one of the nation's most troubled yet remarkable eras had been implicit in Disney's work since the inception of his company more than forty years earlier. Yet the Disney vision (or a general conception—more correctly, misconception—of it) remains, in the minds of followers and detractors, one that instructs children to behave, to conform, to "be good" in the most conventional sense of that admonition. As a close analysis of any one film reveals—*Third Man on the Mountain* serving as a random if serviceable example—precisely the opposite is true. Disney films taught us to question all authority and, when (if) finding it invalid, to strike out against those who would repress youthful freedoms, even if this necessitated employing violence as a last resort.

There will, of course, be those who beg the question, "Yes, but: do you really believe that's what Disney intended?" The best possible response is to cite W. K. Wimsatt, Jr., and Monroe C. Beardsley, who in 1946 coined the term "intentional fallacy." Their theory argues that "the design or intention of the author is neither available nor desirable as a standard for judging the success" of art and/or entertainment.[9] Instead, we ought to scrutinize the piece itself, then determine what, through the discovery of "internal evidence," this particular objet d'art "says" to us. Such an approach derives from a critical movement, flourishing during the twentieth century's first half, known as New Criticism, with I. A. Richards one of the chief founders. Arguing that we must search for the "what" and the "how" if we are to grasp a work's "full meaning," Richards shifted the act of interpretation away from the artist's intent—supposed, stated, or assumed—to the work itself, regarding the text as a self-contained entity that speaks for the artist without any need for surrounding statements.[10]

This concept was transferred from literature to film by Richard Schickel. In an introduction to a collection of essays by Parker Tyler— one of the first major film critics to question the issue of "intent," concentrating instead on issues raised by the work—Schickel insisted:

What it comes [down] to, in essence, is this: There is the conscious movie: the one the people who created it thought they were making . . . then there is the unconscious movie: the one neither makers nor viewers are consciously aware of, a movie that exposes the attitudes, neuroses, desires shared by both parties.[11]

More recently still, Dr. Lester D. Friedman put it this way:

We must recognize that all works of art blend conscious and unconscious ideas and feelings. Once a work is completed, its creator becomes a commentator on it; his version of what his creation means is no more accurate or right than any other critic's interpretation. A creative artist, therefore, can tell us only what he *intended* the work to be, *not* what it is. We need not feel constrained by the boundaries of his limited understanding [of his own creation].[12] (emphasis added)

The only *non*issue when considering the "unconscious movie" (my own approach) is the artist's intention. Yet statements made by Disney over the years will be included, in hopes of convincing the reader that even on what I consider the at-best-dubious level of intent, Disney's vision is notably different from the long-held notion of it.

Another line of attack that must be faced will duly note that Disney did not actually "make" the films. A quick check of any one picture's opening credits reveals that he didn't write, direct, animate, or even produce the vast majority of movies bearing his name. Disney himself was fascinated with this, often relating a favorite story:

I was stunned one day when a little boy asked, "Do you draw Mickey Mouse?" I had to admit I did not. . . . "Then you think up all the jokes and ideas?" "No," I said, "I don't do that." Finally, he looked at me and said, "Mr. Disney, just what do you do?" [13]

Ultimately, Disney's only answer was, "Sometimes I think of myself as a little bee. I go from one area of the studio to another, and gather pollen and sort of stimulate everybody." [14]

Far from suggesting that this disqualifies Disney as the primary artist in what is essentially a collaborative medium, his "signing" of each work ("Walt Disney Presents . . .") establishes the auteurist nature of his process. The more perceptive journalists of the 1930s and 1940s described him as "Leonardo da Disney" [15] and "a twentieth-century Michelangelo," [16] while "his bustling studio was compared to that of Rembrandt." [17] It matters little that during the Renaissance every major artist was augmented by a coterie of apprentices, many of whom dabbed color onto canvases and cathedral walls. Such a then-accepted means of producing work hardly dims the truth: Da Vinci and Buonarroti were the geniuses behind everything recalled today by their names. This holds true for Leonardo da Disney, the twentieth century's Michelangelo.

Finally, some devotees may argue that according to the definition of an auteur by François Truffaut, the film's director deserves to be identified as primary artist. [18] Whether one holds to the *politiques des auteurs* or rejects such an approach in favor of semiotics, structuralism, feminism, deconstruction, or any of the other schools that have slipped in or out of fashion since the auteurist heyday of the 1960s, the fact remains that the director-as-superstar notion was never intended as a hard and fast rule. Andrew Sarris, most conspicuous of all American auteur critics, insisted, after stating that the director will in most cases be the primary artist, "Not all directors are auteurs. . . . Nor are all auteurs necessarily directors."[19] Producer David Selznick, not George Cukor or Victor Fleming, is the auteur of *Gone with the Wind* (1939); *The Longest Day* (1962) conveys the vision of producer Darryl F. Zanuck, not the coterie of directors credited with working on the project. Likewise, overseer Disney's imprint is visible on all his studio's work, not that of any individual writer, director, or producer.

Still, the question arises, owing to the myth of Disney as a craftsman who supplies us with divertissements, so much style without substance: Why should we take Disney seriously? Such an issue was first raised in 1965 by Wood in the preface to his influential book, *Hitchcock's Films.* The volume, via an unrelenting application of the principles of authorship in motion pictures, literally changed the shape and direction of film criticism in America. Hitchcock, like Disney, had never been taken seriously because his films were so entertaining. Such puritanism in popular criticism was based on the erroneous belief that anything that provides fun *cannot* also be art and, conversely, anything that bores us *must* be art. Yet those message movies that win acclaim (and Oscars—Hitchcock was never blessed with the Best Director statuette) in any one era often are swiftly forgotten by the public. Hitchcock's movies, dismissed as perfectly crafted entertainments, remain vivid in our memory, collective and individual. His thrillers proved popular, in those days before home videocassette and now DVD, whenever they were revived in theaters or later on television.

The argument that commercial movies in general were worthy of being considered a viable art form as well as mass entertainment was in itself relatively new when Wood first proposed that we ought to take Hitchcock seriously. His approach had earlier been suggested (in 1954) by Robert Warshow, who noted:

The movies—and American movies in particular—stand at the center of that unresolved problem of "popular culture" which has come to be a kind of nagging embarrassment to criticism, intruding itself on all our efforts to understand the special qualities of our culture and to define our own relation to it.[20]

A decade after Warshow's pioneering of this subject, the barriers between "high" and "popular" culture would entirely break down. Movies, including seemingly light Hollywood entertainments, finally were taken seriously. Such thinking superseded even Warshow, who never dared go quite that far:

There is great need, I think, for a criticism of "popular culture" which can acknowledge its pervasive and disturbing power without ceasing to be aware of the superior claims of the higher arts.[21]

Such a pulled-punch approach, however radical in 1954, seemed naïve a decade later. The diverse arts of Italian opera, Shakespearean drama, and American jazz—considered among the higher forms when Warshow wrote—had in their own eras been treated as vulgar entertainments for lowbrow audiences. The only true difference between a "high" and a "popular" art form exists in perception; i.e., whether that form has or has not yet achieved legitimacy in society's eyes at the time when one happens to receive it. Warshow did, however, wisely note that

such a criticism finds its best opportunity in the movies, which are the most highly developed and most engrossing of the popular arts, and which seem to have an almost unlimited power to absorb and transform the discordant elements of our fragmented culture.[22]

Without ever employing the term, Warshow hinted that the motion picture might at last provide what Richard Wagner hoped to create through his own medium of choice, opera: *Gesamtkunstwerk*, a total union of all preexisting arts. This would be the ultimate and ideal art form, while serving as an *apotheosis* of art itself. It can be argued that Wagner's dream came into being with the invention of film, which—as Hans Richter noted—is an original art form,[23] however potent its relationships to drama and the novel, music and the dance.

Understandably, one Harvard art historian came to the conclusion in 1939 that if film most perfectly serves this function, then Walt Disney was the single filmmaker whose work most fully achieves such an ambition. This writer insisted it was time to admit that we should cease to believe in the illusion that "music, painting, sculpture, and architecture . . . alone are art";[24] the cinema, particularly Disney animation, could fuse these, allowing for a "timeless, spatially unlimited realm" of creativity. His conclusion: The films of Walt Disney comprised "the most potent form of artistic expression ever devised."[25] *Fantasia*, of course, was Disney's most striking experiment in trying to live up to that claim. Its initial abject failure—critical and commercial—caused him to constrain such aesthetic adventuring so his studio might financially survive.

Though the following films had less lofty ambitions, each did address ongoing issues through a technical approach perfectly suited to what was being said. Content and form existed in an organic relationship, necessary in any medium for the transformation of craftsmanship into true style, an achievement that qualifies a work as art rather than mere commercial artifact. Wood had argued that *Vertigo* (1958), *Psycho* (1960), and *The Birds* (1963) singly and together offered Hitchcock's dark and "profound" commentary on contemporary life.[26] The same can be said of *Snow White* (1936), *Cinderella* (1949), and *Sleeping Beauty* (1959).

That all-important notion of "high seriousness"—first advanced by Aristotle—can be applied in our time to the cinema. Or, at least, to those unique films that, on close examination, were fashioned not primarily as an escape from reality (though movies by Hitch and Disney may seem at first glance to be precisely this) but rather as a means of approaching and understanding it. "Homer's criticism of life has [high seriousness], Dante's has it, Shakespeare's has it," Matthew Arnold argued.[27] Believe it or not, Wood dared inform us in 1965, so does Hitchcock's. Likewise, Disney's.

If "the greatness of the great poets" truly does reside in "the power of their criticism of life,"[28] then there is no greater cinema poet than Disney. His contribution is all the more meaningful for being purposefully concealed under an easily accessible surface, as were Shakespeare's plays in their time. Also, Disney's works—and here they are unlike Shakespeare's—are experienced while, as A. A. Milne would put it, we are very young. Reinterpreting the concept of a "criticism of life" specifically for children, Bruno Bettelheim, in *The Uses of Enchantment*, wrote:

Just because his life is often bewildering to him, the child needs even more to be given the chance to understand himself in this complex world with which he must learn to cope. To be able to do so, the child must be helped to make some coherent sense out of the turmoil of his feelings. He needs ideas on how to bring his inner house into order . . . [and] a moral education which subtly, and by implication only, conveys to him the advantages of moral behavior, not through abstract ethical concepts but through [cautionary fables] which seem tangibly right and therefore meaningful to him.[29]

Bettelheim, though, dismisses Disney, subscribing to the aforementioned notion that his films merely water down dearly beloved fairy tales that would have been better left alone. I find this a notable limitation, all the more annoying in a book so rich with perceptions as to how the supposedly simple folk and fairy tales of our youth prove more complex than most adult-oriented narratives.

Gilbert Seldes, in 1956, noted that, despite Walt's then-expanding reputation as purveyor of pleasantries, there existed "a streak of cruelty in Disney," which rendered Disney's work all the more valuable by connecting him to "Grimm and Hans Christian Andersen."[30] Like Disney, these writers displayed just such a darker element, and this is at the heart of our fascination with their work today. Seldes proposed that the key difference between Disney and his competitors in the early cartoon business is less evidenced by the obvious superiority of Disney's technique than "a moral difference, composed of two attitudes: a mischievous impertinence toward the public and a loving kindness toward his own creations."[31] Precisely for this reason, Disney films fulfill Bettelheim's insistence on a literature (in Walt's case, celluloid literature) for children that champions one's growth as an individual entity over conformity to the crowd and its current code. Still, here we encounter the full complexity of the Disney vision. For the individual's responsibility to the social order cannot ever be overlooked, any more than in Greek tragedy. What must be achieved is a difficult, delicate, but necessary balance between the two.

Again, to return to *Third Man on the Mountain:* The film's star, James MacArthur, had only a year earlier appeared in *The Young Stranger*, one of the many teen-oriented films turned out in the wake of *Rebel without a Cause* (1955). MacArthur was among those surly adolescents then attempting to fill James Dean's empty throne following the star's untimely death. Though *The Young Stranger* may be forgotten today, Disney could hardly have been unaware of MacArthur's status then as rebel-prince apparent. Yet there is a key difference between *Young Stranger* and *Third Man*. In the former, MacArthur's character learns the necessity of giving up his argumentative ways; in the latter, experience teaches him that they must never be surrendered. Disney's moral fable—unlike the supposedly riskier film—champions rather than criticizes the rebelliousness of youth.

This is as true of Disney entertainment today as in the past. Attacks on Michael Eisner's regime by the religious right stem from their false assumption that Walt Disney was both conventional and conservative. "Disney [under Eisner] is not Mom and Dad's Disney," Richard Land (president, Southern Baptist Convention) complained in 1997, while organizing a boycott of Disney films, videos, theme parks, and stores, and ABC-TV (currently owned by Disney). "They're not Mr. Disney's Disney anymore. They have moved over to the other side of the spectrum."[32] This, in reaction to the overt sexiness of the title character in *The Little Mermaid* (1989) and a salute to Native American religion (interpreted as "Christian-bashing"[33] by Land) in *Pocahontas* (1995).

Yet even a casual viewing of the original Disney films reveals precisely the same thing. The lovingly presented sexiness of pagan females in "Pastoral Symphony"/*Fantasia* (1940) and the positive depiction of Indian spirituality in *Westward Ho the Wagons* (1958) represented, in

Walt's time, precisely what Eisner and the modern Disney company offer. In fact, then, today's Disney is indeed Walt's Disney. When Land
complains that today's "Disney [company] does not want to have positive portrayals of orthodox Christians,"[34] he reveals a lack of familiarity
with the earlier work to which he compares current Disney films. There
could be no more scathing satire of conventional Christianity than what
we encounter in *Pollyanna* (1960). And it was hardly accidental that
there's no church in Walt's Main Street, USA at his theme parks. By all
accounts, he believed in God but fervently avoided any one religion's
narrow approach, as he did the habit of churchgoing.[35]

The notion of New Age films that are "about the Earth,"[36] in Eisner's words, did not exist in the popular imagination, or commercial
filmmaking, until Disney initiated his *True-Life Adventures* series. In
terms of the generation that emerged from the Woodstock revolution
with new values and an environmental orientation, he was us; we are
him. Disney's films proceed, to borrow from T. S. Eliot, from "a definite
ethical and theological standpoint."[37] An aura of religiosity in Disney's
films—the aforementioned "miracle" in *Third Man*, similar occurrences
in myriad other movies—has been the source of ridicule by many intellectuals. Yet no less lofty a figure than Eliot wrote of "a special religious
awareness" that "we expect of the major poet," claiming: "What I want
is a literature which should be *un*consciously, rather than deliberately
and defiantly, Christian."[38] Disney realized, for the modern mass audience, Eliot's dream. Though the films project all that is best in Judeo-
Christian thinking, they do so while avoiding all parochialism, particularly any notion that one sect has the monopoly on morality.

There was a time when Disney's films were hailed by the critical establishment. Early on, his work, most notably the experimental *Silly
Symphonies*, was praised, even revered. Walt himself was ordained as a
great innovator by opinion makers in influential art circles. But nothing
lasts forever. No sooner did Disney attempt to wow that elite constituency with *Fantasia* than they turned on him, complaining that all he had
managed to offer was a bastardization of the bipolar aural and visual art
forms. Adding insult to injury, the public found this film too highbrow
for its tastes. As Disney retreated into safer projects, including further
fairy-tale films, public response returned but critical respect did not.
The academic elite that had built up Walt's reputation now decided the
time had come to diminish such lofty status. This syndrome is hardly
new; as literary critic Albert Gerard long ago noted in his assessment ap-
plicable to any major figure,

first, the phase of uncritical enthusiasm that accompanies the discovery of a new author . . . [then] the phase of uncritical depreciation that such enthusiasms necessarily provoke . . . only when the second depreciatory phase has run its course [can] a judicial summary [finally] prepare the way for the agreed verdict of history.[39]

Disney's own "phase of uncritical depreciation" was apotheosized in a 1969 volume, *The Disney Version*. Richard Schickel's approach was jubilantly hailed at the time of release for courage and honesty in daring to attack an unofficial national institution. Schickel's thesis can be summed up by a single statement: "Disney's machine was designed to shatter the two most valuable things about childhood—its secrets and its silences—thus forcing everyone to share the same formative daydreams."[40]

That line of attack could also be directed against Carl Jung's theory of the collective unconscious, specifically the sharing of a common myth pool. By implication, Schickel rejects the possibility of an element within the human psyche that, despite each person's unique personality, is composed of universal holdovers from our shared primordial past. That is, certain "archetypes"—key race memories—are common to all human beings.[41] In stories ranging from folk legends, originating in an oral tradition, to the loftiest forms of theater as devised by Sophocles at the height of the Greek Classical Age, such cautionary fables—when experienced in any form, including the contemporary popular cinema—allow for our ritual reconnecting with a half-forgotten human history. Coming in contact with such stories stirs something terrible, troublesome, yet true in a sense of primary knowledge, allowing essential myths to rise once again to the surface of our consciousness.

This constitutes literature, as Kenneth Burke put it, as "equipment for living."[42] In all such stories, the leading character is, in Joseph Campbell's words, one more variation on the hero with a thousand faces.[43] A contemporary author's job, then, is to create a new variation on some ancient archetype, the individual talent expressing itself while partaking of the abiding myth. Sir Thomas Malory (*Morte d'Arthur*), Alfred, Lord Tennyson (*Idylls of the King*), T. S. White (*The Sword and the Stone*), John Boorman (*Excalibur*), and Disney himself (with his own quirky version of White's book) all achieved this in their own eras by approaching the ancient Arthurian legend. The late Campbell firmly believed that George Lucas had achieved precisely this with his *Star Wars* trilogy of the late 1970s and early 1980s, explaining why those myth-influenced movies touched something deep in audiences beyond the more limited possibilities of generic science fiction such as *Star Trek*.[44]

In this light, compare the above plot summary of *Third Man* with Jung's notion of the recurring male initiation-myth:

The hero leaves home and is subjected to a number of tests and trials, culminating in the "supreme ordeal" . . . [his] triumph is rewarded with the "treasure hard to attain" [and] a beautiful princess as a bride.[45]

Rudi faces the "supreme ordeal"—conquering the Citadel—for the purpose of, like Perseus of Greece or England's Arthur, fulfilling his tragic father's unrealized dream. Rudi "must overcome the mother complex"; in so doing, "he 'dies' as his mother's son and is 'reborn' as a man," amounting to "a second parturition from the mother, a final severing of the psychic umbilical cord," which "involves the hero being swallowed into [the mother's] belly."[46] This ritual is replayed when Rudi enters that horrifying yet mesmerizing "secret passage" he discovers by a "miracle," returning to the womb so that he can afterward finally escape it forever, and in so doing make the necessary journey from boy to man.

Third Man appealed, of course, mostly to adolescents. Disney earlier accomplished much the same thing for younger viewers. Walt's Pinocchio, like Collodi's, is swallowed by Monstro and literally finds himself in the belly of the beast. Stepping away from one's experience with such a story—sung and spoken by Homer more than three thousand years ago, viewed in some clammy matinee moviehouse during the 1950s, experienced in a state-of-the-art home theater in the early years of a new millennium—renders the viewer at least vaguely aware of his own ongoing relationship with something eternal. By presenting such an archetype in entertaining terms, the myth—revitalized for a modern audience—provides an education as to how one ought to best proceed on one's life journey. Jung saw this—literature's essential relationship to life itself—as the essence of any single myth's importance:

So it is in actuality: To embark on the adventure of life, a boy has to free himself of his bonds to home, parents . . . and win a place for himself in the world.[47]

Significantly, though, Disney updates one element of the myth. And here he reveals the degree to which man has evolved, as a species, since our race first distinguished itself by forming crude definitions-in-drama of its place in the universe. Rudi couples with his princess-bride, Disney wholeheartedly subscribing to the mating principle inherent in myth. Yet Rudi does not win "the treasure hard to attain"—the prize of being first to scale the Citadel—though he clearly could. More than a decade ahead of its time, this film displays a post-Woodstock notion of the en-

IN THE BELLY OF THE BEAST. The issue of becoming whole and human, merely suggested in Collodi's story, was given a fuller and more modern treatment in Disney's version of *Pinocchio* (1940); only after giving up immediate gratification of the pleasure principle for truly moral behavior, by saving his father from Monstro the Whale, does Walt's incarnation of the wooden puppet find his way in the world and become "a real boy."

lightened, sensitive male—concerned with issues other than his own identity and self-image as conqueror.

A harsh critic of self-interest, Disney subverts the notion of victory, in the eyes of the world and at any cost. In its place, we discover the more modern concept of winning on one's own terms. This is an idea that would prove essential to post-Woodstock cinematic hero-fables, Sylvester Stallone's screenplay for *Rocky* (1976) being a case in point. This is a concept developed by Disney as early as 1949. In *So Dear to My Heart*, Jeremiah's little black lamb does not win the grand prize at the country fair, as Danny did (a most unlikely occurrence) in the Sterling North novel on which the film is loosely based. In Disney, the child viewer encounters a far more complex design for living in which characters must square their inner ideals with the harsh actualities of the world around them.

Be that as it may, in 1969, the *New Yorker*'s revered film reviewer, Pauline Kael, proclaimed that Schickel did a marvelous job of telling "the story of how Disney built an empire on *corrupt* popular art"[48] (emphasis added). No one thought to question how a popular art that fulfilled all the worthy functions of old, eternal myths—while simultaneously employing them to introduce a new, progressive approach to life —could possibly be considered "corrupt." Thankfully, the appraisals and reappraisals did not end there. "Note," Gerard long ago insisted about major artists,

that the third and final phase is not reached by a compromise that splits the difference between too much enthusiasm and too much contempt. Its distinguishing character is rather the newness of its approach, a degree of reinterpretation that amounts to a difference of critical kind.[49]

Without Rymer and his now forgotten attacks on Shakespeare's plays (notably, *Othello*), it's unlikely that Coleridge and Samuel Johnson could ever have reacted to such patently absurd viciousness by offering "a completely new and hitherto unsuspected way of looking at Shakespeare."[50]

As to Disney, a revision has at last begun. In 1997, film historian Steven Watts attempted to free himself of the critical baggage attached to Disney and the concurrent negative reputation. In *The Magic Kingdom: Disney and the American Way of Life*, he described his excitement at seeing Disney's films as a child in the 1950s. Tellingly, though, he guiltily added:

Even much later, when cultural revolution had inspired in me a bushy beard, shoulderlength hair, threadbare clothes, radical political sloganeering, and rock-and-roll musicianship, a trip to Disney World produced a state of fascination bordering on euphoria.[51]

Surely, Watts was not the only hippie to question why, despite his newly acquired post-Woodstock consciousness, he could not set the joys of Disney entertainment aside. Purportedly, such stuff represented the opposite of, even a force antagonistic to, all he now believed in and embraced. The prejudicial view—the widely accepted but incorrect myth of Disney as the enemy of all populist-libertarian thinking—exerted such a huge influence that the scribe felt uncomfortable with his own honest emotional reactions. Individual perception conflicted with common knowledge; the perceived culture clash left Watts confused.

He, and others like him—essentially an entire generation, need not have silently suffered, for the conflict existed only in false common knowledge. "The ordinary filmgoer," cinema historian Peter Noble has commented, "has his whole outlook formulated by the film; politically, socially, [and] intellectually he forms his opinions unconsciously"[52] through experiences—the most important of them in childhood—with popular entertainment. "We saw ourselves in terms of the movies," one American woman who came of age in the 1950s admitted to a sociologist decades later.[53]

Most of what people saw then was indeed conventional, even reactionary. This included films that drew in the youth audience by promising to glorify rebellion. Almost always, such works discouraged rebellious activity in the final reel, from Marlon Brando in *The Wild One* (1954) through James Dean in *Rebel without a Cause* (1955) to Elvis Presley in *Jailhouse Rock* (1957). The abiding irony is that Disney movies—the only films attacked for being too traditional—offered us alternative possibilities *not* in the end rejected by the hero. The screen's first confrontation between a youthful 1960s rebel and an admonishing conservative adult takes place in *Pollyanna* (1960). The Disney film predated, predicted, and, more significant still, defended (if within the safe context of its turn-of-the-century setting) a coming rebellion in which youth stands up to the adult world. At the conclusion, youth is not admonished for doing so. Such a youthful rebelliousness is symbolized by long hair, though this would not become a widespread reality until the Beatles made their first appearances on the *Ed Sullivan Show* in March 1964.

In the film, elderly Mr. Pendergast (Adolphe Menjou) comments on the long, straggly locks on Jimmy Bean (Kevin Corcoran):

PENDERGAST: Your hair's too long! Why don't you get it cut?
JIMMY BEAN: 'Cause I *like* it long!

"Commercial culture," Erica Doss noted, "is perceived as an opiate of illusory satisfactions, an ideological tool that, as Theodor Adorno and Max Horkheimer and more recent Frankfurt School descendants argue, distracts, pacifies, and controls the masses."[54] More often than not, this is the case. To every rule, though, there are always exceptions. While appearing to be the safest (even most antiseptic) examples of popular culture, Disney entertainments serve the function of angering and liberating those masses. When studied individually and then as an oeuvre, his movies offered a homogenized society the big bad wolf of an iconoclastic ideology. Disney films challenged the impressionable audience's acceptance of the status quo, puckishly doing so in the sheep's clothing of soothingly conventional family films.

BIRTH OF THE 1960s YOUTH CULTURE. On the set of *Pollyanna*, Walt Disney introduces a prototype of the upcoming British Invasion (Hayley Mills) to the popular cinema's first rebellious longhair teen hero (Kevin Corcoran).

With this in mind, the realization that radical auteur Jean-Luc Godard's stated intention, "to make 'experimental' films in the guise of entertainment,"[55] is identical with that of Disney (never overtly stated by Walt, of course, yet potent in the work) should seem a little less shocking. This had been the impetus for making *Fantasia*, even as a quarter century later it would be for *Alphaville* (1965).

There have always been rare voices, crying out in the critical wilderness, hoping to fight the great lie. Judith Crist complained about Disney's "*undeserved* reputation for gooery among diabetics, dieters and other thinking members of the adult community" (emphasis added).[56] Even Disney's most fervent fans have, on occasion, furthered the false myth by casually relying on popular prejudices. Writing with great enthusiasm about *Perri* (1957), Leonard Maltin unaccountably concluded that the film about a pair of squirrels contains "the inevitable happy ending."[57] This is not precisely true; *Perri*'s ending isn't happy, in any simplistic sense, nor is there anything inevitable about such a conclusion in Disney films. Properly understood, no Disney film features a happy ending. Snow White does ride away with her prince, but our final image is of the dwarfs, smiling through their tears. Though they are delighted at her good fortune, they'll never see their beloved ward again. Steven Spielberg—our current incarnation of Disney—refers to such an approach (evident in his own Disney-like *E.T.*, 1982) as "an up-cry."

Properly understood, Disney endings are bittersweet. At the conclusion of *Old Yeller* (1957), teenager Travis Coates (Tommy Kirk) must shoot his beloved dog after Yeller contracts rabies. Then he spots Yeller's pup. Travis smiles through his tears, knowing he will love this dog as much as (if differently from) Old Yeller. Life goes on; the cycle continues. If the Disney vision is based on any one key principle, it's that there are no endings in life—happy or otherwise. Only new beginnings—the promise of a positive outcome following difficult, even heartbreaking, experience. Receiving this information in the form of engaging drama leads the viewer, as it did the creator, to a firm belief in guarded optimism.

Was, then, Disney a true and serious (even when working in a comedic vein) artist? He has long been dismissed as something of a lesser order—a superb craftsman working within a commercial concept of film as "product," therefore necessarily lacking the intellectual and/or emotional integrity which defines the essence of true art. But the most heated attacks on Walt's work reveal, on close scrutiny, a naïveté on the part of the mind-set that finds Disney offensive. For example, Crowther of the *Times* launched an all-out critical assault on the very concept of Disney's *True-Life Adventures*, beginning with *The Living Desert* (1953). When Disney created complex montages, augmented by music, transforming raw footage of life in the wilds into wryly humorous entertainment, Crowther huffed: "Mr. Disney and his writers and editors are inclined to do with nature pictures pretty much what they have always done with cartoons."[58] That was precisely the case. Disney is as consistent, vision-wise, in animated movies, nature documentaries, and live-action dramas and comedies as Shakespeare when working in tragedy, history, or comedy.

Such consistency of approach and theme is the very essence of what elevates a mass entertainer into a viable artist. Of course Disney completely transformed the existing material! If he hadn't, he would not qualify as an artist. "In the mind of the poet," Eliot insisted, "experiences are always forming *new* wholes"[59] (emphasis added). Any creative piece should be viewed as "a virtual reality which we invest with value," according to critic Wendy Steiner; "alert to meaning and to pleasure, we go to art for an enlightened beguilement."[60] Everyone knows that Disney offers beguilement. The purpose of this book is to prove that those works were also enlightened in the fullest and richest sense.

A case was once made for Plato being the first Romantic, owing to his idealistic conception of "an ideal world concealed behind the visible, his 'city laid up in heaven,' his daring deduction of all being and knowledge from the idea of *the Good*"[61] (emphasis added). Similarly, each of Disney's nature films implies an ideal world behind all the harsh realities on view. First Disneyland and then Walt Disney World were attempts to create an earthly city, laid up in a heaven. The opening of the first *Disneyland* TV show presented an animated vision of the park (then not yet completed) in precisely those visual terms.

Beginning with *Snow White*, each film proceeds from a worship of Plato's "Good," illustrated in a modern manner. If that sounds a far cry from the half a million longhairs who converged on Max Yasgur's farm near the small town of Bethel, New York, fifty-four miles from the actual place called Woodstock, in August 1969, the difference is largely illusory. Fifteen years after the event, Art Vassmer, co-owner (with his brother Fred) of a small general store, recalled: "We cashed I don't know how many checks, and you know what? Not one of them bounced!"[62] Of course not; the hippies had come to understand, while watching Disney films in their childhood, that you don't do such things. From those films, they grasped the need to respect a continuing notion of the Good while flouting other conventions that had outworn their welcome.

Such a mind-set places Disney firmly in the tradition of such other iconoclastic (and truly American) artists as Mark Twain, Walt Whitman, and Jack Kerouac. They all defy any easy categorizing as liberal or conservative, transcending such labels via a more indigenous identity as homegrown American populists. Novelist Kerouac, as well as political pundit Mort Sahl, folksinger Bob Dylan, actor-director Dennis Hopper, and aforementioned peace candidate Eugene McCarthy—all considered liberals in the sixties—were categorized as conservatives a decade later. This partakes of a long-standing tradition that can be traced back at least as far as John Dos Passos, firebrand author of the socialistically inclined *U.S.A.* trilogy. That immense volume all but defined radicalism during the Great Depression; Dos Passos proved himself an outspoken campaigner for right-wing Republican presidential candidate Barry Goldwater in 1964.

However incongruous all this seems to die-hard liberals and conservatives alike, it remains the essence of American populism. This strain cuts across—indeed, even refuses to acknowledge—old, stifling concepts and constraints of right and left. One of the first Europeans to observe, appreciate, and then defend the emerging American culture, Alexis de Tocqueville, noted with bated breath:

The literature of a democracy will never exhibit the order, regularity, skill, and art characteristic of aristocratic literature. . . . The style will often be strange, incorrect, overburdened, and loose, and almost always strong and bold.[63]

There could be no greater defender of such a uniquely American culture than Robert Pattison. In *The Triumph of Vulgarity*, he describes that element in rock music, convincingly arguing that this contemporary form is our own version of Romantic-era poetry. As to the notion that the original is in any way superior to our version, he scoffs that this

is like complaining that children learn about Snow White from Walt Disney instead of an aged German crone reciting the story from a Jungian store of marchen. The world moves on.[64]

Recently, Harold Bloom has argued that Shakespeare did more than merely create the greatest body of dramatic literature in existence. Beyond that, he presented, in the guise of entertainment, ideas that literally created the modern consciousness, establishing the way we see, think, feel, relate.[65] The thesis of *From Walt to Woodstock:* During the twentieth century, Disney accomplished much the same thing, liberating us from a restrictive worldview that no longer functioned.

True, the Woodstock dream proved notably short-lived. In essence, it died less than four months later, when a free Rolling Stones concert at the Altamont Speedway, near San Francisco, ended with the killing of several concertgoers. For all the supposed dislike of "the pigs" by young people, Mick Jagger himself—noting that the Hell's Angels had been employed as a security force—said: "I'd rather have the cops."[66] In so speaking, he (though British) partook of the American iconoclasm described above, which initially appears radical but may later seem to be reactionary. No question, though, that the dream is vulgar, iconoclastic, and populist at heart.

As Pattison wrote in retrospect:

It is interesting that the Woodstock Festival came to put its stamp on the sixties generation. After all, given some of the negative reactions to the sixties, someone could have dubbed the young people of the time the Altamont Generation. That Woodstock was chosen indicates that, for all its drawbacks and its excesses, the sixties generation struck a responsive chord. People who hated the drugs, the free love, the anti-hero worship, and the anti-establishment sass responded in spite of themselves to the love and the flowers, to the earnest talk of peace and the honest "we-ness" instead of "me-ness," and—the anti-materialism of the sixties notwithstanding—to the no bounced checks at Vassmer's General Store.[67]

All of the above—everything best and worst about what we call the Woodstock generation—was learned from watching Disney films.

And as to the lack of bounced checks at Vassmer's? Had he been around to see that, Uncle Walt would've been *real* proud!

FROM WALT TO WOODSTOCK

1 Sex, Drugs, and Rock 'n' Roll
Disney and the Youth Culture

ROCK AND ROLL IS HERE TO STAY;
IT WILL NEVER DIE.
—Danny and the Juniors, 1956

TUNE IN, TURN ON, DROP OUT.
—Timothy Leary, 1966

In 1954, Bill Haley and the Comets, a Texas-based white group, scored several successes with a style previously written off as "race music," played only on Negro-oriented stations. White disc jockey Alan Freed had already begun to popularize the emerging sound, first dubbing it the Big Beat. After playing two Haley hits—"Rock around the Clock" and

Copyright Walt Disney Productions; courtesy Buena Vista Releasing.

DON'T KNOCK THE ROCK. Early mainstream movies, *Blackboard Jungle* (1955) included, had portrayed rock 'n' roll as the musical choice of juvenile delinquents; Disney broke new ground by having the current clean-cut incarnation of America's Sweetheart (Brit-born Hayley Mills) fully embrace the Big Beat sound in *The Parent Trap* (1961).

"Shake, Rattle, and Roll"—back to back, Freed spontaneously created the term by which the new music would thereafter be known. White suburban kids lapped up rock 'n' roll, particularly after Elvis Presley, the unchallenged superstar of an emerging sound, made his first national TV appearance in 1955. Teenagers immediately perceived Elvis

as a focal point of their [growing] rebellion against social convention . . . he dealt with sex more directly than any previous singer had, and he was the first singing idol that they did not have to share with their elders. After Presley, music and teenagers would never be the same again.[1]

Observers of the pop-culture scene cite this as the beginning of the end to "old" thinking on issues more significant than pop music. That included notions of sexuality, particularly for American women, who, in the mid-fifties, were expected to be more Victorian than the Victorians themselves. Young women began their movement toward liberation— sexual, social, even spiritual—as a result of rock. The new music could be experienced on the radio or the new 45 rpm records, in exploitation movies, in time on TV, and better still live. "Kinsey was a false prophet of the Old Guard," one mainstream woman announced after attending a 1950s concert, noting the wondrous freedom experienced by females while responding. After that moment, the revolution began and "the sexual mutant lie couldn't work anymore."[2] A new youth culture was introduced by Elvis, James Dean, and young (circa 1954's *The Wild One*) Brando—pop-culture revolutionaries whose impact on young people created the concept of a Generation Gap overnight.

As his work illustrates, Disney—alone among Hollywood film-makers—early on understood youth's need for its own identity. In particular, he presaged what would be the central element of youth culture. Disney films, Walt had always lectured his artists, must capture

the dance—the various rhythms that enter into [ordinary people's] lives every day—how rhythmical the body really is. That, in itself, is music. In other words, it could be music in the body.[3]

Disney animation would, as Gilbert Seldes noted, "restore to us our natural impulse to dance," or at least "keep that impulse alive in [twentieth-century] human beings until the conditions of society make it natural for a man to dance [again]."[4]

In addition to the intellectuals, who approved, America's mainstream likewise picked up on this element. Reactionaries, however, complained that Disney's work was subversive and, as such, likely to destroy traditional values. Why, in his movies, were there so much "dancing and sug-

COME ON, BABY, LET'S DO THE TWIST. Despite his ongoing image as a social conservative, Disney, in fact, championed the wild ways of the new American youth culture; in *The Sword and the Rose* (1953), ostensibly set in pre-Elizabethan England, the artistic consciousness behind the project sides with those young people who dare to dance wildly, standing against uptight adults who object to such sexually charged revelry.

gestiveness"? Even in such "should-be innocent subjects [as] Mickey Mouse comedies," one distraught citizen railed, "they are beginning to inject [such] undesirable qualities." Archly conservative parents feared that Disney would forever corrupt "the sense of moral values in their children," leaving the kids "confused and debauched."[5] In truth, Disney did help shape the wild abandon of the new youth's dancing. "The liturgy of rock," one observer noted, "repeatedly calls on the believer to 'dance, dance, dance,' to 'keep on dancin' and a-prancin'.' . . . In rock mythology, this ritual is performed in the streets."[6] Long before the advent of rock, that was the case in Disney films. Dance sequences in *The Three Caballeros* take place in teeming Latin American streets, where white-bread Donald loosens up by joining in the positive, celebratory mood.

Not content to leave such activities in the sacrosanct alternative world of films, Disney soon inspired such giddy abandon in real life or, at least, the "world" he created, allowing everyone an alternative to the era's expected uptight behavior. No sooner had Disneyland been completed (fall 1955) than visitors were encouraged to dance in the streets, alongside costumed performers impersonating beloved cartoon characters. This, Disney hoped, would restore to the typical victim of modern conformist society an emotional, primitive, spiritual, sensual, *natural* sensibility. Ever the iconoclast, Disney constantly instructed his crew to be consciously aware, while preparing upcoming projects, of "how primitive music is—how natural it is for people to go to music."[7]

DANCING IN THE STREETS

STEAMBOAT WILLIE (1928)

GALLOPIN' GAUCHO (1928)

MERRY DWARFS (1929)

THE WHOOPEE PARTY (1932)

THE GRASSHOPPER AND THE ANTS (1934)

ROB ROY (1954)

Dance has always been as essential to Disney films as the music itself. His first synchronized-sound cartoon, *Steamboat Willie*, featured Mickey, making music with whatever he finds handy aboard ship while dancing wildly. The Mouse does not choose to dance, rather does so because he knows no other way to exist other than in total tune with the rhythms of the world. The vision looks forward to young people of the rock 'n' roll generation, who likewise didn't merely listen to their music, rather becoming fully at one with it. Whether or not Disney ever read Nietzsche is unknown. Still, he understood the philosopher's claim that the dancer "straight way imitates and represents bodily everything he feels."[8]

In *Gallopin' Gaucho*, Minnie makes her first appearance, likewise dancing giddily, much to Mickey's (and the audience's) delight. One year later, in *Merry Dwarfs* (1929), Disney provided predecessors to Snow White's companions. They leave off their long day's work to join a street festival, drinking beer and dancing to the music until they happily fall down in the street. The miniature fable's moral is anything but cautionary. This is precisely what working people ought to do, we gather, so long as they have completed their assigned work first. A group of contemporary characters go considerably further in *The Whoopee Party*, dancing and drinking the night away, growing so loud that the police break up the event and arrest everyone. The short film leaves little question with whom an audience is supposed to sympathize. That ancient cartoon creates a sense of déjà vu for anyone who was young in the sixties and involved in that era's equivalent of 1920s whoopee parties: The "happenings"—more often than not ending in precisely the same manner.

More notable still is *The Grasshopper and the Ants*. The Ant Queen (one more of Walt's positive images of women as wise, effective leaders) accepts the Grasshopper's music and dance as a valid form of work. Creativity is as valuable as day labor, if only after he ceases to perform for his own individual enjoyment, doing so for the community at large. Aesop's fable was reimagined to express Walt's values, his highly personal and "complex work ethic [which] he evolved in his early days [including] a pronounced aversion to physical labor."[9] Always, Disney made the point that "creative work, rather than the grind of physical effort, would pave his way to success,"[10] as it does for the Grasshopper in the Disney version. The film's final image is a direct and intentional slap in the face to Disney's father, who, while the boys were growing up, taught Walt and Roy that "the devil was in the fiddle,"[11] dancing to popular music a forbidden activity.

Not, incidentally, without reason. Indeed,

the fundamentalist is right to isolate dancing as the element in rock most indicative of its demonic threat to established [order]. He repeats an observation made by rock's apologists that the music is a return to pagan worship of Dionysos. . . . The ability to dance is equivalent to the ability to feel. It is the ritual celebration of the sentient self imitating the Dionysian infinity.[12]

A ritual celebration that occurs regularly in Disney, who presents dance —offensive to Christian extremists—as essential to our national character. "The American public," Walt noted, "loves dance music."[13] He happily provided that element for a youth culture already in embryo, setting such music against vivid visuals. This constituted, in essence, the birth of today's music video.

The joyful dancing that follows the marriage of *Rob Roy*'s title character (Richard Todd) to his beloved Helen Mary (Glynis Johns) is accurate for the period that is depicted (Scotland in the 1400s), yet it effectively conveys Disney's ultracontemporary attitudes. Here, the highland characters stream out of a church (the outpost of civilization) into nearby woods (the natural world). In this green realm, the merrymakers celebrate their connection to the primitive. In such British costume epics, as in the pastoral American movies (*So Dear to My Heart, Johnny Appleseed, Davy Crockett*), folk dancing plays the same role as in John Ford films—simple peasants acknowledging their connection to the good earth.

SHALL I NOT HAVE THE MUSIC I LIKE?

THE SWORD AND THE ROSE (1953)

Walt's appreciation of dance, and its inherently rebellious implications, is well illustrated here. A true iconoclast, Princess Mary Stuart (Glynis Johns) summons Charles Brandon (Richard Todd) to her private chambers so that he may teach her new and daring dance steps, all the rage on the continent. This includes close physical contact never before displayed in England. The movements embody the sixteenth-century equivalent of early rock 'n' roll's accompanying dance rituals. At the time of the film's release, such chords and corresponding steps were about to captivate American youth. A rebellious teenager in Disney's version, Mary eagerly takes to the new, abandoned style of dancing—*la volta*, a sixteenth-century twist—planning to introduce it at her upcoming ball.

This sequence begins with staid dancing, gradually giving way to revelry as Mary and Brandon, potential queen and her beloved commoner, shock all present with their natural performance. Mary's words in her defense, as older people reel in horror at the sight of such gyrations, are significant:

Shall I not have the music and dance I like at my own ball?

Two years later, all across America, teenage girls would ask that question of parents—begging them to allow rock 'n' roll to be performed, and danced to, at sweet-sixteen parties. Some adults "got it," others didn't. The Disney family, during the boys' formative years, were among those who didn't; any and all dancing was considered "just evil"! [14] Walt's embrace of dance implies his rejection of their narrow view.

In the film, courtly superstraights are dismayed. Cold, calculating Queen Catherine of Aragon (Rosalie Crutchley) is horrified enough to hurry away. Not all adults are so uptight. Her husband, Henry VIII (James Robertson Justice), proves himself a natural man, if closeted in regal robes, when he gleefully attempts to perform the dance. A believer in free love, Henry employs the wild dance as an excuse to flirt with a young noblewoman. The audience is induced to like Henry, despite his vulgarity, because he *feels;* retro woman Catherine, incapable of emotion, fades into the woodwork. Moviegoers were encouraged to scoff at her, sympathizing with Mary, Brandon, Henry, and his new inamorata. Wild dancing and rebellious behavior are positively portrayed, here as in all Disney films, as is that rare woman who dares initiate them in a social context, be it in Henry's England or Eisenhower's America.

DON'T KNOCK THE ROCK

MAKE MINE MUSIC ("ALL THE CATS JOIN IN") (1946)

Until the mid-1950s, "both popular-music musicians and their audiences were overwhelmingly middle-class and white."[15] During and after World War II, a mass African American migration occurred, poverty below the Mason-Dixon Line and a simultaneous opening of new factory jobs in the North among the economic factors responsible for this sea change in society and, in due time, popular culture. Negroes (the polite term at the time) brought their music with them, and it was soon heard on minority radio stations that white kids eventually listened to. As a result, Anglo "pop" singers, beginning in 1952, recorded cover versions of black R&B records; wholesome Pat Boone performed a supposedly more respectable version of Little Richard Peniman's "Tutti Frutti." These discs were marketed directly to teens, who—owing to the new prosperity of the early 1950s—had more money and spare time than was previously the case: "By 1958, 70 percent of all the records sold in the United States were purchased by teenagers."[16] Almost exclusively, these recordings fell into a new genre: Black music, reinterpreted by white performers—rockabilly types in the South, big-city street cruisers in the North.

With rock came a sense of identity. At last, "teenagers . . . felt that they had a music of their own, a unifying force that gave them a common consciousness and set them off from their elders."[17] So was born the American—and, in time, international—youth culture. Many adults reacted with abject terror, particularly to rock's black origins. Rev. John Carroll (Boston) insisted, "rock 'n' roll inflames and excites youth like jungle tom-toms readying warriors for battle."[18] Early critics were remarkably unguarded about their bias. An official warning was issued by the White Citizens Council, insisting that if rock were not stopped in its tracks by whatever means necessary, the new music would destroy the middle-class Anglo-American teenager, owing to an invasion of subur-

EMERGENCE OF THE YOUTH CULTURE. The very concept of "the teenager," as we employ that term today, came into being during the postwar years, when the affluent offspring of Eisenhower-era conformists rebelled against their parents, seemingly (as one famous 1955 film put it) without a cause; while most Hollywood studios approached the phenomenon with caution, and then in a highly critical vein, Disney consistently celebrated the new youth culture, beginning with *Make Mine Music* (1946).

bia by vestiges and values of minority cultures.[19] Asa "Ace" Carter complained that rock appealed to the "base in man," inciting "animalism and vulgarity."[20] The official industry publication, *Music Journal*, concurred, vilifying "this throwback to jungle rhythms," likely to incite youth to "use it as an excuse for the removal of all inhibitions and the complete disregard of the conventions of decency."[21] Resistance to rock 'n' roll paralleled the simultaneous opposition to integration; many people

objected to its racial background and content, even claiming, as many southerners did, that rock 'n' roll was a plot jointly sponsored by the Kremlin and the NAACP, and that . . . it was "nigger music," and as such was designed to tear down the barriers of segregation and bring about sexual promiscuity, inter-marriage, and a decline in the morals of young whites.[22]

A new term—"juvenile delinquent"—was added to our pop lexicon. Self-appointed guardians of public decency irresponsibly bandied the concept about, using it to describe any young person who enjoyed rock. In Hollywood, producers churned out movies like *Rumble on the Docks* (1956), depicting an escalating rock 'n' roll–inspired youth menace.

Disney alone dared openly oppose such attitudes:

Despite all the publicity about delinquency, [I think] America's youngsters are a pretty good lot. One of the things I want to do is make a picture that shows the good side of teenagers. I get so put out with all these pictures about delinquency. . . . I don't think they show a true picture of young people today.[23]

Walt illustrated that attitude early on, in the "Jazz Interlude" segment of *Make Mine Music*. Released in 1946, at the onset of postwar modernism, the sequence (alternatively known as "All the Cats Join In") not only predicted rock 'n' roll a full decade early, but presented it as a viable extension of the Big Bands—as such, a natural evolution in popular music rather than, as social conservatives would have it, a temporary aberration. Benny Goodman and his orchestra provided the score, segueing from traditional jazz in the sequence's early moments to an ever more radical sound as the "Interlude" continues. In essence, Goodman—the least likely artist to be associated with rock—introduced the new sound to American audiences, in collaboration with Disney.

The film unfolds sketchbook fashion, as if we were watching a hand that flips pages, revealing still pictures that appear to move. Exhibiting a primitive predecessor of the movies, this serves as Disney's means of establishing that earlier forms of a medium pave the way for the following stage, in movies or music. We see a cat—a feline, though also a hepcat in 1940s terminology—bouncing to the beat. Before our eyes, he transforms into a teenage boy, Disney's visual reminder (and not unlike teenager Tommy Kirk's transformation into the title character in the upcoming *Shaggy Dog*) of man's connection with the animal kingdom, his surrender to "the beast within." For a Romantic like Disney, that beast is, more often than not, positive.

That's the case here, as the boy—crew-cutted, in varsity sweater—can't stroll down the street without mimicking the music that exists in his mind. For the new youth, music continues to mentally play even when no longer actually listened to. At the malt shop, he calls his girlfriend, asking her to join him. She's a predecessor of the type so popular in the following decade, when a song called "Dungaree Doll" would reach number ten on the pop charts in February 1956.[24] She hops into a car overflowing with teenagers, who drive wildly on their way to the impromptu hop. A decade later, writer-director Nicholas Ray would revive that image as Natalie Wood leaps into an identical carful of kids in *Rebel without a Cause* (1955). The difference is, Ray's rebellious teenagers are perceived, even by the film's young hero (James Dean), as juvenile delinquents. In Disney, and Disney alone, teen rebels are positively portrayed.

On the dance floor, they begin their shenanigans innocently enough, jiving to a jazz tune. Moment by moment, however, the beat becomes bigger. As it does, their movements grow ever wilder. The boy flips the girl about in movements that pass far beyond anything that could be considered jitterbug, resulting in a vivid, accurate depiction of the rock 'n' roll to come. By record's end, their movements set the pace for the shimmy-bop, mashed potato, and Peppermint Twist. Walt's full acceptance of the new music makes perfect sense, considering that rock "has little to do with the objective facts of time and age. It has everything to do with mythic realms of imaginary youth, and these are open to adolescents of all ages."[25] Rock, then, derives from the Disney vision in films and on TV, as well as the theme parks that actualized Walt's "world." Members of the first generation of children to enter "the happiest place on earth" soon created the music that would address the same aspect of human existence—the Romantic sensibility that speaks less to children than the everlasting (some would say arrested) adolescent in each of us.

ROCK 'N' ROLL IS HERE TO STAY

THE MICKEY MOUSE CLUB (1955–1959)
THE ABSENT MINDED PROFESSOR (1961)
BABES IN TOYLAND (1961)

Initially, Hollywood's recognition of the new music was confined to cheap exploitation flicks like *Shake, Rattle, and Rock* (1956), *Rock, Rock, Rock!* (1956), and *Rock around the Clock* (1956). Their commercial success proved the youth market that now existed for music could also be tapped by movies. Shortly, early Elvis Presley vehicles—*Loving You* (1957), *Jailhouse Rock* (1957), shot on a grander scale—were created for this target audience. Yet the first major studio film to include rock, Richard Brooks's seminal *Blackboard Jungle* (1955), employed Bill Haley and the Comets performing "Rock around the Clock" to identify that postwar problem, the juvenile delinquent. When the idealistic teacher played by Glenn Ford leaves his slum school to visit an upscale institution, the clean-cut students he encounters do not listen to rock. The first adult movie by a serious auteur to acknowledge rock set firmly in place what would be the abiding mind-set toward the new music.

Dick Clark would spearhead a push in the opposite direction, laboring to change rock's negative image via his ABC programs, *American Bandstand* and *The Dick Clark Show*. Initially a local phenomenon on ABC's Philadelphia station in 1952, *Bandstand* was picked up for national broadcast in August 1957, originally telecast on 67 stations. By December 1958, Clark was reaching more than 20 million viewers over 105 stations.[26] Neat, well-dressed, polite teens were seen responding to rock 'n' roll by impressionable youthful viewers across the country, providing a corrective to previous presentations. Clark's only major ally in his crusade was Disney, who might have shared Clark's title of America's oldest living teenager. During the mid- to late fifties, *American Bandstand* served as ABC's lead-in to the *Mickey Mouse Club*. Instead of contrasting, as expected, the shows merged.

As the Mouseketeers—initially children, average age ten—matured, Disney replaced the pop music they originally danced to with rock 'n' roll. Most popular among them, Annette Funicello was launched, with Walt's blessing, on a career as a rock 'n' roll vocalist, charting hits like "Lonely Guitar" and "Tall Paul." By 1957, most of the *Mickey Mouse Club* serials were oriented not to small children, but teens. Disney matched Annette with Tim Considine and David Stollery, who competed for her attentions, the loser often being passed along to Roberta Shore or Darlene Gillespie. Having long since shed her mouse-ka-ears, Annette ran the boys ragged in *The Further Adventures of Spin and Marty* and *Annette*, then did much the same thing to Considine and Tommy Kirk in *The Shaggy Dog*. In each show or film, wholesome-looking teenagers would slip a stack of records on the player, then jubilantly dance to rock 'n' roll music. By early 1957, few viewers could tell precisely where *Bandstand* ended and the *Mickey Mouse Club* began. The ultimate segue took place when Annette, before performing her daily duties on the prefilmed *Mouse* show, appeared as a guest on *Bandstand*, performing her latest "single" live.

If Disney's afternoon-TV programming was geared to preteens and teenagers, the feature films were intended for a broader market, including parents. In *The Absent Minded Professor*, Walt was able to convey to adults in the audience that rock 'n' roll was indeed here to stay, and that they ought to relax and enjoy it. Fred MacMurray, firmly established as a symbol of suburban uprightness thanks to his ABC series, *My Three Sons*, played the college professor hero. At one point, he attends an on-campus party, where students dance to rock 'n' roll while faculty members maintain a polite distance. No sooner has Ned Brainard arrived than he begins dancing with the kids, all clean-cut types, despite their love of rock. They cheer him on, "Go, prof, go!" Rock 'n' roll emerges in the film's context as a harmless celebration of youthful energy that can also be enjoyed by the young at heart. Adult moviegoers were induced to warmly laugh with Brainard, satirically laughing at his uptight colleagues.

The following year, Disney mounted his production of a perennially popular holiday musical, Victor Herbert's *Babes in Toyland*. Annette played the female lead, Mary Contrary; opposite her, as Tom Piper, appeared Tommy Sands, who had skyrocketed to fame three years earlier playing a thinly disguised Elvis in the live TV drama *The Singin' Idol*, repeating the part in a filmed adaptation. This had hardly endeared Sands to those reactionaries still damning Presley. Nonetheless, the Disney film—which opened in New York City at Radio City Music Hall, accompanied by the annual Rockettes' family-oriented Christmas extravaganza—further helped legitimize rock. For this rated as the first large-scale mainstream musical to include a performer of new music. By diminishing the distinction between rock and what its fans' parents listened to, Disney musically bridged the Generation Gap, demarginalizing rock 'n' roll.

Simply, the general consensus was that if the new music had Mr. Disney's blessing, it couldn't be all that bad after all. True, neither Disney nor Dick Clark had featured African American youths in the early years of their afternoon shows. Though both men were ready and willing, the network remained fearful. Nonetheless, having Anglo kids perform what was primarily black music for other Anglo kids broke down the first barrier. The next logical step was for African American teenagers to be incorporated into *American Bandstand* and *The New Mickey Mouse Club*. By taking the cautious, quietly progressive route, Disney and Clark set into motion the eventual racial integration of television through rock music and its accompanying dance steps.

Where Disney ventured first, others would follow. Shortly, the Presley musical ceased to be geared only to young audiences, transforming with *Blue Hawaii* (1961) and *Viva Las Vegas!* (1964) into a reimagined version of Hollywood's traditional family-oriented musical. Annette herself would shortly move on to slightly dirtier dancing with another of the era's rock 'n' rollers, Frankie Avalon, in a series of surf movies that began with *Beach Party* in 1963. However fervent their initial opposition to rock, mainstream adults had been gently persuaded to accept it as mainstream entertainment.

ROLL OVER, BEETHOVEN

THE PARENT TRAP (1961)

The Parent Trap rates as a significant film in the history of rock 'n' roll's absorption into popular cinema. Additionally, the film offers another example of Disney, owing to his cachet as a purveyor of innocent entertainment, approaching subjects still taboo for adult-oriented filmmakers. *Parent Trap* is about divorce. Throughout the 1950s, movies that dared mention divorce were frowned upon as dangerous. The multi-Academy-Award-winning *From Here to Eternity* (1953) had been denounced by the Catholic Church as "objectionable" owing to the Deborah Kerr character's considering a split from her husband, though such a break never occurs. Yet Disney dared mount a family-oriented situation comedy in which a divorce has taken place *before* the film begins. As if intentionally adding insult to injury, he included in the title sequence a song performed by Annette and Tommy Sands, Disney's own rock 'n' roll royalty.

Disney's values are traditional, so *The Parent Trap* not surprisingly assumes an adamantly *anti*-divorce position. The point is not that he takes an ultraliberal stance, condoning such activity, but rather that he rejects the know-nothing brand of conservatism that, like an ostrich with its head in the ground, hopes and believes that an unpleasant fact of life will, if ignored, go away. As a true progressive, Disney openly addresses the issue while offering the then-controversial musical form known as rock 'n' roll as a means of solving the problem. The film's premise, the reunion of a Bostonian blueblood, Maggie McKendrick (Maureen O'Hara), and her former husband, rugged western rancher-millionaire Mitch Evans (Brian Keith), again raises Disney's love of relationships that cut across class barriers. Their twin daughters, Susan and Sharon (both played by Hayley Mills), meet by accident at a summer camp. Each has been living with one parent, utterly unaware that she has a sister. First, they trade places so each can get to know her absent parent. Then they bring the two together again before Mitch can marry Vicky Robinson (Joanna Barnes), a young gold digger. Another example of Disney's farsightedness: Shallow, pseudosophisticated Vicky is the only person in the movie who smokes, most adult filmmakers then still visually equating smoking with maturity.

Parent Trap opens with an animated image of an old-fashioned framed adage, with one word added: "God Bless Our *(Broken!)* Home." At film's

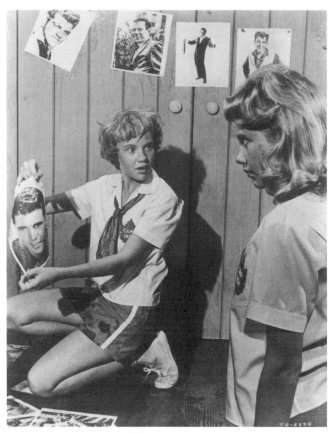

Copyright Walt Disney Productions; courtesy Buena Vista Releasing.

LEGITIMIZING THE YOUTH CULTURE. Throughout the late 1950s, rock 'n' roll stars remained as controversial with adults as they were popular with teenagers; in the family-oriented feature *The Parent Trap* (1961), Disney permanently removed the negative stigma by having two nondelinquent girls (Hayley Mills and Hayley Mills) express their attraction to Ricky Nelson, without damage to their positive image, thereby educating parents in the audience as to rock's positive potential.

end, that italicized word has been eliminated. In the animated title sequence, two cupids, their naked derrieres pointed at the audience, attempt to remake that aforementioned sign. Susan and Sharon will later assume the cupids' place, contemporary incarnations of the mischief-making little devils from ancient mythology.

For a quiet dinner Mitch and Maggie will share on his ranch, the girls re-create an Italian restaurant where their parents shared their first date. The twins provide entertainment, their show enacting Chuck

Berry's "Roll Over, Beethoven," considered a slap in the face merely three years earlier to adult fans of mainstream music. Disney legitimizes Berry's statement for the mass audience. First, Sharon steps out on a makeshift stage, costumed as Beethoven, performing the Fifth Symphony on a piano. Then, Susan—a protohippie California girl, mop-topped and wearing the regalia that flower children would opt for five years later—marches in with a guitar. Her words to the more conservative performer:

Let's compromise. *You* give a little, *I'll* give a little.

What they devise is the first example of fusion between rock and classical, a musical marriage that would be reworked during the 1960s, most popularly in Mason Williams's "Classical Gas," most artistically in Procol Harum's "A Whiter Shade of Pale."

As their parents smile in appreciation, the twins musically bridge the Generation Gap. They are revolutionary—not for the hell of it, rather rebels with a cause: "I think what you and Daddy did to us is awful!" Susan complains. During the course of the story, the girls grow ever more willing to stand up to their parents, refusing to continue as victims of adult problems. Ultimately, they determine their own destinies, which —however extreme a notion in 1960—is what Disney proposes as the right approach for youth. They couldn't achieve this without rock 'n' roll, here depicted for the first time in a Hollywood movie as an agent for positive social change.

The film's rock 'n' roll title song, performed by Sands and Funicello over the credits, informs teenagers in the audience that they must do the same thing, the preservation of a parental marriage ultimately the responsibility of the kids:

If their love's on the skids,
Treat your folks like kids,
So to make them dig,
First you gotta rig,
The parent trap.

The song continues:

If they lose that thing,
And they just won't swing,
Then the problem falls on *you!*
Then *you* must prepare
The parent trap.

In Disney's hands, rock 'n' roll can convey positive ideas to a non-delinquent teen constituency, within a mainstream film intended to appeal equally to adults. Shortly after the film's release, all discussion as to whether rock had a right to exist abruptly ended.

THE ULTIMATE TRIP

FANTASIA (1940)

Rock 'n' roll has always been conceived as an outgrowth of the 1950s. Drugs, on the other hand, are associated in our abiding pop mythology with the sixties. In fact, drugs were hardly an unknown quantity during the early days of the youth culture, in real life and in the movies. *High School Confidential* (1958) initially seemed to be shaping up as one more rock 'n' roll exploitation flick, with Jerry Lee Lewis performing. Quickly, it transformed into a crime caper about a drug ring operating in a typical American high school. Nonetheless, in 1960, only a relatively few students—self-styled bohemians—had actually abused illegal drugs. Ten years later, the rage on campus was to tune in, turn on, and drop out.

That phrase had been coined by Dr. Timothy Leary. In August 1960, the inquisitive thirty-nine-year-old Harvard psychology prof journeyed to Cuernavaca, Mexico. There, in the presence of several Indians, he ate from their bowl of sacred mushrooms, employed to heighten individual consciousness during the Native American vision quest. Leary experienced a life-altering high that lasted nearly four years, producing "a dramatic conversion to visionary drugs as key to understanding and inner peace."[27] Shortly, Leary and a growing coterie of followers became aware of synthetic drugs, newly created substances capable of mind expansion. The military had been experimenting with such stuff on unknowing soldiers since the 1950s, LSD included. Leary came to consider drug use a political statement, providing a clue as to why a considerable number of the era's college students swiftly leaped on the drug bandwagon. "Since drugs were illegal, using them also represented a rebellion against established authority."[28] Such use was thus natural for students who had already embraced anti-Establishment activism to protest what they considered an immoral war.

Exploitation films like Roger Corman's *The Trip* (1967), starring Peter Fonda and Dennis Hopper and written by Jack Nicholson in their pre–*Easy Rider* days, attracted young viewers with vivid psychedelic imagery. Then, Stanley Kubrick's *2001: A Space Odyssey* (1968) appeared, quickly emerging as a movie milestone. The film's simulated flight through time and space (which, however unconsciously, drew heavily on Disney's Tomorrowland shows) provided the visual equivalent of a drug trip. The following year, *Fantasia* was rereleased and, for the first time, scored at the box office. *Fantasia* would shortly become the potheads' movie of choice, second only to *2001*. Theaters located near universities were filled with long-haired freaks, surrounded by sweet-smelling fumes worthy of a Grateful Dead concert. As Leonard Maltin has noted:

Walt Disney did not live to see his film be taken up by the younger generation of the 1970s, who adore the film (and who have caused no little embarrassment for the Disney image by using it as an adjunct to pot-smoking). No doubt he would be pleased to see that these kids, some thirty years after the film was made, have finally given it the praise it so richly deserves.[29]

As to any supposed "embarrassment," it's clear the studio not only anticipated, but hoped to exploit, the drug culture's reaction, judging by its advertising slogan for *Fantasia*'s rerelease: "the ultimate trip!"

Disney's ambition for the film had, from its outset, been to create a (to borrow a term from 1960s youth culture) "mind-blowing" experience, combining "animation and classical music, cartoon humor and classical mythology, geological science and religious piety, whimsy and intellectual seriousness" via "bizarre images that dug deep into the unconscious."[30] Even in 1940, the more perceptive critics noted the film's desire to bypass any normal viewing experience, striking directly at the audience's "psychic stream," thus allowing moviegoers to "glide through the space of consciousness"[31] and, in Walt's words, broaden "the field of abstraction."[32] Aptly describing the film, these phrases also serve to explain most of the significant cultural artifacts of the late 1960s, exemplified by the Beatles' *Yellow Submarine*. That song was transformed into an animated film by Peter Max, hailed as "the Disney of the 1960s." The 1968 movie was favorably compared to *Fantasia*, overflowing with gentle emotion and psychedelic imagery—as essential to the Woodstock generation as to Walt's ongoing vision.

Yet another critic, writing at the time of *Fantasia*'s initial release, intuitively grasped Disney's desire to create the psychedelia that would be so central to pop culture some thirty years later:

Here come comet-like shapes shooting across the screen, lines agitated into sensuously beautiful patterns, undulating surfaces, areas of color penetrating each other. . . . The whole thing is a succession of beautifully colored abstractions. . . .

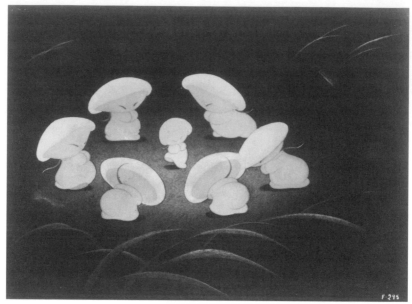

TURN ON, TUNE IN, DROP OUT. Dr. Timothy Leary was inspired to experiment with mind-expanding drugs after munching on "magic mushrooms" in the early sixties; Disney's *Fantasia* (1940) presaged this and, when rereleased in 1969 as "the ultimate trip," showed a profit at the box office for the first time.

We have no need to talk again of the substance of abstract art—to point out the beauty of form and color per se.[33]

Such appreciations were rare in 1940. Disney's film, combining popular and classical culture in entirely new ways, was mostly written off as offensive. Critic Dorothy Thompson, in lieu of a normal review, instead described her sad emotional state after watching *Fantasia*:

I left the theater in a condition bordering on nervous breakdown. I felt as though I had been subjected to an attentat, to an assault [by Disney and conductor Leopold Stokowski, who] were responsible for the brutalization of sensibility in this remarkable nightmare. . . . Since the chief characteristic of this . . . century is the collapse of the civilized world . . . *Fantasia* is [best taken as] a social symptom [of that collapse].[34]

Academics and the intelligentsia railed against what they found vulgar. No better word exists to describe the film, though, as Robert Pattison would note; vulgarity in our post-rock arts marks the ultimate step in America's democratization of culture. Moreover, the "convergence of elite and mass cultures in our age" and the concurrent triumph of vulgarity "[do] not mean the extermination of elite culture but the reinterpretation of that culture in a popular mode."[35] In this light, *Fantasia* paved the way for all contemporary culture, particularly those elements which Susan Sontag would define as camp: pop artifacts, initially considered to be in remarkably bad taste, yet generating such surprisingly lasting appeal that they force a redefinition of aesthetics, in time allowing them to be hailed as classics. Thus, hippos dancing gaily to Ponchielli's *Dance of the Hours*—a horrific image to the 1940s critical elite—literally initiated the modern sensibility.

Though Thompson perceived Disney's assault as fascistic, it was in fact democratic. Classical music was restored to its original audience, the public at large. No wonder Pare Lorenz, a critic and filmmaker of populist sensibility, encouraged Disney to ignore such attacks: "You can dismiss the complaints of the little hierarchy of [elitists] who try to make music a sacrosanct, mysterious, and obscure art."[36] Walt's attitude, expressed thirty years before Woodstock, would have been at one with that of the hippies: "It isn't highbrow to like good music."[37]

The cinematic equivalent of abstract art was employed for Bach's Toccata and Fugue in D Minor, followed by a set of magic mushrooms, dancing about hippie-style during a non-Christmas version of Tchaikovsky's *Nutcracker Suite*. Instead of tinsel, viewers witnessed free-flying bows, playing on floating strings, and light shows featuring synthetic colors that never existed in life, much less, until then, on the screen. Patterns of nature from around the world seem to have been ground through a cinematic synthesizer, flowering into original compositions that in 1960s terminology were "perception altering." A jam session by jazz artists provided a transition between scientific renderings of creation and stark conceptions of how ancient evil might rear its head once again, to the tune of Stravinksy's *Rite of Spring* and Mussorgsky's *Night on Bald Mountain*.

The potential of the motion picture was advanced as much here as in *Citizen Kane*, released all but simultaneously, likewise a commercial flop. And like Orson Welles, Walt was far ahead of his time. Though this has always been the public's perception of Welles, the same cannot be said of Disney. Perhaps, though, he would have appreciated the unique praise offered by two hippies, passing a joint back and forth in 1970 while viewing *Fantasia* in a full auditorium of young people, grooving on the movie and the music: "You know, man, this would be a great flick, even if we *weren't* stoned!"

THE ENERGY DANCE

DUMBO (1941)

Even before the rerelease of *Fantasia* in 1969, on-campus film programs, which rented 16 mm prints of European imports by Bergman and Fellini for screenings, began to regularly request such Disney classics as *Dumbo* and *Alice in Wonderland*. Initially, suppliers assumed a growing interest in the art of animation among college students. In fact, the emerging youth culture, recalling those films from childhood, wanted to watch them in a new light. Quietly but quickly, the Disney company withdrew both films from distribution.

In *Dumbo*, the psychedelic sequence occurs at mid-movie, when the large-eared baby elephant is at his low ebb. "Pink Elephants" begins with Dumbo falling into a trunkful of spiked water. The sequence serves as a prelude to (and, perhaps, inspiration for) Ken Kesey's Merry Pranksters, who drove across America, dropping "acid" in reservoirs, as detailed by Tom Wolfe in *The Electric Kool-Aid Acid Test* (1968). Dumbo's companion, Timothy the Mouse, literally dives in after his friend, issuing a challenge. How uniquely can Dumbo shape bubbles blowing from his trunk? Out slips a pink elephant, then

that elephant blows another elephant out of his trunk, and soon there are four elephants using their trunks as trumpets to herald the song "Pink Elephants on Parade." This begins the surreal fantasy of design, space, color, light, and gags, all to the tune of this minor-key march.[38]

"Pink Elephants" is the single sequence from the golden age of movies that, viewed in a new social and cultural context, projects Leary's 1966 attitude about the mind-expanding potential of hallucinogens: "The 'turned on' person realizes that SHe is not an isolated, separate social ego, but rather one transient energy process hooked up with the energy dance around hir."[39] Dumbo and Timothy, like Leary's hippies, hook up with the universal "energy dance" as the sequence continues. Considering that Dumbo will shortly learn to fly, a comment from William Burroughs, the era's other leading drug guru, seems appropriate: "The program proposed is essentially a disintoxication from inner fear and inner control[,] a liberation of thought and energy to prepare a new generation for the adventure of space."[40] Disney was also interested in preparing a new generation for that adventure, as *Man in Space* (1956) and *Mars and Beyond* (1957) reveal.

GO ASK ALICE

ALICE IN WONDERLAND (1951)

Dumbo's single psychedelic sequence pales in comparison to the entirety of *Alice*. Disney's film (like Lewis Carroll's "Alice" novels [1865–1872], on which it is based) serves as a prototype for the sixties drug experience. Walt's incarnation of the heroine foreshadows, two decades before the fact, every straight girl who went crooked over drugs and lived to regret it. "Every action of a human being," Leary claimed, "reflects his state of consciousness. Therefore, every person is an artist who communicates his experience."[41] Disney's unique rendering of Carroll's character is precisely that, an imaginative child whose Freudian dream expresses, in surreal terms, frightful impulses just beneath the surface of a creative being who for years has survived in conventional society.

The film opens with a shot of Victorian London, Disney's period-piece counterpart to the equally uptight America of his own time. A few tall buildings are recognizable over the trees and bushes of Hyde Park, a spot of nature (i.e., freedom, liberty) amid encroaching civilization (cultural suffocation, restrictions on individual rights). Though London is large and the park (in contrast) relatively small, the camera angle suggests that this outpost of the natural world is actually immense, as any and all vestiges of civilization sink into oblivion on the frame's left edge. An aural parallel is achieved by having Alice's older companion reading (while still offscreen) to the child from a history book; before we glimpse the woman, we know her to be associated with the past. Though the credits identify her as Alice's sister, the film itself contains no specific designation as to who she might be—older sister, youngish mother, au pair—perfectly suiting Disney's purpose. Such ambiguity allows her to emerge as representative of the uptight Victorian society, the sort of person Alice is expected to become.

Whether that will ever occur is questionable. When a slow pan to the right finally allows us to see the two females, Alice's companion sits upright, prim and proper, reading with perfect elocution, her voice devoid of emotion. She's oblivious to the fact that Alice has long since lost interest. Wordsworth's child-as-swain incarnate, Alice has climbed up into a tree, always a prime symbol of nature in Disney. There, motored by Romantic emotion rather than Neoclassic intellect, she braids a garland of flowers, placing it on her cat's head, turning the pet into a mock satyr. Rather than Carroll's typical late-Victorian child, Disney's Alice seems more a progenitor of America's flower-power hippie girls. "*My* world," Alice sighs when her companion attempts to draw her from a solipsistic existence and back into the everyday world.

Though her companion dismisses Alice's ramblings as nonsense, the child refuses to kowtow:

If I had a world of my own, *everything* would be nonsense.

An embracing of everything the mainstream considers nonsensical connected the counterculture to both Disney and Carroll. Jefferson Airplane's "White Rabbit" invoked author and auteur, while at one major university the popular on-campus club, where rock music was performed amid much pot-smoking, was named Jabberwocky.

Alice dreams of a Dali-esque world in which Neoclassical and wildly Romantic iconography commingle:

In my world, cats and rabbits would reside in fancy houses.

Then, prototype of the hippie to come, she adds:

Flowers would have extra special powers!

They already possess precisely that, in Disney films. One *Silly Symphony*, *Flowers and Trees*, presented Disney's über-image of nature, sans man, as the good garden, flora and fauna communing. Shortly, Alice will (at least in her dreams) chase after the White Rabbit. She slips down a deep tunnel toward the very center of the earth, which, in this post-Freudian nightmare variation on Carroll, signifies her own psyche. Significantly, in Disney's version, the tunnel to Wonderland exists not "through the Looking Glass" (despised narcissism), but by crawling inside a tree—always a magical portal to enlightenment in Disney films. For Walt, trees provide the door to a pantheist's final sense of primal mystery lurking just behind nature's façade.

Alice finds herself faced with a door resembling those Aldous Huxley envisioned in *The Doors of Perception* (1954), the selfsame doors that inspired the name for Jim Morrison's band. Too large to slip through the mouth/keyhole, the adventurous protohippie does not hesitate after spotting a drug bottle on the glass table bearing the label: "DRINK ME." The situation is not very different from the 1960s answer to everything, according to Timothy Leary: "'Tune in' means arrange your environment so that it reflects your state of consciousness, to harness your internal energy to the flow around you."[42] This is what Alice manages every time she changes drugs. High now in every sense of the term, she opens a box instructing her to "EAT ME!"

THE DOORS OF PERCEPTION. From Aldous Huxley to Jim Morrison, the key icon of self-knowledge has been Freud's concept of the *door*; Lewis Carroll presaged all that in his *Alice* stories, even as Disney brought such a surreal conception to the screen in 1951. Walt's Alice passes through the doors to literally become the first flower-power person while in the Red Queen's garden.

As Grace Slick would put it in 1967:

One pill makes you larger,
And one pill makes you small.
And the ones that Mother gives you
Don't do anything at all.
Go ask Alice:
When she's ten feet tall!

Alice's sojourn among the flowers provides one of her few pastoral interludes. At one point, she's literally seen "grazing in the grass," as one pop record of the late sixties put it. Disney's Alice admits: "You can learn a lot of things from the flowers," a conclusion with which most of her hippie-era descendants would concur. Through all that occurs, Alice blithely continues on, living out one more of Leary's dictums: "If the outside environment doesn't harmonize with hir state of mind, SHe knows that SHe must move [on] gracefully to get in tune."[43]

Finally, Alice reaches the giant mushroom, upon which the Caterpillar lounges, sucking in substances through his pipe. His words, half nonsense and half poetry, make clear the Caterpillar is stoned out of his mind. Alice not only eats of the mushroom to alter her state, but packs pieces of it away for further experimentation. "Marijuana," Yippie leader Jerry Rubin would claim, "is the street theater of the mind."[44] Likewise, animator Ollie Johnston has been quoted as saying: "It has become a cult picture, and now they ask us, 'What were you guys "on" when you worked on *Alice?*'"[45]

Shortly, Alice becomes embroiled in the film's ultimate street theater, the Mad Tea Party, at which point the drug-induced state becomes utterly unbearable. Until then experiencing all with youthful curiosity, Alice becomes truly threatened for the first time. "It would be so nice," Alice muses, "if something would make *sense* for a change!" Pushing Romantic thinking to the limit has proven as unbearable as was its opposite; "weird" has finally lost all charm for Disney's heroine as the drug trip turns bad.

As it would for the hippies, for the drug culture swiftly ran out of control. As early as 1967, while most of young America still held to the myth that their drugs were relatively harmless, William Burroughs, one of their heroes, warned:

The strong hallucinogenic drugs (including LSD) do present more serious dangers than their evangelical partisans would care to admit. . . . States of panic are not infrequent. . . . These drugs can be dangerous and they can give rise to deplorable states of mind.[46]

Or, as Alice—having survived her own state of panic—puts it:

I went along my merry way,
And never stopped to reason.
I should have known that
There would be a price
To pay, someday!

Alice is last seen leaving London's refuge of nature behind, heading home with her companion. They are going to have, we hear, "a spot of tea." Alice still carries remnants of the magic mushroom, and there's no reason to believe she won't continue to consume the pieces, if now in moderation. Additionally, the colors that characterized Wonderland, a bizarre and unreal combination of soft blues and electric pinks, now appear over seemingly staid London town, as if to suggest a pothead haze is permanently settling on the modern city. Though she hardly seems likely to embrace her sister's Neoclassicism, Alice realizes a happy medium between that woman's reactionary life and her own brief flirtation with cultural revolution that would be the closest one can come to per-

THE CULTURE OF CONFORMITY. Conventional and capitalistic, the aptly named Mr. Banks (David Tomlinson) reels in culture shock as his uptight value system is severely shaken by a natural woman (Julie Andrews) and his nonconformist children (Karen Dotrice and Matthew Garber) in *Mary Poppins* (1964).

fection. This, the logical conclusion from a filmmaker whose own progressive impulses were always balanced by traditionalist leanings.

STRAWBERRY FIELDS FOREVER

MARY POPPINS (1964)

Even as the British Invasion was occurring, *Mary Poppins*—with its English setting and hippie-ish heroine—arrived on theater screens. An

Earth Mother, Poppins (Julie Andrews) draws the children away from the drab, conventional existence of their parents into a wildly colorful natural world. Disney's imagery for the animated sequences might have been inspired by an LSD trip: One pastoral setting actually includes strawberry fields which appear likely to roll on forever, as well as talking animals that might, at any moment, announce: "I am the Walrus!"

The ultimate drug-inspired sequence, however, occurs when Mary brings her wide-eyed wards to the home of Uncle Albert (Ed Wynn). They engage in yet another mad "tea party," the term hippies would shortly co-opt for smoking marijuana to get high. That's precisely what happens here, quite literally. No sooner does one taste Uncle Albert's tea (an inspiration for a later Beatles tune) than a user finds him- or herself scraping against the ceiling. No wonder *Mary Poppins* proved, in the mid-sixties, to be that rare film able to bridge the Generation Gap, drawing in older and younger viewers in equal numbers.

2 Little Boxes Made of Ticky-Tacky
Disney and the Culture of Conformity

LITTLE BOXES,
MADE OF TICKY-TACKY,
AND THEY ALL LOOK
JUST THE SAME.
—Malvina Reynolds, "Little Boxes," 1962

AS FAR AS I'M CONCERNED, I AM THE TRUE LIBERAL.
—Walt Disney, 1957

As a boy in rural Marceline, Missouri, young Walt noted that "everything was done in a [spontaneous spirit of] community help."[1] Years later, he included the notion of human goodness deriving from commu-

Copyright Walt Disney Productions; courtesy Buena Vista Releasing.

DISNEY AND THE WORK ETHIC. The central piece in *Fantasia* (1940) is "The Sorcerer's Apprentice," which may be interpreted by viewers as Disney's allegory for the work ethic; like his creator, Mickey Mouse does not enjoy physical drudgery, though he learns that only after an alternative, intellectual form of labor—hard study of ancient tomes—will he be safely freed from drudgery.

nal activity in *So Dear to My Heart* (1949), a theme that continued to his final study of small-town America, *Those Calloways* (1965). In live-action and animated films, denizens of isolated areas, living as rugged individualists for most of their lives, in the end rally around one of their own when he or she proves unable to overcome adversity alone. Such a political attitude is identical to what we find in the films of Frank Capra. At the conclusion of *It's a Wonderful Life* (1946), the masses toss their money into a common pot, bailing out George Bailey (James Stewart). He, in response, verbally pays homage to Karl Marx: "Any man who has *friends* is truly rich." This group action was performed to rescue a benign capitalist-turned-comrade from a ruthless practitioner of the worst sort of self-serving individualism (Lionel Barrymore).

Like Capra, Disney despised America's money culture and the mindless conformity it engendered. As collaborator Ben Sharpstein recalled, "Walt never had any reverence for" bankers.[2] Disney said of businessmen: "They are all a bunch of schemers," making him feel "like a sheep amongst a pack of wolves."[3] He came by such attitudes through experience, watching from the sidelines as hardworking neighbors were evicted from family farms. A formative philosophy was intensified by conversations with his father, a lifelong socialist.[4] Elias instructed the family on the excesses of capitalism so raw that it turns evil: *not* the making of money to survive within the American system, which they themselves (Elias included) were always engaged in, but rather the *worship* of money. That is, the acquiring of wealth as an end unto itself, gold as false god. Not surprisingly, then, the child Walt's very first sketch ridiculed a "big, fat capitalist with [all] the money," cruelly lowering "his foot on the neck of a laboring man."[5]

In this, we may note a parallel to the career of Sergei Eisenstein, chief architect of Soviet cinema, whose initial creative offering had also been a caricature of big-money types. Specifically seeking out Disney during his single trip to Hollywood, Eisenstein insisted that Walt's films imply "a revolt against partitioning and legislating, against spiritual stagnation and greyness."[6] Visiting the studio, he confessed to being overwhelmed by Disney's ability to transform an assembly-line process into a vital and primitive art form, drawing on our rich American heritage of folklore and our European-inherited affinity for the fairy tale. Always, though, Walt converted such basic fables into works that played as contemporary in tone if not setting. The wide range of Disney films strongly appeals to the Jungian myth pool of our collective unconscious and speaks directly to the post-Marxist proletariat.[7]

Eisenstein's adoring reaction contrasts with that of Frank Lloyd Wright. Because some of Wright's ideas ("a house should not be on a hill, but of a hill") appealed to Walt, a firm believer in man's ability to live in harmony with nature, Disney extended an invitation to visit. The architect did stop by, recoiling in horror at the freewheeling collaborative approach. Hurriedly exiting, the exasperated Wright hissed: "Democracy? That's not democracy, it's *mob*ocracy!"[8]

CAPRA-CORN FOR KIDS

THE SPIDER AND THE FLY (1931)
MICKEY'S GOOD DEED (1932)
THE THREE LITTLE PIGS (1933)
THE GRASSHOPPER AND THE ANTS (1934)
THE GOLDEN TOUCH (1935)
MICKEY'S SERVICE STATION (1935)
MOVING DAY (1936)
SNOW WHITE AND THE SEVEN DWARFS (1937)

An implied defense of socialism appears in the earliest cartoons. Based on an old nursery rhyme, the very title *The Spider and the Fly* proves a misnomer in Disney's version. Here, we meet not a single fly, helplessly stuck in the web, but an entire community rushing to his rescue. An individual, standing alone, has no hope of defeating the powerful enemy; working together, they overcome. Disney practiced what he preached. The Burbank Studio (completed in 1940) actualized his desire "to build a kind of worker's paradise."[9] Walt's own proud words about his relationship to this artistic collective reflect a Leninist notion of leadership: "We all work together, no one of us any more important than the other."[10] Disney's attitude did not go unnoticed. "Even in Soviet Russia, where group effort is paramount," one leftist noted, it would have been difficult to discover "such heterogeneity of effort" leading to an equal "homogeneity of accomplishment."[11] The films offered Capra-corn for kids, populist politics presented in the easily accessible guise of animated entertainment.

In *Mickey's Good Deed*, the Mouse, a street person with no companion but his dog, sells Pluto to a rich family. He does this not to buy food for himself (individual survival) but to help a mother cat and her starving brood (communal responsibility). The rich family is horrible, their boy an impossible problem child; Pluto escapes the elaborate but empty home, rejoining Mickey on the street. A conventionally moralistic ending would call for the return of either Pluto or the money, but Mickey loudly laughs at having outwitted the moneyed class. Intellectual observers of the time pointed out that Disney "satirizes the 'survival of the fittest' idea"[12] when, in the guise of Social Darwinism, this natural phenomenon is applied to human situations. In such a light, *Mickey's Good Deed* can be read as an allegory for Roosevelt's New Deal.

Such populist thinking likewise serves as the political subtext in *The Three Little Pigs*. Some critics accused Disney of sentimentalizing the old story by having the two silly pigs survive rather than be eaten by the wolf. An alternative reading takes the film as a call for community. Together, the three pigs defeat their common enemy, even as Americans might conquer the Big Bad Wolf of the Depression. Such a concept recurs in *The Grasshopper and the Ants*. Again, Disney was accused of removing the fable's hard edge. Rather than allow the Grasshopper to die of cold and starvation, his Ant Queen instructs her minions to drag him inside their hall. Had Disney stuck to the source, his film would play as socially Darwinistic. Instead, we see a democratization of the myth. The liberal-minded community, headed by a wise, benign female leader (Disney's support for feminism), does the progressive thing, rehabilitating the Grasshopper. He's allowed to stay, though only if he agrees to fiddle as a form of work, forsaking music-making as an escape from labor. The Grasshopper rejects his former attitude ("the world owes me a living"), arcing to a more enlightened plane ("I owe the world a living!").

No animated short more clearly offers an anticapitalist cautionary fable than *The Golden Touch*, Walt's most personal project among the *Silly Symphonies*. In Disney's version of the Midas tale, the king dooms himself by rejecting wine and women. However socialistically inclined, Disney's films never reject life's sensuous side, as *Fantasia*'s orgy sequence makes clear. The tragedy is not that Midas possesses gold, only that he obsesses on it. The filmmaker's signature touch appears when his incarnation of Midas gives up his riches for a hamburger, the American working man's meager reward. Just as leftist is *Mickey's Service Station*. Mickey, Donald, and Goofy portray hardworking blue-collar types communally (the title notwithstanding) running a garage. Perennial villain Pete, a rich man in an expensive suit, tears up in a sports car, giving the boys ten minutes to find and fix a squeak under the hood, "or else!" The good workers, through communal effort, get the job done. Yet even machines, it would appear, hate the upper class, the only people who, during the Depression, could afford them. In the fade-out, the car rebels, attacking

TOWARD "A NEW AMERICAN POLITICS." Anticipating the Woodstock era, Disney films imply the need to transcend earlier, restricting notions of conservative and liberal; whereas the Republican concept of individualism is present owing to Disney's insistence on creating distinct personalities for each dwarf in the 1938 feature (not the case in the original fairy tale), the dwarfs accomplish positive things only when working as a tight Democratic community.

its owner, though it worked fine when still in the hands of the ragged threesome—i.e., the working class.

The following year, Walt offered his most Steinbeckian piece, *Moving Day*. A family, hardworking but without jobs, cannot pay their rent and are forced out of the house. It would be easy to believe John Ford was influenced, if only unconsciously, by this brief animated piece while planning the parallel sequence in *The Grapes of Wrath* (1940). In one of the first articles to argue that film ought to be regarded as a legitimate art form,[13] Gilbert Seldes insisted Disney was not only a remarkably gifted technician but also the American cinema's only true social revolutionary, "both extending and ultimately undermining the rationalist ethos of modern society."[14]

The features bear this out. While planning *Snow White*, Disney realized that he would have to retain the diamond mine to satisfy those familiar with the fairy tale. Still, he grew uncomfortable with the implication that his little heroes were raw capitalists. Following a brainstorming session, Walt told his story department that the seven should discover a discarded doorknob amidst the pile of gems, "look at it with interest, keep it and throw the jewels away."[15] What motivates them is the pleasure they derive from labor, not any financial payoff.

Disney's film was hailed by the nation's leftist fringe press. Such politicized critics adored the movie medium, owing to its collaborative quality, insisting this naturally inclined cinema toward socialist art. Red scribes were particularly overwhelmed by "Walt Disney's contribution to Marxist theory,"[16] disseminated to the masses via film, recalling Eisenstein's efforts two decades earlier at Lenin's behest. America's political critics perceived Disney's dwarfs as "a miniature communist society," the swirling vultures as "Trotskyites," the poison apple as the endless antisocialist editorials in William Randolph Hearst's publications.[17]

THE WORLD'S FIRST HIPPIE

THE GRAIN THAT BUILT A HEMISPHERE (1942)
DER FUEHRER'S FACE (1943)
VICTORY THROUGH AIR POWER (1943)

Disney's leftish rhetoric can be found even in films made on behalf of the U.S. government, covering such seemingly nonpolitical issues as the emerging scientific approach to agriculture. According to *The Grain That Built a Hemisphere*, the dissemination of corn throughout the Americas created "a common bond of union and solidarity." Not surprisingly, Disney recoiled at the emergence of fascism. No sooner had his lifelong idol (political and professional) Charlie Chaplin unveiled *The Great Dictator* (a controversial film in 1940, when most Americans still favored isolationism and appeasement) than Disney was off and running with *Der Fuehrer's Face*. Donald is cast as a naïve, apolitical little-man. He learns, through harsh experience, the true horrors of Hitler's vision for the world. The hope, apparently, was that this brief cartoon might, like Chaplin's epic-comedy, inspire an apathetic nation to realize that if we weren't careful, it could indeed happen here.

As World War II drew to a close, "liberal" was transformed from a (pun-intended) *red* badge of courage to a dirty word. Even in the poisonous atmosphere of McCarthy-era America, Disney pushed his progressive agenda. "These are times for *radical* departures" (emphasis added), Walt insisted, in defense of crusading in *Victory through Air Power* for the creation of an independent air force, much to the chagrin of conservatives within the military.[18] Disney's enthusiastic accommodation of radicalism is best illustrated in his wholehearted support of Ward Kimball, despite the puckish animator's bragging about his pinkish politics and his penchant for creating outlandish pornography involving Snow White and the dwarfs.[19] Walt's reaction—only "one man who works for me I am willing to call a genius," this being Kimball; he alone "can do anything he wants to"[20]—indicated full support for an animator who claimed that "the crazies keep the world going."[21]

It was Kimball who persuaded Disney to edge their imagery ever closer to surrealism, enabling the studio to visually capture the escalating atmosphere of paranoia in atomic-age America. For this, and other offbeat elements, Ward would be hailed by one observer as "the world's first hippie."[22] That artistic approach suggests a parallel between the politics of Ward and Walt, expressed in animation, and those of the counterculture, discovered in what would decades later be referred to as "the new music":

The essential points stressed again and again in rock's liturgy are the growing, healthy self, the infinite extent of human energy when freed from restraint, the corrupt and inhibiting nature of the world's social organizations, the equality of men at the level of feeling, the aversion to institutions, especially political and class institutions, and the inestimable value of allowing each self to make its own approach to the infinite.[23]

RIGHT TURN?

PINOCCHIO (1940)

NO HUNTING (1955)

SUSIE, THE LITTLE BLUE COUP (1952)

THE NEW NEIGHBOR (1953)

FATHER'S WEEKEND (1953)

PETER PAN (1953)

THE NIFTY NINETIES (1941)

THE SIMPLE THINGS (1953)

Yet Disney in time came to be perceived as spokesman for conservative values and the status quo. Critics only had to dismiss *Snow White* as an aberration, focusing instead on his next film, *Pinocchio*, a male-oriented coming-of-age story that emphasizes the individual over the collective. In it, society at large is corrupt, the characters composing it cynical, exploiting the title figure for monetary gain. Pinocchio realizes, in time, that he can rely only on his family. Joining them in the belly of the beast (Monstro the Whale), Pinocchio—nearly Nietzschian as he learns that

that which does not kill him makes him strong—achieves his desired goals through a triumph of his will. Though the film's heroes are common people, *Pinocchio* can be (and has been) read as rightist populism, having more in common with the views of George C. Wallace than Henry Wallace.

Through one of its house organs, B'nai B'rith accused Disney of being nothing less than an "arch reactionary."[24] Such a harsh indictment has less to do with any significant shift in the artist's values than with a misreading of his work. Walt's films of the era actually reveal an increasingly liberal agenda, one far ahead of its time. *No Hunting* scathingly portrays Donald and other hunters, resulting in the first antigun cartoon. *Susie, the Little Blue Coup*, concerning a charming car that is eventually discarded because of her years, is anti-ageist. During the 1940s and 1950s, Disney transferred his cast of recurring characters from their rural cartoon setting to the new suburban sprawl. This was widely considered a cop-out. The onetime defender of authentic grassroots types now served as the abiding celebrant of conformist culture. Such a change in subject matter was, in fact, necessary to assure that Walt would not, like the world he had once inhabited, become an anachronism. The shift in situation was, significantly, accompanied by a corresponding shift in tone, Disney's appreciation of a life lived close to the earth giving way to sharp satire on the shallow, affluent middle-class society attacked by William H. Whyte, Jr., in *The Organization Man*.

The New Neighbor presented Donald as a suburbanite, and, in *Father's Weekend*, Goofy attempts to entertain his son on a Saturday afternoon. Disney portrayed such activities, typical during the fifties, from a critical point of view. Donald's new neighbor turns out to be every middle-American conformist's worst nightmare. Goofy, having worked in the city all week, has lost touch with his child. Playing with him for a few hours in the backyard on Saturday afternoon cannot compensate for an authentic closeness, squandered while Dad busied himself with pursuing the almighty dollar. The world, as Wordsworth said, is too much with us; precious time given over to involvement with modern institutions would have been better spent actively engaging with other humans.

The short film's portrait of Goofy is consistent with those of other money-minded types offered by Disney during the fifties. Adults so absorbed with business that they can't concentrate on the abiding, beloved institution of family are consistently held up for ridicule. In *Peter Pan*, Mr. Darling is initially described as "a practical man," precisely the way Walt perceived his own stern father, Elias. In Never Never Land,

Mr. Darling will metamorphose into the monstrous Captain Hook, both characters voiced by actor Hans Conried. Hook, then—in the Disney version, if not in James Barrie's original—is a purposefully grotesque caricature of the already exaggerated image of a businessman/husband/father who, subservient to "the world," as Wordsworth conceives it, has unknowingly lost touch with everything that is truly important in life—that which is familial and spiritual.

Disney kick-started the nostalgia craze and the back-to-nature movement, offering an alternative vision of how we ought to live—in contrast to the 1950s conformist culture surrounding his audience—in *The Nifty Nineties* and *The Simple Things*. In the former, Mickey and Minnie slow down to recapture the joys of a less-pressured society; in the latter, Mickey and Pluto, solid suburbanites, regain their sanity by heading for forest and seashore. If Disney's commingling of nostalgia and nature seems a reactionary approach to existing social problems, then every Romantically inclined activist from Henry David Thoreau, with his Walden Pond, to the hippies, with their Woodstock, must likewise be dismissed. What occurred in such unique (and uniquely American) instances was a phenomenon beyond any easy labeling as "right" or "left." Emerging from a consciousness first expressed by Thoreau and eventually popularized by Disney, the counterculture would subscribe to a new politics of nonviolent cultural subversion in which "the goal is to amalgamate people in a new universal order without attacking the existing social structure."[25]

LOOK FOR THE UNION LABEL

TOMORROWLAND (1954–1957)
PEOPLE AND PLACES (1954–1961)
IT'S A SMALL WORLD (1964–PRESENT)
*DAVY CROCKETT, KING OF THE
WILD FRONTIER* (1954–1955)

An anti-Disney movement among academics emerged even as the Depression crawled to its close. To the horror of the Old Left, Disney bitterly opposed the unionization of his studio, fervently denouncing an extended strike (beginning May 29, 1941) by once-loyal workers. This marked "the beginning of the end of good relations between the producer and his most articulate appreciators," those "liberal intellectuals who found this demonstration of their [former] idol's political views at surprising variance"[26] with his waning progressive reputation. Less vividly remembered is that Disney simultaneously enraged the era's rightists by opposing all financially controlled monopolies, including those within his own industry. He, and he alone, crusaded against the ownership of theater chains by big studios. Still, some of Disney's statements from that time do suggest that the filmmaker had navigated a sharp right turn: "I am positively convinced that Communist agitation, leadership, and activities have brought about this strike."[27]

Such stridency derived from pressures that nearly forced Disney out of business. The government seized his studio for the war cause, something it hadn't done with any other Hollywood company. This made it nearly impossible to work at precisely that moment when his old adversaries, the banks, demanded that Disney pay all monies owed. Walt had no one to rely on but long-loyal workers. When they appeared to betray him at his most vulnerable moment, Disney's reaction was understandably extreme. The ideal workplace he had created, for his employees as much as for himself, appeared to be on the verge of foreclosure, and with their complicity. Besides, as Disney perceived the situation, his company offered the socialist-ideal-made-real: "I want to be just [another] guy working in the plant."[28] He opposed unionization for the same reason Lenin would have been outraged to learn that a mini-union would henceforth speak for his staff. However short-lived, Lenin's ideal society was based on the creation of a perfect work situation; unions, necessary in such unenlightened places as capitalist America, were rendered moot. In such a socialist utopia, the lowliest cleaning lady at the office would presumably be paid as much as the leader.

For Disney, too, that was how things ought to work. Ub Iwerks, required to produce the lion's share of animation, was paid considerably more than Walt, who ran the place. Why unionize, Disney reasoned, when he had, unlike other Hollywood honchos, provided the perfect shop? Considerably less publicized is the fact that, whatever his qualms about unions, Disney early on gave in and agreed to accept one. The ugly impasse came about only when he suggested, as a happy compromise, that his employees be allowed to vote by secret ballot for whichever type of union they wanted. The already-existing Screen Cartoonists Guild, fervently hoping to extend its growing power, refused; it, and it alone, would unionize Disney, or the Guild would shut Disney down. What outraged Walt was less the concept of a union per se than the removal of the democratic right of individuals to determine their collective future. No wonder he complained of "disillusionment and discouragement"; however threatening those overseas Nazis might be, as he came to see it, "the real fight for Democracy is right here at home,"[29] where unions that paraded their supposedly leftist values in actuality assumed a position that he considered cryptofascist in its hard, cold grab for absolute power, the will of the people be damned.

Hardly a party-line rightist now, any more than he'd earlier been a party-line leftist, Disney was an equal-opportunity hater of *all* brands of authoritarianism. The great threat, which had hailed from fascism in the thirties and early forties, now (in his eyes) came from communism in the late forties and early fifties. The very nature of the totalitarian beast, without regard to its polarized political origins, was what Disney deeply despised. As to this marking his break with liberalism, Walt's words in attacking postwar communism belie that. He most feared this system's threat to "all the good, free causes in this country," those being "all the *liberalisms* that really are American" (emphasis added).[30]

As to supposed evidence of a reactionary bent, Disney did indeed join the Motion Picture Alliance for the Preservation of American Ideals when that organization first met on February 4, 1944. This occurred while World War II raged; as the organization's first vice president, Disney was responsible for the Motion Picture Alliance charter's wording, calling for a "revolt against a rising tide of Communism, Fascism," as well as *any and all* other political philosophies that "seek by subversive means to undermine" the existing American way of life.[31] When, in the postwar years, the Alliance was transformed into a narrowly rightist group, targeting suspected communists through a guilt-by-association approach that played into the hands of red-baiters, Disney insisted that his name be stricken from the list of officers.

America, in Disney's broad view, is not liberal or conservative, progressive or traditional, Democrat or Republican. The genius of the system resided in a symbiotic relationship of each complementary opposition—an ever-shifting balance between rugged individualism and commitment to community. Most Americans, unlike party diehards, regularly change loyalty back and forth between the extremes, as the constant alteration of presidential and congressional power proves. For any artist (filmmakers included) to be considered truly American, he or she must offer an expansive view, expressing "a new political order, so different from what passes for politics in the European tradition [or its imitative American counterpart] that it looks [on the surface, at least] apolitical."[32]

Such a delicate balance must likewise exist in the work of a filmmaker who is to be considered truly American rather than specifically partisan.

ERASING THE BARRIER OF "CLASS." In Disney entertainment, neither the rich nor the poor as a class of people is idealized or attacked; rather, individuals from each class become better people by coming to understand those who hail from differing strata of society. This concept is clear in both the live-action and animated Disney versions of Mark Twain's *The Prince and the Pauper*, as well as in the most popular of all *Mickey Mouse Club* serials, *Spin and Marty* (1955), starring David Stollery and Tim Considine.

This was the case in Capra's films, as well as those of John Ford and Howard Hawks. The diverse Americans encountered in Ford's *Stagecoach* (1939) and the cowboys in Hawks's *Red River* (1948) surrender their individualism when attacked by such outside forces as Indians or outlaws. To survive, they become a community. At the end of each film, however, the group dissolves, as each narrative's protagonist (both men played by John Wayne) walks alone, as a rugged individualist, to a final confrontation with his own unique destiny.[33] The delicate balance between community and individualism, when successfully achieved, must be considered what is best about America.

Orson Welles expressed this view in *Citizen Kane* (1941). The title character is simplistically labeled by political extremists, who project their own paranoia onto this essentially apolitical person:

LIBERAL SPOKESMAN: As to Charles Foster Kane, he is today what he always has been: A *fascist!*

CONSERVATIVE SPOKESMAN: To my way of thinking, Charles Foster Kane is nothing less than a *communist!*

CHARLES FOSTER KANE: I am now what I always have been: an *American!*

Long considered a thinly disguised image of newspaper magnate William Randolph Hearst, Kane is also Welles's autobiographical figure. Welles's vision of himself as all-inclusive American holds true for Walt.

That Disney did not desert liberalism during the 1950s is best understood by studying the work he oversaw at this time. About the *Tomorrowland* TV shows, he explained: "We are trying to show man's dream of the future" as part of a human continuum, therefore the logical extension of "what he has learned from the past."[34] That fusing of polar opposites was furthered in the concept for his *People and Places* series, Disney claiming that "the old must steadily give way to the new," revealing his progressive bent. Then he swiftly added that "our purpose has been to capture and preserve [fast-fading] stories before they become only dim memories,"[35] making clear his adherence to the balancing factor of traditionalism. Viewed from this angle, Disney seems something other than the cliché rightist that he would, during the twentieth century's second half, be cast as. A true conservative—political or cultural—anticipates "the future with skepticism, for it holds only more change—and change is what trashed the glories of the past."[36] Conversely, Disney's *Tomorrowland* programs glorified a wonderful promise for the future, fully accepting the need for and inevitability of change. If leftists believe that "human behavior is learned and can be changed" by education,[37] then Disney must be considered the liberal's liberal. His populist-inclined insistence on educating the masses while entertaining them at his theme parks was essential to this concept.

While rightists "emphasize the difference among people," leftists "tend to emphasize the similarities."[38] Disney's pet project for the 1964 World's Fair was *It's a Small World*, which introduced the concept of multiculturalism long before anyone ever came up with that term. Visitors were spirited past audio-animatronic dolls representing youth from different countries, their skin color and ethnic costumes clearly distinguishing each unique people. All, though, sing the same song, if in various languages. Disney delights in diversity, yet his key point is that what draws us all together in a human community must ultimately and always be seen as primary.

As for the issue of the individual in relationship to his or her community, Disney's vision is conveyed in *Davy Crockett*. During the night sequence preceding the final assault on the Alamo, Davy (Fess Parker) strums his guitar and sings "Farewell to the Mountains."[39] Initially, the camera holds close on the hero. But as Davy continues his song, best friend Russel (Buddy Ebsen) joins in; they are contained in an expanded two-shot. The camera angle then shifts again, allowing us to note their nearby Indian companion, Bustedluck (Nick Cravat), the ever-expanding community including minorities as full members. One by one, other Alamo defenders (including Hispanics) begin to sing. As they do, the angle continues to broaden until Crockett, initially dominating the shot, is reduced to one of many. The mise-en-scène's implication is that by sharing Davy's song (one recalls the communal quality of music in *Snow White* and other animated classics, so similar to that in Ford's films), these men come to share Crockett's positive spirit. Each "is" Crockett, just as every gladiator, in producer/star Kirk Douglas's politically leftist epic, "is" Spartacus.

Disney reinforces this attitude with the final chorus, deemphasizing Crockett (the subject of all previous verses) in favor of *the group as hero*:

> History books tell,
> *They* was all cut low,
> But the truth of this is,
> It just ain't so.
> Cause *their* spirit'll live,
> An' *their* legend grow,
> Just as long as *we* remember
> The Alamo.
> Davy, Davy Crockett,
> and *Crockett's company*. (emphasis added)

Like these Alamo defenders, all Disney's groups constitute a makeshift "alliance of outsiders":[40] The unloved rich boy, befriended by poor blacks in *Song of the South* (1946); the unwanted orphan girl, taken in by local labor leaders in *Pollyanna* (1960); the freakish elephant, befriended by the symbolically ethnic birds in *Dumbo* (1941). We see the balance of America's yin/yang complements, unique individualists who choose to become a community for the purpose of common survival.

Still, *Time* chose to portray the Crockett craze as evidence of America's shift to the right, a part of the abiding McCarthy-era mentality. According to this reading, Crockett provided evidence that the country was ready to embrace a conservative hero. The series had been cleverly calculated to rally the nation, made insecure by the Soviet threat, or so the magazine's anonymous scribes insisted. The caption accompanying a photo of Parker in coonskin cap insisted Davy's "grinnin' down a b'ar" symbolized a regathering of America's strength, will, and courage, necessary to fight and subdue the Russian bear: "Let Moscow Do Its Worst!"[41]

Difficult to square this assessment with a concurrent story printed in the *Communist Worker*, praising *Crockett* as leftish propaganda, the story of a working-class man, propelled into politics less by ambition than a desire to do right by common-man friends of all races.

Earlier, Davy is, if not an outright pacifist, then certainly a peacenik, abhorring violence, believing in reconciliation with Indians; i.e., the film's "Reds." Their leader is even called Red Stick, and though there was no historical Creek chief of that name, this was a term applied to a segment of the Choctaw subtribe, owing (according to historians of differing persuasions) to their carrying of dyed-red tomahawks or the wearing of dyed-red sticks alongside the feathers in their warbonnets. Later, Crockett dares to stand against the sitting president, Andrew Jackson (Basil Ruysdael), on issues involving civil rights.

In Disney's dramatization, the film's two Tennesseans-turned-politicians serve as foils. Crockett remains true to grassroots ideals, while Jackson is corrupted by big-money forces, transformed into a capitalist as offensive as the one played by Lionel Barrymore in Capra's *It's a Wonderful Life*. Davy resembles the decent, fair-minded characters James Stewart played in that film and Capra's *Mr. Smith Goes to Washington* (1939). Executives at ABC, which initially broadcast the Crockett shows, were clearly aware of the resemblance. When his contract with Disney ended, they persuaded Parker to star in a weekly half-hour TV version of *Mr. Smith Goes to Washington*.

LET'S GET TOGETHER

BON VOYAGE (1962)
LADY AND THE TRAMP (1955)
THE SWORD AND THE ROSE (1953)
ZORRO (1957–1959)
THE PRINCE AND THE PAUPER (1962)
THE PRINCE AND THE PAUPER (1990)
SPIN AND MARTY (1955)

No matter how wealthy he became, Disney refused to live in trendy Beverly Hills, nor did he mix with Hollywood's self-styled elite. This genial eccentric preferred to make his home in a quiet, pleasant neighborhood, spending most of his time with immediate family and a few old friends, partly explaining why he never lost the common touch. Not surprisingly, then, Disney's films project his attitudes about the class system in America, particularly his deep distaste for pretension and faux sophistication.

Consistently, the city that symbolizes this in the canon is Boston. *Bon Voyage*, a comedy-drama, concerns an Indiana family's trip to Europe, the Grand Tour almost ruined before it even begins. No sooner have Harry (Fred MacMurray), an uneducated plumber, and his Boston-born wife, Katie (Jane Wyman), stepped into their stateroom than her blue-blood relatives arrive to see them off. Katie's family has never grasped her attraction to the simple (if financially successful) working man. They callously if unconsciously insult him while making small talk. Shallow and superficial, the Bostonians are unable to grasp that Katie recognizes honesty, decency, and authenticity when she sees it, and she sees it in Harry. He, as was so often the case with characters played by MacMurray during the 1960s, emerges as Disney's onscreen projection of himself. He remained vividly aware that his own commercial success could never protect him from those privileged arbiters of public taste who had condemned *Fantasia*.

Not surprisingly, Disney films convey a sharp sensitivity to such elitist attitudes, projecting an egalitarianism that is, at heart, democratic in a uniquely American sense of that term. In *Lady and the Tramp*, Disney's attitudes about the moneyed concept of "class" in the fifties were propounded objective-correlative style: i.e., by safely setting such contemporary concerns in Walt's favorite time frame, turn-of-the-century small-town America in transition, before the First World War darkened our geopolitical landscape. The film deals with life's haves and have-nots. If Disney was now firmly entrenched with the former, he still thought like the latter. *Fortune* could point out in May 1966 that he was one of the best-compensated executives in the United States. Disney retorted: "I neither wish nor intend to amass a personal fortune. Money—or rather the lack of it to carry out my ideas—may worry me, but it doesn't excite me. *Ideas* excite me."[42] The film's human heroes, the Darlings, are not written off as decadent simply because they have achieved a better life than most. Their "goodness" is evident in their clear love for one another, their dog, and, in God's good time, their child. The pure-bred cocker spaniel Lady lives a life of leisure, luxury even. No pampered rotter, though, Lady is motivated by the work ethic. A monstrous rat, unbeknownst to the family, can't strike so long as Lady stands guard. Only when a well-intentioned but wrong-minded aunt arrives, tying

Lady to her doghouse (at which point she is indeed reduced to decorative object), does the rat become threatening.

In contrast there is Tramp, freedom-loving mongrel from the other (wrong) side of the tracks. A street-smart "operator" (he plays humans to get what he wants), Tramp is a womanizer (his past affairs constitute an issue that Lady, after romantically falling for him, must deal with). Circumstances cause Tramp, while avoiding the local authorities, to seek refuge in Lady's neighborhood. "Snob Hill," he disdainfully calls it—a bit of "bad" Boston in each and every American city. Most impressive is Disney's evenhandedness—refusing to take sides, or to allow the child audience to do so, as Lady and Tramp meet. We do not watch as, in morality play fashion, the street tough is won over by the symbol of civilization, or vice versa. Rather, we witness a combination of the two. Lady must toughen up. She does, entering Tramp's dangerous haunts, learning to survive there. He must grasp the worth of traditional values, committing to family in general, fatherhood in particular. At the end, each has met the other halfway.

This notion would, in a different context, be expressed when, in *The Parent Trap*, Hayley Mills (playing twins) sings "Let's get together!" Successful survival in Disney is about the art of necessary, willing, and happy compromise replacing a power struggle leading to the domination of one or the other, male or female, rich or poor. Walt's is the liberal view, arguing in favor of cooperation rather than competition.[43]

Scooped up by the dog catcher and placed in a pound, Lady—like more than one Dickensian aristocrat—discovers firsthand how horrible life is for those trapped in society's lower echelons. Though the story, obeying an ancient unity, takes place in one town, this is truly a tale of two cities, that of the upper crust and that of the underclass. Lady's fellow "prisoners" are, she (and we) learn, quite decent. As in Chaplin's *Modern Times* (1936), Disney's dregs are not "that way" owing to inner failing or inborn defect but because the system failed to provide them with any abiding hope—the liberal view. A great deal is made about Tramp's being a mongrel, particularly by Jock, the little Scottie living next door to Lady. Though he's positive in many ways, Jock's flaw is prejudice. He believes that, having a pedigree, he is superior. A mongrel (allegorically, for the human audience, the result of a racially mixed marriage), Jock insists, will reveal his low instincts, sooner or later. When Tramp sneaks into the Darling home to fight the rat, the now-leashed Lady unable to do so, Jock assumes Tramp is up to no good. When it's

SCENES FROM THE CLASS STRUGGLE IN BEVERLY HILLS. A recurring theme in both live-action and animated films is Disney's desire to break down all pre-existing class barriers, as well as his belief that this can be best achieved through mixed marriages; this notion appears in such diverse films as *The Sword and the Rose* (1953), *In Search of the Castaways* (1962), and (seen here) the aptly titled *Lady and the Tramp* (1955).

revealed that Tramp killed the rat, Jock admits: "I've misjudged him, *badly!*" Tramp proves himself a thoroughbred in terms of character if not breeding. Accepting this, Jock relents—and, more important, arcs.

Child viewers were, then, taught a lesson of liberal bent: the tragedy of prejudicial thinking, contradicting those philosophic conservatives who place an emphasis on "lineage and the advantage of coming from 'a good family.'"[44] Not that there's necessarily anything wrong with a good family, as Lady and her decent owners make clear. "Leftists identify with the poor, the disenfranchised," so they often "romanticize rebels and outsiders"[45] like Tramp, while "rightists tend to identify with the Establishment,"[46] such characters as Lady and her family.

Disney avoids any polar approach. Individual character determines everything, here as in the live-action *The Sword and the Rose*. A period piece, that film offers the same paradigm presented in *Lady and the Tramp*. An individualistic highborn woman, Mary Stuart (Glynis Johns), falls in love with a commoner, Charles Brandon (Richard Todd). Mary defies social convention to marry Brandon, Disney—the artistic consciousness behind the project—clearly approving, and wholeheartedly. Similarly, in *Zorro*, highborn Senorita Elena (Eugena Paul) falls for a humble, hardworking vaquero. Only villainous Monastario (Britt Lomond), the *comandante* of Spanish Los Angeles, considers this outrageous, loudly complaining about the need for racial purity. The impressionable young viewer is trusted to consider the source, then side with the hero, Diego (Guy Williams), an enlightened aristocrat who enthusiastically approves of the match. At the end of each theatrical film or television program, the marriage of characters with racially pure backgrounds and those of mixed and/or uncertain ancestry is celebrated in true liberal fashion.

This cutting across class barriers exists in nonromantic situations as well. The Disney studio twice adapted Mark Twain's politically charged *The Prince and the Pauper* (1881). The adventure yarn contains a subtext of social criticism, disguised by its author (in the same manner Disney would subsequently employ) within a pleasing fable for children. First came a three-part television miniseries for NBC (March 11, 18, and 25, 1962); twenty-eight years later, a twenty-five-minute featurette starring Mickey Mouse in the dual roles of Henry VIII's son and a poor boy resembling him. Each learns about the other side of life, and as a result about himself. The natural (and, for Disney, true) aristocrat, the audience realizes, is anyone who can survive, democratic-style, in the most difficult situations.

A similar theme underlined the *Mickey Mouse Club* segment *Adventures of Spin and Marty*, based on *Marty Markham*, a children's novel focusing on the problems of a spoiled rich kid sent to spend the summer with rough-and-ready fellows at a camp. Though Disney liked the concept, he insisted on magnanimity, enlarging the role of another boy, Spin Evans, a poor teen who works several jobs during the year to afford his stays on the ranch. Marty (David Stollery), the modern prince, learns to love the cowboy lifestyle, becoming considerably less pretentious while living close to nature. Spin (Tim Considine), a contemporary pauper, realizes bluebloods are all right, once they accept their connection to the brotherhood of man. Initially, Spin is seen bussing the tables of other boys, Marty assuming that this is Spin's job. Marty will learn that on this ranch, every boy must take turns doing such lowly physical work, himself included. Though he initially recoils at the notion that he, a born aristocrat, might actually serve the others, he embraces such duties as he arcs from despised Bostonian blueblood to a true (in Disney's view) aristocrat. By the finale, all the boys, rugged little individualists at first, have transformed into a working community, led by the title characters—now comrades who realize the class one is born into means nothing and one's character, as displayed by words and deeds, everything.

GO WEST, YOUNG REPUBLICAN

DAVY CROCKETT, KING OF THE WILD FRONTIER (1955)
WESTWARD HO THE WAGONS (1956)
THE SAGA OF ANDY BURNETT (1957–58)

During the latter years of his life, Disney registered as a Republican, growing as ardent in his support of that party as he had been a formidable voice for FDR and the Democrats in his youth. Still, Disney's politics, as expressed in his movies, remained entrenched in an abiding dislike of the raw capitalism that twentieth-century Republicans had associated themselves with. Even in later years, Disney more resembled the liberal Republican tradition that first reached national prominence in the mid-nineteenth century with John Charles Frémont's presidential candidacy (1856) and ended with the final days of Theodore Roosevelt's presidency in the twentieth century's early hours, soon to be replaced by the more money-oriented mentality of Coolidge and Hoover.

In Disney's first western, the despised money culture is signified by the offscreen presence of Amos Thorpe, the (fictional) Establishment type who runs against Crockett in rural Tennessee for state representative. Davy's corrupt political competitor wears a fancy suit. As film historian William Everson has noted, bad guys in westerns are not, as is commonly believed, identified by black hats; numerous heroes, from the fictional Zorro to the reality-based Wyatt Earp, wear black. Rather, the villain's iconographic costume is the dress suit, key symbol of the Eastern moneyed class.[47] Davy, on the other hand, campaigns in buckskins, a populist hero in embryo.

Earlier in the film, we met and loathed Tobias Norton (William Bakewell), a (fictional) martinet–military officer who, during the Creek War, strutted about in hand-tailored uniforms. Crockett's Smoky Mountain volunteers—Rousseau's natural men, thus his best men—wore buckskins. Norton reappears in Washington as an overdressed political lobbyist, representing shady businessmen. Eventually, he corrupts President Jackson by luring him into exploitive money/land deals at the Indians' expense, despite a treaty Jackson earlier executed.

Other westerns further developed this theme. In *Westward Ho*, the

Oregon-bound 1840s caravan's horse herd is jointly owned by two men, elegantly attired Spencer Armitage (Lesley Bradley) and unpretentious Obie Foster (Morgan Woodward). "We lost five horses," Armitage bitterly complains following a Pawnee raid. "Under the circumstances, not too bad," the caravan's wagonmaster, James Stephen (George Reeves), sighs, thankful no lives were lost. When the caravan is endangered by yet another war party, Stephen determines to stampede the horse herd, distracting the Pawnee, who are out for profit, not blood. "Our horses or our hides" is how buckskin-clad frontier scout Hank Breckinridge (Jeff York) sums up the situation. Concerned only with his finances, ruggedly individualistic Armitage bitterly objects: "Not *my* horses, you don't!" His common-man foil believes in community values; Obie turns all the horses loose for the common good. As they run free, Armitage darts behind rocks, in danger of being trampled and killed by the source of his raw capitalism.

The film's most complex figure is Bissonette (Sebastian Cabot), French-Canadian owner/manager of Fort Laramie. Bissonette sells rifles to Indians, an act that in most westerns—Raoul Walsh's *They Died with Their Boots On* (1941), John Ford's *She Wore a Yellow Ribbon* (1949)— identifies any such Anglo as a villain. In Disney's more complex view, Bissonette combines self-interest ("To sell is my business; these are my customers, too") with raised consciousness ("Guns are good for hunting as well as fighting"). In other films, the white man who says this is a self-serving hypocrite; in Disney's, the man really means what he says. These Indians, we must understand, are not hostile Pawnee but peaceful Lakota, dangerous only when provoked by insensitive whites. Otherwise, they are, as Bissonette (in context, Disney's spokesman) insists, equal as human beings and as such worthy of being treated equally.

The *Saga of Andy Burnett* miniseries dealt with the gradual initiation of the title character (Jerome Courtland) into the tight fraternal organization of mountain men. Andy hopes to be accepted by a particular group of independents led by real-life trappers Jack Kelly (Andrew Duggan) and Old Bill Williams (Slim Pickens). They share contempt for entrepreneur John Jacob Astor's American Fur Company, a heartless conglomerate that tries to force small independent groups like theirs out of business. In episode two, *Andy's First Chore* (October 9, 1957), a onetime independent, Bill Sublette, informs this group of trappers that he's formed an alternative to Astor's monopoly, called the Rocky Mountain Fur Company. At first, the boys are tempted to join Sublette; quickly, they realize that power (particularly money power) more often than not corrupts. In conversation, Kelly senses that Sublette, likable enough when he, too, was an independent contractor, has already begun to sound as profit-hungry as Astor. Telling him "thanks, but no thanks," they head off on their own.

AN EPITAPH ON THE EISENHOWER ERA

POLLYANNA (1960)

All at once, the Kennedy years were upon us, offering an emphasis on youth and the promise of a New Frontier. In such an altered sociopolitical context, who might want to see a sentimental film glorifying the good old days—one that, in Walt's own words, "sounded sweet and sticky"?[48] But Disney's unique take on Eleanor H. Porter's sentimental salute to a bygone America avoided (even undermined) those expected qualities. The film satirizes small-town America, revealing the superficiality, hypocrisy, and pretentiousness just beneath its apparently wholesome surface. Properly understood, *Pollyanna* qualifies not only as Disney's initial film for the new decade but the first significant breakthrough movie of the sixties.

For Disney, the 1912 setting serves as yet another objective correlative for the fast-fading fifties. Thanks to its English-accented star, Disney's film presages the British Invasion, offering a protohippie who believes in the power of love to conquer all. Disney's Pollyanna is just such a wide-eyed youth, her deceased parents having been missionaries. She now carries their peace-and-love message to Harrington, a typical American community, where Pollyanna rebels against its stultifying system. Similar to Oedipus's Thebes or Hamlet's Elsinore, this microcosm is a poisoned city, desperately in need of catharsis. Pollyanna's upbeat attitude appears less a case of some goody two-shoes, gazing at the world through rose-colored glasses, than of a realist's strategy for surviving in a world mismanaged by uptight adults.

Pollyanna accomplishes this, in a tradition that runs from Plato to Chaplin, by searching for evidence of any small instance of "the good." Bleak as things become, particularly after her life-threatening accident, Pollyanna finds it. Like Hamlet, she chooses to believe, if tenuously, that there is indeed providence in the fall of a sparrow. Disney's film thus offers an epitaph on the Eisenhower era, as well as a preview of things to come. Like folksinger Melanie Safka, Pollyanna owns a brand-new pair of roller skates, searching for some bold lad with a brand-new key.

In the opening, little boys dive into the ol' swimmin' hole, as a locomotive from the East (a reference to the one in the first sequence of *So Dear to My Heart*) chugs by. Seemingly Rockwell-esque, the image will be sharply undercut by a swift realization. These are orphans, living in a dilapidated home, endangered by water pipes that threaten to explode at any moment. Disney's camera eye immediately persuades us to identify with the have-nots. Unconventional orphan Jimmy Bean (Kevin Corcoran), second cousin to Twain's Huck Finn, rolls a big wheel down a dirt road, moving from right to left, the natural direction for a film's radical characters.[49] He runs several conventional girls (pushing dolls in baby carriages, symbolizing early absorption into conformist society) out of his way. They'd been moving toward the right, politically (one presumes) as well as physically. Our iconoclastic heroine never associates with those girls, having nothing in common with them. Instead, she becomes best friends with Jimmy, despite arriving to live with Aunt Polly (Jane Wyman), the town's wealthy matriarch.

This woman must deal with a young subversive in the house. Pollyanna slips out to join those working-class radicals who dare oppose Aunt Polly's arrogant aristocracy of wealth. These blue-collar types—older farmers and young factory workers, setting differences aside for solidarity's sake—organize. In time, they launch a nonviolent (though incipiently socialist) revolution. This, three years before Martin Luther King would make his politics abundantly clear from a cell in the Birmingham jail:

Why direct action? . . . Isn't negotiation a better path? Nonviolent direct action seeks to create such a crisis and foster such a tension that a community which has constantly refused to negotiate is forced to confront the issue. It seeks so to dramatize the issue that it can no longer be ignored.[50]

This is precisely what the film's radicals attempt in their emphatic, if emphatically nonviolent, protests against Aunt Polly's Old Politics. As a result, Pollyanna renounces her biological inheritance to become their comrade.

Disney is too complex an artist, and too far-seeing a thinker, to reduce his vision to a youth-versus-adult diatribe. Many youth-culture heroes (from Eugene McCarthy to Timothy Leary, Allen Ginsberg to Ken Kesey) were well over thirty; conversely, those National Guardsmen who fired on protesters at Kent State were in their early twenties. Disney recognized that true youth has more to do with attitude than age. So some of the film's positive characters are advanced in years, most notably Mayor Warren (Donald Crisp), who opposes his town council when members refuse to fund a new, safer orphanage. Aunt Polly prefers financing cosmetic improvements to the shabby building, a shrine to her late father's memory.

As one upscale resident, Tarbell (Edward Platt), admits:

A lot of us have got vested interests in her companies. Our wives belong to her ladies aid groups. My wife would skin me alive if I went against her.

Sinclair Lewis knew this man well; Tarbell is Disney's Babbitt, a once decent person who, as T. S. Eliot might have put it, has gone hollow inside by subscribing to the emerging conformist society. Tarbell speaks for the newly affluent townsfolk, twentieth-century Coolidge/Hoover (rather than nineteenth-century Frémont/Roosevelt) Republicans. The film's situation might well have been created by Frank Norris, or another of those muckraking authors so admired by Walt's father. However well scrubbed Harrington's whitewashed fences are, a dirty mentality exists behind the façade.

Even the newspaper editor (like his counterpart in Henrik Ibsen's 1882 *An Enemy of the People*) refuses to print the truth, for fear that Aunt Polly will ruin him by withholding advertising dollars. Though he was specifically addressing problems of the black community, Stokeley Carmichael might well have been speaking of all such situations when, in 1966, he wrote:

the form of exploitation varies from area to area but the essential result is the same—a powerful few have been maintained and enriched at the expense of the poor and voiceless . . . masses. This pattern must be broken.[51]

Yet if wholesale subscription to the culture of greed is to be despised, wealth in and of itself doesn't necessarily indicate evil. Born into money, Dr. Edmund Chilton (Richard Egan) is anticapitalist, at least in the raw (offensive) sense of that term. Edmund returns to Harrington following a five-year absence; he's been running a free clinic in Baltimore rather than amass profits by attending to Boston's upper levels. Aunt Polly's well-paid servants, seemingly loyal, secretly support the ever-growing sense of working-class solidarity. When Mrs. Lagerlof (Reta Shaw), the cook, steals from her employer (using flour and other items to make cakes that will be sold at the communal bazaar), her decision is played as light comedy. The tone conveys to a child audience that in some cases, stealing—when practiced against a cold capitalist institution, for the good of the group rather than personal gain—is right, even moral.

Certainly, more right and moral than Aunt Polly's conventional charity, frigidly viewed as "a duty and a job that must be done." Her gifts

AN ENLIGHTENED CAPITALIST. In Disney films, money is *not* the root of all evil, for what he attacks is an attitude in which money is worshipped rather than employed in the service of "the good"; *Pollyanna* (1960) posits the case of Dr. Edmund Chilton (Richard Egan), whose inherited wealth frees him to attend to poor people without needing to charge them, and who—in the Romantic tradition of Wordsworth—derives pleasure not from cash but from the world of nature, where he dallies with the child-as-swain heroine (Hayley Mills).

stem from an American aristocrat's Queen Victoria–like vision of herself, burdened by a responsibility to provide uplift for the masses she continually condescends to. Such people resent Polly's imperial approach. "Do-gooders," one old-timer hisses, throwing away his jar of calves' foot jelly.

Such people adore the bazaar, where class distinction is destroyed. All elements of society (save only Polly, alone in her mansion on the hill) engage in this American folk tradition. Here, Disney reveals a loose alliance of pantheism and socialism through the least likely of means: A performance of "America." Pollyanna and several other children, dressed in red, white, and blue, stand together, forming a living American flag. Onscreen, we see a symbol of Disney's bipolar America. The individual temporarily surrenders a sense of self for the community's greater good. Eagerly stepping up, iconoclastic Pollyanna stands in the wrong spot. Once adjusted, she then sings, Disney's camera cutting to close-ups at key moments for a visual emphasis that indicates his interpretation. "God shed His grace on thee" implies pantheism, spirituality existing in the natural world around us, if we only notice; "and crown Thy good with brotherhood" likewise emphasizes the importance of the fraternal social bond.

A traditional song has been effectively co-opted for progressive purposes, as Pollyanna pushes for Disney's vision of an American utopia. Walt's original conception for his Florida Epcot Center was to have been an actualization of such a dream for a progressive, perhaps (dare we hope?) perfect working and living community.[52] In this, Disney resembles the hippies who transformed a three-day rock festival into a makeshift utopia called Woodstock:

The rocker may become a rebel, but rarely a revolutionary. A revolutionary wants to capture the system he opposes and remake it in his own image [though for the rocker, the] point is not to capture but to avoid. The rocker objects to the City of the World, but he is already a citizen of another better city.[53]

In ancient times, that would have been Saint Augustine's City of God. For contemporary Americans, its secular alternative is Disneyland and/ or Walt Disney World.

The parks' creator, as their names make clear, is as willing to write celebratory "songs of myself" as Whitman. Disney theme parks are the progressive populist's notion of a perfect world—an incarnation of values rejected by key conservative thinkers, including Irving Babbitt, who scoffed that

various Utopists may come together as to what they wish to destroy, which is likely to include the whole existing social order; but what they wish to erect on the ruins of this order will be found not only in dreamland, but in different dreamlands.[54]

Likewise, Disney's "dreamland"—his ideal made real—was divided into Frontierland, Tomorrowland, Fantasyland, and Adventureland. Other *demi-mondes* would be added over the years to "the happiest place on earth." Disney is in tune with all aspects of society, from elderly conservatives to young rockers. For all Americans, the "most cherished goal [is] happiness."[55] There is no distinction, then, between the counterculture's realliance of interests into a new politics, best expressed by the Re-Flex Band when they hail "the politics of feelin' good," and the earlier vision of Walt Disney, as stated by his alter ego, Uncle Remus: "My, oh, my, what a wonderful day."

3 The Man Who Says "No"
Disney and the Rebel Hero

In satirizing raw aspects of capitalism, Disney firmly placed himself (however unconsciously) at the epicenter of a radical artistic movement. "American society," as Henry Steele Commager noted, "may have been

Copyright Walt Disney Productions; courtesy Buena Vista Releasing.

"BE ALWAYS SURE YOU'RE RIGHT, THEN GO AHEAD!" The character of David Crockett, portrayed by Fess Parker in five hour-long Disney TV installments (which were then reedited into two feature films), remained essentially true to the real-life prototype; what Disney emphasized, however, was Crockett's rebellious nature, those anti-Establishment attitudes that caused him to have more in common with such other mid-fifties pop icons as James Dean and Marlon Brando than with traditional western heroes like Roy Rogers and Gene Autry.

habituated to money standards, but it found few literary spokesmen to justify . . . business enterprise of the acquisitive society."[1] With the exceptions of certain popular writers (John Hay, Booth Tarkington) producing slick stories for glossy magazines and the Book-of-the-Month Club readership,

most authors portrayed an economic system disorderly and ruthless, wasteful and inhumane, unjust alike to workingmen, inventors, and consumers, politically corrupt and morally corrupting. This all but unanimous repudiation of the accepted economic order by its literary representatives is one of the curious phenomena of American culture. . . . Yet their findings did not correspond with those of . . . Hollywood producers . . . most of whom pictured a society that was prosperous, virtuous, harmonious, and contented.[2]

Most, but not all—Disney was the major exception. Like Frank Norris, Upton Sinclair, Theodore Dreiser, John Steinbeck, and other serious novelists, Disney—all but alone among Hollywood producers of the twentieth century's first half—dared attack the dark underside of our country's economic foundation. Better still, he did so in the guise of giddy popular entertainment. Disney's work resembled the legendary wolf in sheep's clothing. Those aforementioned muckraking writers, after all, preached mainly to the converted.

Still, it was not enough to merely attack the system in print or on film. Conversely, Disney had to also glorify that man who, in the words of Albert Camus, says "no," risking all by standing up to the culture of conformity. This "subversive tradition," with its underlying theme of rebellion, "is a fundamental one—perhaps *the* fundamental one— in American literature" (emphasis added).[3] Nonetheless, it was, during the century's early years, confined largely to the finest (if not always most widely read) literary works. Tinseltown, for the time being, mainly served to comfort what H. L. Mencken dismissed as the great American unwashed with colorful cinematic confections.

Until, that is, the first stirrings of a counterculture. Late-sixties films—*Wild Angels* (1966), *Bonnie and Clyde* (1967), *Easy Rider* (1969), *The Wild Bunch* (1969), even the lighthearted *Butch Cassidy and the Sundance Kid* (1969)—glorified social bandits, as one might expect from movies of so turbulent a time. In fact, such themes were initiated during the fifties, that drab era in which the man in a gray flannel suit reigned as our primary popular social icon, a genial former general and golfing aficionado, the easygoing president. But this was also the era of Marlon Brando in a black leather jacket on a motorcycle in *The Wild One* (1954),

James Dean in red windbreaker behind the wheel of a hot rod in *Rebel without a Cause* (1955). The rebellion that would explode volcano-like one decade later actively bubbled in the fifties. Nowhere were its implications more clear than in Disney films.

REIMAGINING THE GREEN MAN

THE STORY OF ROBIN HOOD AND HIS MERRIE MEN (1952)

Originally, Disney's decision to shoot in England was dictated by financial necessity. He and his distribution company, RKO, discovered that their profits from films released in the United Kingdom had been frozen in pounds, which could be spent only in the British Isles.[4] Why not take advantage of castles and countryside by making movies there, spending that money to hire local talent? Once this decision was made, Disney as always forsook arbitrary choice of projects. *All* the British films glorify social bandits involved in revolutionary activity against an existing power structure based on the rawest form of capitalism. A decade later, the children who had seen them—now teenagers and young adults— would put Disney's attitudes on rebellion, though portrayed in the safe context of period pieces, into contemporary action.

The live-action *Robin Hood* opens with Disney's characteristic dual narrative device. Employed in tandem are the two essential elements of cinematic storytelling, sight and sound. As we see an old storybook open, we simultaneously hear a wandering troubadour warble a folk ballad about the same subject. In this manner, the formal (upper-class) literary approach is fused with the informal (working-class) ballad tradition. By beginning his film in such a manner (as he already had with *Pinocchio* and would soon do again with *Davy Crockett*), Disney suggests his true intention: Make films that played not to one segment of the audience (thereby dividing us), but to the public at large (thereby bringing us together by crossing all class barriers).

This stylistic decision mirrors the content. In Disney's unique reading, the romance of Robin and Marian represents a marriage of blue-collar lad and woman of privileged background. Their victory over all odds advances the notion of the necessity for idealistic youth to rebel against restrictive notions of class. In this, Disney presaged "a cultural phenomenon of the late sixties which writer Tom Wolfe tagged 'radical chic': a desire on the part of the upper classes to identify with what they imagined to be the exotic, more vital lifestyle of the lower classes."[5] By film's end, aristocratic Maid Marian joins the outlaw gang, entirely composed, in Disney's version, of working-class men.

Allan-a-Dale, so often eliminated from film versions (he does not appear in Warner Brothers' 1938 epic incarnation starring Errol Flynn, directed by Michael Curtiz), is here (as played by Elton Haytes) central to the story. For he immortalizes the hero's acts of rebellion even as they occur. The balladeer functions on another level—a period-piece projection of Bob Dylan, Donovan, and all the other shaggy-dog practitioners of walking-talking blues whose anticommercial, anti-Establishment guitar strumming would in time provide a perfect accompaniment to the mid-1960s antisocial activities of Abbie Hoffman and other prominent figures of the counterculture. In Disney films, as in the unique lifestyle of the short-lived Woodstock Nation, music does not merely provide background to action, but serves as a meaningful conduit of all that occurs.

For hippies, music drove as well as reflected their new politics. Bob Dylan would write and sing of an American variation on Robin Hood:

John Wesley Hardin was a friend
To the poor.
He traveled with a gun
In every hand.
But he was never known to
Harm an honest man.

Dylan's words might have been unconsciously drawn from those heard in his own moviegoing youth, as sung by Allan-a-Dale in Disney's film:

Long did he fight,
For the right,
And so, I pray,
May *you!*

By "right," Allan clearly means, as the movie will establish, the *left*. This direct address to the audience establishes Disney's desire: His *Robin Hood* serves as a call to arms. We, like the film's hero, ought to rebel, at least when the social situation warrants militant action. That, of course, is when capitalism has been so corrupted that the working man is no longer able to survive.

The film opens in 1190, as King Richard I (Patrick Barr) passes through Nottingham on his way to the Crusades. Immediately, we meet two middle-aged (and decent) men: the upper-class Earl of Huntingdon

(Clement McCallin), an enlightened capitalist and idealist who plans to travel with the king, and working-class Hugh Fitzooth (Reginald Tate), a realist who opts to remain home, caring for his immediate concerns. The realists, in Disney's take on life, are by far the wiser of the two. Richard's departing on a holy war, and the decision of the good sheriff to join him, leave the countryside in the corrupt hands of Prince John (Hubert Gregg), as well as John's own cruel appointee for the sheriff's position (Peter Finch).

Then we meet the film's notably youthful heroes. Maid Marian (Joan Rice) is accompanied by a nurse, Tyb (Louise Hampton), a lovable meddler who recalls the similar character in *Romeo and Juliet* (1596). Her name here is apparently intended to recall that play, in which Shakespeare's unnamed nurse mentions more than once that she is best friends with one of the Capulets, Tybalt. Unlike that comic bawd of a nurse, however, this one is traditional and serious. Likewise, instead of the prim and proper Juliet, Disney's Marian is anything but a typical image of the perfect late-feudal, early Renaissance woman, as incarnated by Olivia de Havilland in the Curtiz *Robin Hood*—always quietly obedient to elders, particularly men. Disney's Marian is a dungaree doll living eight centuries before denim was invented, a teenage rebel and a Romantic one in *every* sense of the term. She slips away from the castle, and all those civilized values it symbolizes, into the woods. Once there, she surrenders to pagan impulses, with no criticism—stated or implied—from the film's author.

Early in the film, Marian teases youthful Rob Fitzooth (Richard Todd), a charming commoner. Such a situation offers a sharp contrast to the 1938 film, in which Robin is introduced as Lord of Locksley Hall. The aristocratic approach to the character, so prevalent in previous Robin Hood movies, would not have served Disney's political agenda. Playfully causing Robin to miss his mark at archery, Disney's Marian rolls about with him on the ground, revealing a great deal of leg and garter, wrestling with the man who, later, will openly be referred to by other characters as her "lover." As always in Disney, the woman proves to be the initiator of sexual contact. This, much to the chagrin of her nurse. Tyb discovers the two entangled on the ground (Marian clearly in charge) and begs the girl to return and bid her father farewell before he leaves with Richard. Marian's rebellious values are shared, in a positive portrayal, by the film's other key female, elderly Eleanor of Aquitaine (Martita Hunt). Upon realizing that her own son John rules England in a corrupt manner, the good protofeminist queen sides with the revolutionaries, aiding and abetting their plans (in Disney's version) for a violent overthrow of her own government.

That would not be necessary, were Richard still around. Before departing, Disney's incarnation of the Lionheart insists: "The strength of England resides in the well-being of our *humblest peasant!*" Any revolution against such a wise leader (though a born aristocrat, Disney's Richard reveals himself as democratic, fully appreciating the common man) truly would be revolution for the hell of it, and Disney will, in fact, have none of that. His rebels always have a social purpose, which would also prove true for most national leaders of the sixties counterculture. Though the concept provided Abbie Hoffman with a title for his best-known book, such thinking was rejected by almost all the era's icons, including—truth be told—Hoffman himself. "There are two types of laws: just and unjust," Martin Luther King wrote in his rightly famed 1963 letter from a Birmingham jail. "One has not only a legal but a moral responsibility to obey just laws. Conversely, one has a moral responsibility to disobey unjust laws."[6] Months later, Mario Savio, leader of the Free Speech Movement at Berkeley, offered a similar assessment:

If you accept that societies can be run by rules, as I do, then you necessarily accept as a consequence that you can't disobey the rules every time you disapprove.... However, when you're considering something that constitutes an extreme abridgement of your rights, conscience is the court of last resort.... In our society, precisely because of the great distortions and injustices which exist, I would hope that civil disobedience becomes more prevalent than it is.[7]

Robin Hood reveals this was Walt's theory, an attitude consistent with his whole body of work.

No sooner has Richard departed than John and the sheriff raise taxes and enforce trespass laws, preventing the lowest class of citizenry from hunting deer. Initially, Robin is less radicalized by such events than his father, who here splits the arrow at the archery tournament. Ordinarily, that action is assigned to Robin, more often than not toward the end of any film variation on the Robin Hood legend. Disney's alternative approach allows for a dose of the wisdom that enlightened adults—a rebellious working-class cognoscenti—share with impressionable children in Disney films.

After Robin hits the bull's-eye and apologizes to his father for denying him a chance to win, Hugh replies: "No man is beaten till he admits it!" Hugh Fitzooth then splits Robin's arrow, first teaching the boy

THE YOUNG AND THE RESTLESS. Most film adaptations of the Locksley legend, including Michael Curtiz's famed 1938 Warner Brothers production, portray the love of Robin and Marian in the stiff, formal, papier-mâché historical manner; in Disney's 1952 version, Robin (Richard Todd) and Marian (Joan Rice) are everyday (and surprisingly contemporary) oversexed teenagers who sport in the forest until a grumpy adult arrives to break up their charming tryst.

a moral lesson by practicing what he preaches, then magnanimously choosing to share his prize with the lad. Here we see the Generation Gap successfully bridged when adults maintain the values of their early years—mentally, emotionally, and spiritually remaining forever young.

Such a refusal to admit defeat had already been presented as the essence of Disney's moral vision, in the "stick-to-it-ivity" animated sequence in *So Dear to My Heart*. Just as significant, youth does not rebel against adults when they are clearly in the right. Robin adores his father, whose wearing of the green and living in the woods, far from corrupt civilization, makes clear that this older man's primal sympathy remains intact. What radicalizes Robin is the murder of his father by the sheriff's men, after Hugh has made his rebellious nature known to the Establishment. When the sheriff offers Hugh a position among his posse, Hugh replies: "You'll not tempt me to raise my bow against my neighbor." Truly a man of the people, he cannot be corrupted by money, so dedicated is the film's Hugh Fitzooth to working-class solidarity.

Ambushed by corrupt forces of authority, Hugh dies in Robin's arms, the youth then heading into the forest. Once there, he transforms into a combination of that legendary English figure, the Green Man, and Rousseau's natural man—as such, a role model for the impressionable young audience. As the wandering balladeer puts it:

> Robin, who was called Fitzooth,
> Is living in the woode.
> His coat is changed to Lincoln green,
> His name to Robin Hood.

The sheriff, a capitalist in the rawest sense, believes money will and must corrupt the populace.

> With 40 marks on his head,
> His best friend will turn him in.

No one does. One poor farmer, beaten in front of his family as their humble home is confiscated in lieu of taxes, is promised leniency if he will disclose Robin's whereabouts. He spits on the sheriff's man, knowing full well that he and his family will suffer terribly.

The film's full title reveals Disney's communal values, rather than (as is the case in other Robin Hood movies) an emphasis on the title character as primary hero and rugged individualist. Conversely, the sheriff's men anticipate the description which Eldridge Cleaver would, in 1968, employ to describe those authority figures who entered ghetto neighborhoods: "The police department functions like an occupying army in the black community, and it intimidates black people."[8] Disney's Robin has more in common with Kirk Douglas as the title character in Stanley Kubrick's *Spartacus* (1960) than with Charlton Heston in Anthony Mann's *El Cid* (1961). In the latter, the common men are helpless without their pro-Establishment leader and must have him to follow even after he is dead if they are to function. In the former, each and every one of the rebel band can rightly claim, "I am Spartacus!", their anti-Establishment champion. The difference is between an elitist-imperialist vision and a progressive-populist one. Disney's film is identical in vision to Douglas's and, like it, opposes the worldview expressed by Heston.

Music, in Disney, serves as the means by which people can communicate with one another in a more basic, honest, and direct manner than spoken language, too often used in dishonest ways by dishonest people. So Disney here offered a characteristic addition to Robin Hood lore: the memorably delightful "singing arrows," by which members of the band send messages to one another. All the expected sequences are included, if in the context of an original structuring of the story. Robin's duel with Little John (James Robertson Justice) upon a log over a river; Rob's friendly enmity with Friar Tuck (James Hayter), as they force each other to provide piggyback rides across yet another river. Here, though, all such moments eventually culminate in a far more politicized vision than even the 1930s version, in which the working people carried hammers and sickles into Sherwood.

In the Disney version, the sheriff refers to the Merrie Men not as "outlaws" (as in other Robin Hood movies) but as "rebels," Disney lionizing such anti-authoritarian behavior. As Allan-a-Dale gleefully puts it:

He robs the rich to aid the poor,
A most unusual practice.
But now that he has been outlawed,
He *needn't* pay his *taxes!*

As in old folk tales and ancient ballads, the sheriff is at one point captured, blindfolded, and brought into the green wood. Once there, he is forced to join the Merrie Men at dinner and drink a toast to absent King Richard. In Disney's version, though, the sequence takes a radical turn not present in any other version. Unmasked, the sheriff encounters not the gaily dressed outlaw band of Curtiz's film but the dregs of society, including Red Gill (Archie Duncan), still scarred from the torture he received at the sheriff's hands. A point-of-view shot, forcing us to see the gang as the sheriff perceives them, reveals anything but a whitewashed incarnation. Rather, these are working-class people who have been pushed to, then beyond, the limit.

Or, as mid-sixties radical James Farmer put it:

The nonviolent militants, seeking to mount a revolutionary force . . . need those folk who are not yet wedded to nonviolence, who are wedded, indeed, only to their own fierce indignation. They need them from the pool halls and taverns as well as from churches, from the unemployed and alienated and the rootless.[9]

This statement, issued in 1964, predated the violence that would overtake the civil rights and antiwar movements only a few years later. Similarly, at this point in Disney's *Robin Hood*, the gang has avoided killing anyone, though that will shortly change.

In 1968, Roy Innis replaced Floyd McKissick as national director of CORE. Extremely militant, Innis ushered in an era of the "young turks." At this point, the movement "began to turn away from the concept of nonviolence and to consider seriously the idea of armed struggle."[10] With the birth of a new militancy, the "Mississippi Summer Project was almost *calculated* to produce violent confrontation."[11] As James Forman recalled in 1972, "There was never any doubt that I was psychologically prepared to kill my oppressor by whatever means I had."[12] Likewise, Disney's rebel band turns to violence only after Maid Marian is imprisoned, at which point they kill people (including the sheriff) without remorse in order to save her.

Significantly, the onetime child of privilege had run away from the castle, joining Robin in the green wood, exchanging her silk and satin civilized clothing for the rough linsey-woolsey sheath of the common people. Her outer garments clearly reveal an inner change. As much the center of activity as Robin himself (in previous versions, Maid Marian is merely a decorative addition), she informs the rebels that King Richard is now being held prisoner in Austria. Immediately, all the gang members produce their individual holdings of money and stolen jewels, throwing them into a single sack for the common good. Like the small-town people who similarly toss their coins into a communal pool for the sake of James Stewart in Frank Capra's *It's a Wonderful Life*, they care little about personal riches, preferring to enrich their country by helping to return the rightful king.

It is here that Richard, having returned largely due to their efforts, confronts the outlaws. The sequence ends the story in a way only Disney could have conceived. First, with Marian not present, Richard informs Robin he will henceforth be the Lord of Locksley Hall; the working-class man has attained position after proving his value in open acts of violent rebellion. Aristocracy, in Walt's films, is something that must be earned through hard work, in this particular case the unique labors of the rebel as enlightened bandit.

Then, Marian—informed that she, as a noblewoman, must marry the Lord of Locksley—proves her budding feminist sensibility by standing up to her king. Refusing to marry in the old style, Disney's Marian makes clear that she too is a Romantic rebel, as well as a singularly individualistic woman who will marry only for love. Finally, Richard reveals to her Robin's ennoblement, and so Marian has no objection to such a match. She, Disney's ideal woman, believes in an aristocracy, so long as it is an aristocracy based on achievement, not the old aristocracy of birth and/or class. Robin, Disney's role model, has won acceptance in society by attacking authority at its most corrupt.

A SMALL WORLD, AFTER ALL

ROB ROY, THE HIGHLAND ROGUE (1954)

Rob Roy is not an adaptation of Walter Scott's 1817 tome but an entirely original work. Disney blended historical research on Scotland's Mac-Gregor clan with his own ongoing interest in discovering historical justifications for violent revolt. As to why this particular story, long neglected, had been chosen, Walt made that clear in his introduction to the TV screening (October 3 and 10, 1956): "A great love of *liberty* and *beauty*" was, in his view, the quality that most characterized the Scottish rebels. Two fundamental ideals in Romantic thinking, such values coalesced with Roy's "Robin Hood–like exploits." Disney could hardly resist reviving the legend of a folk hero all but forgotten except in Edinburgh's annual festivals. The social outlaw was clearly becoming Disney's stock-in-trade. "English history," he explained with a wry smile before *Rob Roy* rolled, "tells us he was a *rogue;* the Scots tell us he was a *hero!*" One man's terrorist is, simply, another's freedom fighter.

The film's scrolling-text prologue informs us that "the flicker of rebellion" was lit when, in the seventeenth century, proud Scots became infuriated upon learning that England would be ruled by German-born George I, rather than their own beloved James Stuart. They reacted, we are told, by "throwing down bagpipes, pulling out swords," leading to a bloody protest that Disney's film supports. The opening sequence depicts a pitched battle between uniformed English troops, marching in perfect formation, and Rob Roy's Bluebonnets, leaping from hiding with a fervor worthy of Che Guevara's 1960s militants.

"The price of rebellion, MacGregor," the opposing commander sighs to Rob Roy when he is captured. This is not an Englishman, though, rather a fellow Scot. Indeed, one who is related to Rob (on his mother's side) by marriage: the Duke of Argyll (James Robertson Justice). Rather than portray him as a traitor to the cause (precisely how the admirable but limited Rob perceives Argyll), Disney reveals the legitimacy of this man's approach. Argyll believes that Scottish resistance to German George is largely prejudiced, something Disney consistently criticizes. Given a chance, nonviolent compromise can be achieved. "I'm fighting for Scotland, too," he confides at one point, "but in a different way."

The villain of Disney's piece is not Argyll or (as might be expected) an Englishman, but yet another Scotsman, the Duke of Montrose (Michael Gough). This simpering social climber covets the decent Argyll's position as Secretary of State for Scottish Affairs. Montrose would like to deal directly with England, though not, like Argyll, for Scotland's good, but his own. It is the political opportunist, not the English, who emerges as the heavy in this socially, politically, and morally complex version.

In keeping with Disney's ongoing vision, it's not surprising that Montrose aspires to "class" (he affects English styles in clothing and wigs). On the other hand, Argyll—of the Campbell clan—is as rugged as Rob himself. A self-serving raw capitalist, Montrose—through his agent, still another Scotsman, Killearn (Geoffrey Keen)—imposes a vicious tax policy. The now-peaceful crofters will repeatedly have their taxes doubled until someone breaks, revealing the whereabouts of Rob. As in *Robin Hood*, though, those who administer such policies are mistaken in their judgment about simple folk, for there is no Judas among them. The approach backfires, causing violent rebellion to begin again, as Rob and his men lay siege to the British outpost at Inverness, while Argyll hurries to London in hope of yet achieving a peaceful settlement.

Shortly, we meet Rob's mother, Margaret Campbell MacGregor (Jean Taylor-Smith), yet another of Disney's strong and significant older women. Upon learning that her son is a prisoner and will be spirited away for eventual execution, she announces with a wink: "He's not hanged yet." It is she who makes the escape plans that Rob's loyal followers pursue in their risky but successful attempt to save him. Also met early on is young Helen Mary (Glynis Johns), whom Rob will court and marry. She, like her older counterpart, is as courageous as the men when need be. At one point, as soldiers attempt to arrest Rob again, she fights beside him, as an equal partner—anything but a trophy wife despite her notable beauty.

In addition to incipient feminism, *Rob Roy* features a sense of reflexivity that predates the depiction of social outlaws in Woodstock-era films, particularly Arthur Penn's *Bonnie and Clyde* (1967). This becomes most obvious in that sequence during which the title characters peruse their own considerable press coverage. As Argyll, hoping to achieve amnesty for Rob, reaches London, he discovers the city in the throes of a Rob Roy craze. The streets teem with people of all classes purchasing penny-dreadful novels about "the good badman." In particular, Danel Defoe's paperback *The Highland Rogue* captures the interest of an Austrian countess (Ina de la Haye), current consort to the king (Eric Pohlmann).

This romanticized version, however fanciful, is naïvely accepted by George as the final word on the subject. When Argyll arrives, the countess—though the king's mistress, she is presented here with great respect—is able to translate (Disney's recurring theme of communication between people of like heart over divisive language barriers) between Argyll and the king. Yet another strong and positive woman, the wise countess subtly creates an understanding between the two seemingly irreconcilable men, as well as a desire on the king's part to meet the Romantic rebel.

This occurs to the chagrin of Prime Minister Robert Walpole (Michael Goodliffe) and General Cadogan (Martin Boddey). Their haggling over the war presages high-level meetings on Vietnam, when the Pentagon begged for more soldiers while officials worried about the national budget:

GENERAL CADOGAN: All you can think about, Walpole, is money, money, *money.*
ROBERT WALPOLE: I'll never mention it again if you'll show me the way to get along without it.

"I give you back your sword, and your *name,*" his majesty informs Rob when the fighting is finally done. Personal identity is significant and can only be achieved through communication; national chauvinism, here as always in Disney, stands as a wall that must be demolished. Any talk about a Stuart king is long forgotten once Rob Roy and King George achieve a sense of each other's fundamental human decency. German,

English, and Scot—all the positive characters representing those varied ethnic groups—come together in a loose confederation, respecting each other's uniqueness owing to the achievement of a common chord.

It's a small world, after all.

DISOBEYING ORDERS AG'IN

DAVY CROCKETT, KING OF THE WILD FRONTIER (1955)

Pop-culture critics have largely written off the great Davy Crockett "craze" of 1954–1955 as the last hurrah for old-fashioned American values, a final solid hero in the Hopalong Cassidy tradition of a few years earlier—i.e., a true American whom kids could root for with full parental blessing. According to this line of thinking, something incalculable then happened. Those Crockett fans did a sudden turnaround, embracing Elvis Presley as their new icon by mid-1956, much to the chagrin of their elders. Yet close analysis of the *Crockett* TV episodes and subsequent film version belies that notion. Davy, or at least Disney's incarnation of him, offered a clear predecessor to the rebel heroes of the late fifties. Overlooked in most all discussion of the Crockett series, then and now, are Davy's anti-authoritarian attitudes. These often take the form of outright contempt for Establishment figures whom, if the conventional mentality of family-oriented western heroes were present, he would be expected to respect.

In 1813, moments after arriving in Andrew Jackson's encampment, Davy (Fess Parker), like his historical counterpart, disobeys orders, crossing the river into Indian country to hunt game for the starving soldiers. Davy's commanding officer, the fictional Major Norton (William Blakewell), follows with a dictate from General Andrew Jackson (Basil Ruysdael) to bring Crockett back. When Norton loudly interrupts Crockett's attempt to "grin down a b'ar," Davy upbraids the uniformed officer in front of his troops, who gaze on in disbelief. None of them would dare speak this way to the arrogant symbol of authority, though in secret all would like to do as Davy does.

This is but the first of many such transgressions. When winter comes, Crockett and his volunteers desert the camp, crossing over a bridge (despite soldiers who point a cannon at them to halt the leave-taking), and head home to tend to their families before winter. Personal commitment, particularly to family, takes precedence over public responsibility in all Disney films. "If he's allowed to leave," Norton complains to Jackson, "it will destroy the discipline of the whole camp." The destruction

THE REBEL IS THE MAN WHO SAYS "NO!" Disney's incarnation of the historical Crockett (Fess Parker) embodies Camus's notion of the rebel as hero; in this scene from the 1955 western, Davy—role model for a generation of impressionable children—gleefully disobeys the orders of his military-martinet commanding officer (William Bakewell).

of such discipline is clearly held in high esteem by Davy and Disney, for Norton is contemptuously treated as an arrogant fop. Meanwhile, Davy's act of rebellion has a ripple effect. The soldiers then refuse to obey orders and to shoot their comrades down, as Norton orders them to do. Though the incident was drawn from Crockett's autobiography,[13] it plays in context like a similar incident in Eisenstein's *Potemkin* (1925); the marines aboard that fated battleship, when commanded by a pompous upper-class commander to fire on misused sailors who have turned rebellious, refuse to do so.

Eventually, Davy and Georgie (Buddy Ebsen) return for active duty in the Florida swamps, the Choctaws having fled there to hide with their Seminole cousins, fellow members of the greater Creek nation. At once, the frontiersmen volunteer to go scouting. Jackson has been called to New Orleans to fight the British; Norton—now in command—forbids any such action. "Guess we'll have to start disobeyin' orders again," the natural men casually inform him, leaving camp without another word.

Later, in Washington, D.C., when Norton (now an oily politician) orders Congressman Crockett to support President Jackson's corrupt plans for relocating peaceful Indians to the far West, to satisfy Jackson's raw capitalist backers, Davy responds even more intensely.

NORTON: Crockett, if you go in there and speak against President Jackson's bill, you're through in politics.

CROCKETT: Here's what I think of *your* kind of politics!

He punches Norton, suited symbol of Establishment corruption, committing political suicide. Then, of course, Crockett travels west to greater—and final—glory at the Alamo.

RADICAL MODERN YOUTH

THE LIBERTY STORY (ABC-TV; MAY 29, 1957)

JOHNNY TREMAIN (1957)

The justification of open and violent rebellion against unjust authority had, in the English films, served as an objective correlative for Disney's views. Now, though, the safety of such a distancing device was eliminated, and revolution played closer to home. Still, the period-piece approach would artistically shroud such a call to arms against intolerable situations, while ironically allowing Disney to express such incendiary material in the guise of patriotic jargon.

Esther Forbes's 1943 novel *Johnny Tremain* concerns the exploits of a fictional lad who becomes involved in the early years of the American Revolution. Such a book would prove well suited to Walt's purpose. His version was released on July 4, 1957, suggesting that what he offered here constituted a traditional flag-waver. The movie's release was preceded by an hour-long TV show explaining the reasons why Forbes's modern classic had then been chosen for Disneyfication.

In recent years, historians have explained the youth movement of the hippie era in general, antiwar activity in particular, by placing such situations in a historical context:

In the United States, student movements have a long history, going back to colonial times; student movements played a part in the American Revolution. . . . The student movements of the 1960s were, in one way, simply the reappearance of an age-old phenomenon.[14]

Disney predicted the demonstrations of the counterculture, in almost precisely those same words, before they occurred. He opened *The Liberty Story* by presenting scenes from his earlier *Robin Hood.* Now, Walt concentrated not on the romance and adventure that had made the earlier film a box-office success, but on selected moments that vividly expressed his political slant. Robin Hood, Disney insisted, "remains an inspiration to all men who love freedom," particularly those who object to "tax upon tax" levied by corrupt leaders like King John to "keep himself in power."

Images of downtrodden working men, circa 1050, finally pushed to the point of open rebellion, accompanied Disney's spoken commentary: "they stood together" in solidarity, thereby achieving through group effort "the rights of the individual." That line perfectly expressed Disney's view of a balanced America. Only by engaging in communal (Democratic) activity can we ensure the continuation of individual (Republican) rights. The Magna Carta, signed by King John, was offered by Disney as the prototype for our own Bill of Rights, providing the show's host with a perfect segue from the British backdrop to an American incarnation of necessary social discord.

"Even as we shoot down British soldiers," James Otis (Jeff York) shortly says in a clip from the forthcoming film, "we will be ensuring the rights of future generations of Englishmen." The patriot's words provide Disney with his justification of the fatal activity to come. His version of *Johnny Tremain* would not be anti-English, any more than his *Rob Roy* had been. Rather, Disney offered a defense of violence (if only and always as a last resort) against any system that denies basic human rights.

The necessity of not only mature adults, but also idealistic teenagers, to become personally involved in American revolutions, whether in the mid-1770s or the mid-1960s, is fully explained. "Liberty is for the *young*," Samuel Adams (Rusty Lane) confides to his fellow middle-aged men. The Boston Tea Party of 1773, depicted without commentary in the theatrical film, is in the TV special accompanied by a telling voice-over: "In fact, many of the participants were Harvard students," Walt intoned, chuckling. "A college boy is always ready for a prank, and to these 'merry pranksters,' this was the joke of the age!" Merry pranksters would be the term seized upon by the counterculture's own James Otis, Ken Kesey, to describe the young people with whom he traveled the country, making politicized mischief.

Likewise, Norman Mailer, the future Sam Adams of the hippie era, would contemplate those young people protesting in Chicago's streets during the Democratic National Convention of 1968 and note in a TV interview that "they are my street soldiers." Not surprisingly, then, Disney's version strips away much of the sentimental melodrama from

Forbes's story, in order to more clearly provide impressionable viewers with a case study in the making of a violent revolutionary. Johnny (Hal Stalmaster) undergoes an arc from a self-serving individual to a dedicated member of the radical community. The initially wholesome, easy-going teenager is last seen killing agents of the Establishment and doing so with great relish.

Still, the magnanimous Disney tacitly avoids any simplifications in his depiction of the occupying force. Admiral Montagu (Lumsden Hare) and General Gage (Ralph Clanton) are positively portrayed—the former in the first half, culminating in the Boston Tea Party, the latter in the second, chronicling Paul Revere's ride and the early battles at Lexington green and Concord bridge. Assigned the task of monitoring Boston's waterfront, Montagu maintains a sense of humor. Noticing that Rab Silsbee (Dick Beymer), one of the armed radical youth, carries his rifle sloppily, the genial British officer shows the teenager how to properly display a gun, thereby winning the lad's respect. Likewise, Gage secretly admits that he agrees with Lord Chatterton, who begged George III to end military occupation. Gage is nonetheless a soldier and must do his duty. Until combat becomes inevitable, though, Disney's Gage clings to hopes of a peaceful solution: "No blood has been shed by my command so far," he insists, "and no blood *will* be spilled!"

When the fighting begins, it is not one of Gage's men who initiates bloodshed. The true enemy—here, as in all Disney works—is the cold-blooded capitalist who aspires to outworn notions of "class." Such sentiments are symbolized by Jonathan Lyte (Sebastian Cabot), his values immediately expressed by the fact that he alone among the Bostonians on view keeps a black child in servitude. The lad must perform, in an exaggerated manner, demeaning gestures of respect toward his lordly owner. Johnny is (at this point) himself a budding capitalist. Though aware that his deceased mother was Lyte's sister, he never contacted Lyte because Johnny "wanted to make my own way in the world," planning to achieve this through hard work at his trade. When his hand is damaged while doing a job for, ironically, his uncle, this is no longer possible, so Johnny does what his mother commanded and approaches Lyte as a last resort. The rich, as signified by Lyte, prove less than charitable; in contrast, the poor silversmith (Will Wright) to whom Johnny was apprenticed offers to let him stay on. But Johnny—Walt's Johnny, if not Esther Forbes's literary incarnation—cannot accept charity. He turns down free bed and board in typical Disney fashion: "Not if I can't

THE MAKING OF A VIOLENT REVOLUTIONARY. In the 1960s, social critic James Forman would detail a series of experiences that transformed the nation's conventional youth into radicals willing to take on the Establishment; Disney's 1957 reinterpretation of Esther Forbes's historical novel *Johnny Tremain* presented the similar metamorphosis of two idealistic teenagers (Dick Beymer and Hal Stalmaster) into hardened killers, fighting for the cause of individual freedom.

earn it." When, after his infirmity keeps Johnny from winning a job, he desperately approaches Lyte with proof of his familial relationship (Jonathan Lyte Tremain owns a silver christening cup, inherited from his late mother, bearing the family crest), Lyte knowingly lies, telling a constable the boy stole it.

Lyte demands the death penalty for what he calls "an example of modern *radical* youth." Johnny, at the moment, is anything but, though that epithet well describes Rab, Johnny's foil early on. At their first meeting, before Johnny's accident, he happened on Rab printing the *Observer*, a journalistic voice of the Committee (the elder group of revolutionary thinkers) and the Sons of Liberty (the youth who put their ideology into action). The former parallel the Old Left of the 1930s; the latter anticipate the New Left of the 1960s. In particular (and in keeping with Disney's own view as expressed in earlier English films), it's the unfair tax laws that these patriots most object to. Despite Rab's attempts to win Johnny over to their cause, he will have none of it:

You can keep your politics. I'll stick to my trade and mind my own business.

Johnny is, at this point, an example of apathetic youth. He doesn't want to get involved, can't see how any of this affects him. The movie will chronicle his growing radicalization through experience.

Johnny's blithe attitude is soon challenged when he finds himself unjustly arrested. Rab brings Josiah Quincy (Whit Bissell), Dr. Joseph Warren (Walter Coy), and other patriots to Johnny's jail cell. There they explain that they will provide a lawyer. Johnny's moral education continues:

> JOHNNY: I can't *afford* a lawyer.
> QUINCY: Any innocent man can afford *me*.
> RAB: When we're *together*, we are *strong*.

Johnny's first lesson in solidarity makes a great impression on the boy. Once freed by a fair-minded magistrate, he realizes the system does work, though only when men of like mind communally insist on the rights of any person, however humble.

The bread of liberty is not baked by men alone. It must, in any Disney retelling, have women, as Johnny also learns. He would not be set free if Cilla (Luana Patten), teenage daughter of silversmith Lapham, didn't appear in court on his behalf. The magistrate is most impressed that she would speak out against her father's landlord. Cilla does the right thing, though her action could entail hardships for her family. This is but the beginning of Disney's inclusionary attitude toward women. Cilla joins the Sons of Liberty (in Disney's version, the group could more correctly be called the Sons *and Daughters* of Liberty), taking a job as barmaid so as to listen in on conversations between British officers, then regularly report to the Committee. Whenever the radical youth gather onscreen, we see women as well as men present.

For the time being, the young (and emotionally charged) rebels, like their more thoughtful adult counterparts, continue to work within the existing system. In so doing, they presage those college students who kept their hair short and clothes neat while campaigning for Eugene J. McCarthy in 1968, during the "Look Clean for Gene" period of guarded yet idealistic hopefulness. Only when McCarthy was denied any influence at the Democratic convention, his young followers among those openly beaten on the streets of Chicago by Mayor Richard Daley's police force along with the more radical Yippies, did youth turn violent. Which precisely describes what happens here, when teenage revolutionary street soldiers don Indian clothing (they look remarkably like the hippies of a decade later, renowned for their own Indian accoutrements) for the Boston Tea Party after mature rebels are unable to achieve a peaceful solution to the growing problems.

The sequence, as it plays out onscreen, directly anticipates a statement by James Farmer about the modern movement for human rights:

What happened . . . after Montgomery was a kind of wedding of two [social] forces . . . the means-oriented idealists of pacifistic turn of mind, for whom nonviolence was a total philosophy, a way of life, and the ends-oriented militants, the postwar angry young men who saw in direct action a weapon.[15]

True to his artistic vision as well as his own unconventional ideas, Disney needed to find an accurate historical object that would serve as the film's visual icon—some striking symbol for his ideas on both the need for revolution and the glories of nature. As the Romantic Rebellion had stressed the link between man (at his revolutionary best) and the green world around us, a perfect answer to that question arose: the concept of a Liberty Tree in downtown Boston. In Disney's dramatization of the Boston Tea Party, the young rebels have reverted to nature in the best sense—following their revolutionary instincts, yet not harming anyone aboard the ship. Now, they march (and sing, such activity always a positive venue of emotion in Disney films) as they circle the Liberty Tree, a single vestige of nature in the otherwise civilized city.

Director Robert Stevenson choreographed their movements so the group closely resembles the Scots in *Rob Roy*, leaving the church behind on the rebel hero's wedding night, preferring to return to primitive nature. Within the *Tremain* sequence, Disney crosscuts to Lyte and Montagu, watching the proceedings from the window of an expensive house. They serve as perfect foils for one another. Lyte is aghast, having planned to buy the tea at cut-rate prices, thereby making money by exploiting the idealists, whom he angrily curses as "radicals"; Montagu, an old "good soldier," delights in the action below, noting that "these 'Indians' seem to prefer principle to profit!"

Johnny himself, by this point released from jail, has joined in close company with Paul Revere (Walter Sande):

JOHNNY: You all helped me so much. I'd like to help you!

From then on, the onetime would-be capitalist never mentions a normal job again, in the sense of earning money for personal gain. All "work" is in the cause of the coming revolution, learning to ride a horse so he can assist Revere. That occurs when General Gage must send troops to Concord, confiscating the growing store of arms there, despite the insistence of revolutionary leaders that "free men will never give up the means to defend their liberties."

At this point, armed confrontation clearly becomes inevitable, and the ailing James Otis at last addresses the Committee, which he helped found. Otis here becomes Disney's spokesman, raising the film's key question: What justifies violence? Other Committee members suggest that the unfair taxes and unwanted presence of British soldiers are more than enough. Otis waves them away, insisting that these are only unpleasantries that could yet be tolerated. Johnny calls out, "The rights of Englishmen," and Otis's old eyes light up, delighted to realize that the voice of youth would intuitively come so close to his own way of thinking.

"But why stop with *Englishmen?*" Otis asks Johnny. Only in the fight for the rights of all men, including those yet unborn, can violence be tolerated. Then, the film's incarnation of the historical Otis predicts two coming revolutions:

The peoples of all the world; the peasants of France, the serfs of Russia!

This, at the height of the McCarthy era! Democracy and socialism, in Disney's view equally acceptable means of opposing authority. Bold words, considering the temper of the times during which Walt made this film, the blacklisting of filmmakers who dared express such views in their work still in full sway.

Disney's depiction of the early battles, while historically accurate, also serves his particular purpose. The revolutionaries lose at Lexington, when they fight the British in a civilized manner. Then, they win at North Bridge near Concord when resorting to Indian—*natural*—tactics of guerrilla warfare. These are the very strategies, one can note with due irony, with which the equally ragtag Vietcong would fight the immense invading American force to a standstill. As one sage long ago pointed out, those who do not learn from history are doomed to repeat it—if, in this case, from the other side of the fence.

Better still, we can learn from Disney's artistically rendered—and politically loaded—version of history. In the end, the defeated yet highly respected General Gage pays the rebels their greatest tribute: "We have been vanquished by an *idea*—a belief in human rights." Whether the real Gage would have said such a thing is doubtful; the Gage of Disney's artistic imagination could say nothing else.

ALL MY SONS

THE SCARECROW OF ROMNEY MARSH (1964)

According to Whibley, all Romantic thinking can be traced back to the serpent in the Garden of Eden, "because he was the first inciter to rebellion against law and order."[16] If that is true, then most all of Disney's heroes are embodiments of the serpent, including the title character of this period drama. Originally broadcast as a television serial (April 9, 16, and 23, 1964), released in Europe as a theatrical feature under the title *Dr. Syn*, the project marked Disney's return to the English-lensed rebel-hero films of the early 1950s. This time, however, Walt pushed the envelope further by having the title character, one more enlightened aristocrat who leads a working-class rebellion against his own class when the commoners are being taxed into poverty, be a man of the cloth. Again, like Eisenstein before him (and the famed Berrigan brothers to follow), Disney believed the proper role of the church was not to act as an arm of the Establishment, keeping the common folk subdued at a time of social upheaval, but to be an agent of what Lenin called the only righteous war: revolution.

"There comes a time," Dr. King wrote in his letter from a Birmingham jail, "when the cup of endurance runs over, and men are no longer willing to be plunged into the abyss of despair."[17] In this case, the inhabitants of England's southern coast, circa 1775, rally around Dr. Syn (Patrick McGoohan), who disguises himself as a scarecrow and rides wildly through the night. Syn's antagonists are General Pugh (Geoffrey Keen), sent to crush the insurgency by King George, and Squire John Banks (Michael Hordern), the leading local aristocrat (unenlightened, a raw capitalist), hoping to maintain good relations between his citizenry and Pugh's troops so as to further his own business interests.

In a parallel plot that provides romantic interest while allowing Disney to raise the Generation Gap issue, the elderly squire objects to the courting of his daughter by a young British officer. Though a decent, courageous fellow, he's rejected for being "too rebellious"—in the squire's mind, a negative attribute, though in Disney's, this is clearly a highly positive quality for youth to possess.

Indeed, the young man's very rebelliousness will shortly aid Dr. Syn's cause and help the squire, who ironically objects to it. The squire's son, it turns out, has deserted from the Royal Navy as a result of continuing battles of an imperialist leaning that he believes to be morally wrong. This episode was broadcast as a Sunday evening NBC family-hour program precisely when American soldiers were first attempting to deal with the equally dubious morality of our presence in Vietnam. The rejected officer rescues the squire's son, who otherwise would be hanged by that very general whom Squire John regularly wines and dines at his home.

Also spirited out of the country are several other draft dodgers who are sent by Dr. Syn to Canada, the very place where our own youth—likewise, draft dodgers and deserters—headed to avoid the war in Southeast Asia. Only when the current regime's corruptness hits home—when his own son finds himself in grave danger—does the squire finally wake up to the reality that a "my country, right or wrong!" mentality is in itself wrong. As always in Disney, family loyalty takes precedence over national chauvinism. To borrow from the title of an Arthur Miller play, the squire comes to recognize working-class kids, along with his own boy, as "all my sons."

Despite his advanced age, the squire turns away from Establishment thinking. He now supports the young rebels who protest what was once their beloved Motherland, but which has become a cold, heartless aggressor. In the final shot, the young lovers are reunited—with the newly enlightened squire's blessing. And, not surprisingly, the officer informs his bride-to-be that he plans to quit the military, which he had long planned on for his career, to find a more liberating way of life for their family.

Peace, he implies, is the answer. Peace and, as we can tell from the looks in their eyes, love.

4 Toward a New Politics

Disney and the Sixties Sensibility

WE KNOW THROUGH PAINFUL EXPERIENCE THAT FREEDOM IS NEVER
VOLUNTARILY GIVEN BY THE OPPRESSOR; IT MUST BE DEMANDED BY
THE OPPRESSED.
—Martin Luther King, "Letter from Birmingham Jail," 1963

WE WERE RESOLVED TO FIGHT. IT WAS A TIME WHEN WE OVERCAME
OUR OWN MIDDLE-CLASS TIMIDITY AND FEAR OF VIOLENCE.
—Columbia student Mark Rudd, 1969

In our popular mythology, the sixties began on an optimistic note, with
the election of a youthful president, the creation of the idealistically
named Peace Corps, and a firm belief that, thanks to the space program,

Copyright Walt Disney Productions; courtesy Buena Vista Releasing.

THE EGGHEAD AS HERO. During the 1950s, Americans had chosen genial general
Dwight Eisenhower as president over the more intellectual Adlai Stevenson; Disney, however, favored the smart and innovative iconoclast, as embodied by the aptly named
Brainard (Fred MacMurray) in *The Absent Minded Professor* (1961) and (pictured here) *Son
of Flubber* (1963).

an exciting new area had opened for us to explore and, in time, conquer. Then, with the assassination of John Kennedy in late November 1963, we learned Yeats had been right: The center could not hold; things fall apart. The constantly escalating war in Vietnam, violent ghetto burnings at home, the emergence of an ever-expanding hard-drug culture, a rash of assassinations (Dr. Martin Luther King and Senator Robert Kennedy killed within weeks of one another in 1968) all attested to a darkening of our society, unimaginable during the decade's innocent opening years. These and other events conspired to temporarily radicalize our country's youth, resulting in a counterculture that would culminate at Woodstock.

The truth, in fact, was considerably more complex. Though Students for a Democratic Society (SDS) is widely (if wrongly) believed to have been formed in the turbulent late sixties, the organization was created early in 1962 as "an outgrowth of a socialist organization known as the Student League for Industrial Democracy, which operated from 1905 to 1948."[1] Certainly, though, the SDS was a reimagined version of that organization, specifically created by and for the generation that had come of age during the 1950s:

The Baby Boom had created a huge population, and . . . postwar prosperity in the 1950s had allowed many of those Baby Boomers to grow up in a world of financial security. It was these secure Baby Boomers who began to enter college in the early 1960s, more than doubling the U.S. college population between 1960 and 1964.[2]

This was a generation composed of young adults who, in terms of popular entertainment, had been raised on Disney's films and TV shows. Also, and every bit as significant,

they comprised the first generation that was exposed, through television, to the evils of the world at large: racial segregation in the South, the Korean conflict overseas, strife and war all around the globe. They were also the first generation that grew up with the knowledge that the world could be destroyed by the atomic bomb.[3]

SDS, originally organized at the University of Michigan (a young Tom Hayden was one of its founders), made its values known in a series of agendas and concepts collectively referred to as the Port Huron policy statement:

We are people of this generation, bred in at least modern comfort, housed in universities, looking uncomfortably at the world we inherit. Our work is guided by the sense that we may be the last generation in the experiment with living. We ourselves are imbued with urgency.[4]

If nuclear war did not bring a swift end to the world, then contamination of the environment would likely achieve precisely that, if more slowly and painfully. It didn't sit well with such educated youth to learn multimillion-dollar companies like Dow, targeted by the growing number of activist students as a key polluter of America's environment and values, were financially married to the very universities these students attended. Generous "research grants" from megacorporations linked them with academia. Increasingly, then, young people came to realize that their schools were anything but sacrosanct ivory towers of unsullied intellectualism.

The SDS attitude, as it turned out, proved to be anything but an isolated aberration. Simultaneously, the Free Speech Movement arose among West Coast students. They had been taught as children by parents, schools, and churches that, as John Donne had put it, all's right with the world. They realized that things were, in fact, awry—our supposedly benign government and higher-education systems deeply involved with the dirtier aspects of everyday life. Perhaps surprisingly, the national leader who first warned us about the monolith he called "the military-industrial complex" had been an elderly Republican conservative. That phrase was coined by President Eisenhower on the eve of leaving office; nonetheless, it became a catchphrase of the Democrat-controlled decade's emerging youth.

The concept proved particularly keen for budding social radicals, informed that they could not openly practice what their university and government preached—i.e., free speech, something they'd been loudly doing on the sidewalks outside college buildings. Shortly, students found themselves arrested for expressing their values in public. One such concerned student named Mario Savio insisted:

In The Berkeley Ghetto . . . you question the mores and morals and institutions of society seriously. This creates a feeling of mutuality, of real community. Students are excited about political ideas. They're not yet inured to the apolitical society they're going to enter. But being interested in ideas means you have no use in American society . . . unless they are ideas which are useful in the military-industrial complex. That means there's no connection between what you're doing and the world you're about to enter.[5]

Essentially, "the student movements of the 1960s were . . . simply the reappearance of an age-old phenomenon. The difference was in the issues being raised, and in the size and intensity of the response."[6]

Hollywood, for the most part, chose to ignore the ticking of this social time bomb. The studios continued to provide the type of escapist fare that had been de rigueur in the fifties: John Wayne westerns, giddy comedies starring Rock Hudson and Doris Day. If Disney had been the exception to the rule during the Eisenhower era, he would now spearhead the transition toward a new American cinema first evidenced by Stanley Kubrick's *Dr. Strangelove* (1964), later solidified in 1967 with the simultaneous releases of *Bonnie and Clyde* and *The Graduate*.

HOW I LEARNED TO STOP WORRYING AND LOVE THE BUM

THE ABSENT MINDED PROFESSOR (1961)

SON OF FLUBBER (1963)

Romanticism, so despised by Irving Babbitt, is, as previously mentioned, characterized by a "reactionary spirit against whatever preceded it."[7] In this sense, those who accuse Disney of being a reactionary are correct. He did react against the contemporary equivalent of what British Romantics had, in the early 1800s, found offensive: England's Age of Reason. That period roughly paralleled our own Eisenhower era. Disney ruthlessly satirized its most offensive elements, lionizing those freethinkers who, following the 1952 defeat of presidential candidate Adlai Stevenson, were dismissed as "eggheads."

Such people are vividly depicted by Fred MacMurray as Ned Brainard, his last name a reference to the Democratic man of intellect abandoned by a middlebrow, middle-of-the-road populace. Brainard embodies Disney's preferred type of nonconformist, for he never affects the bulky black sweater and goatee of the Beat Generation. Ned's nonconformity, like that of all Disney protagonists, has less to do with appearance than reality.

Brainard doesn't drop out of society or commit outrageous acts of self-conscious rebellion. Indeed, he isn't even a rebel in his own mind, though he seems one to others. This is an individual who accepts himself as he is, operating as he must in the world. Never does he attempt to shock the straights. They are shocked, though, by the presence of a person who truly, if softly, treads his own lonely road, without being self-congratulatory about it. For Disney, individualism at its best occurs not with a purposeful pose but with a forceful frame of mind, coupled with an emotional state of well-being. As such an individual, Brainard emerges as another of Disney's key autobiographical figures—the genial eccentric and closet genius, character and author defined by naïveté, absentmindedness, determination, and (in an appealingly self-critical vein) occasional stupidity.[8]

The essence of the plot, what little there is: College prof Brainard accidentally creates flying rubber ("flubber"). A patriotic citizen, he plans to turn his discovery over to the powers-that-be. But when he calls Washington, Brainard is caught up in endless bureaucracy. Since flubber is unique, no one in authority can figure out whom Ned ought to deal with. Whether such a storyline qualifies Disney as liberal or conservative by our current standards is difficult to say. Clearly, though, Disney consistently scorned a sprawling, monolithic government in which concepts become so subdivided into specific niches that no one can conceive of the greater good. As the situation grows ever more absurdist, Brainard finds himself in a surreal conversation with someone at the Department of Agriculture, willing to help if the professor will first explain how flubber impacts farmers. Significantly,

this was not the last Disney film to poke fun at the government, which also came in for a ribbing in the sequel to this picture. Some have found a parallel between Brainard's rejection and runaround from the government and Disney's own career, in which he repeatedly had to do things on his own, without the support of others.[9]

Brainard, like Disney (and such other typically American filmmakers as Capra and Ford), embodies a pair of fast-fading icons: the late nineteenth century's liberal Republican and the early twentieth century's conservative Democrat. Disney forever champions the individualistic man of personal vision who, despite catcalls from the conformist crowd, eventually must stand alone.

Or, more correctly, *nearly* alone. Disney's heroes (like Capra's and Ford's) are always blessed with a woman of substantial character who stands by her man. Here, it's Betsy Carlisle (Nancy Olson), secretary to the president (Leon Ames) of Medfield College. The most eligible mature woman on campus, Betsy is pursued by a conventional fellow, Dr. Shelby Ashton (Elliott Reid). A symbol of shallow conformity, Shelby teaches at nearby Rutland, an Ivy League institution catering to the sons and daughters of the wealthy. Medfield, in contrast, is locally run; Brainard prefers to teach the common man's offspring. Shelby consistently appears nattily attired. Always, he says and does the conventionally right thing. Yet Betsy will not give in to Shelby's pleas to marry, even after Brainard stands her up at the altar for the third time. This is not intended as an insult. He's so involved with his latest project—at once creative and scientific, edgy in concept yet brimming with potential for the mainstream if only people will approach the idea with an open mind—that he forgets to show up for the wedding. No question that he loves Betsy as much as he can ever love any woman.

In truth, Ned Brainard loves his work more than anything. One wonders how closely this parallels the situation between Walt and his own wife, Lillian. In the film, Betsy becomes Ned's anchor in reality; he, her flight from conformity—in this case literally, riding high into the sky in his flubberized Model T, an antique car embellished by modern science. The vehicle proves a potent symbol, and one that all but defines the Disney vision in a single image, as the best of the past merged with a potentially wonderful future.

The film's impact would be muted if Brainard were sentimentalized, but Disney knows better than to slip into such maudlin characterization. While piloting his flying car, Ned becomes an overgrown boy, deriving mischievous pleasure by terrifying cows in the pasture below. Later, he harasses his competition for Betsy's hand, flying above Shelby's automobile. Brainard honks his horn and smashes his tires down on the other vehicle's roof, causing Shelby to crash into a police car. Disney's soft-spoken alter egos are anything but homogenized; always, there's a touch of the bad boy in them.

If Shelby serves as Ned's conformist foil, the outright villain is Hawk (Keenan Wynn), rawest of raw capitalists. His source of income makes clear that the money of the appropriately named Hawk is dirty: The Auld Lang Syne Finance Company repossesses refrigerators, cars, and the like from decent locals who have fallen upon hard times. What a marvelous contrast between our hero and Hawk, a supposedly "respectable" businessman who hires goons to procure the flubber secret. Hawk becomes so obsessed with money that he bets against Medfield when the basketball team plays Rutland, though his own son attends Medfield. Apparently, Bill Hawk (Tommy Kirk) is the only rich kid at the humble school, attending because his greedy father didn't want to splurge on an Ivy League education.

Now, Hawk is consumed with a great new dream: replacing the small town of Medfield entirely, in particular its charming Main Street and adjoining college, with a modern housing tract. If he succeeds, Medfield will become a Levittown, its appealingly individualistic homes replaced by little houses made of ticky-tacky, and they'll all look just the same. Upon learning of flubber, Hawk attempts to prevent Brainard from doing the decent thing and selflessly sharing flubber with his country. Hawk hopes to partner with Brainard and bring in as much money from flubber as possible. Though Brainard has nothing against money, he finds the notion of making money for its own sake offensive. Brainard created flubber not owing to a profit motive, but because he wanted to experiment. Similarly, Disney has said:

Money is something I understand only vaguely, and think about it only when I don't have enough to finance my current enthusiasm, whatever it may be. . . . I have little respect for money as such; I regard it merely as a medium for financing new ideas.[10]

Disney includes a finale that presages Stanley Kubrick's *Dr. Strangelove*, with its criticism of the military and the irresponsible use of nuclear weaponry. As Brainard and Betsy sweep over Washington, planning to deliver their discovery to the president, officers in charge of strategic defense offices assume the Model T to be an unidentified flying object. Shortly, missiles armed with nuclear warheads are pointing upward at harmless eccentrics. The black-and-white photography, previously characterized by the bland look of a TV sitcom, now takes a harshly lit documentary approach. Marked by low-key lighting, this is precisely the style Kubrick would assume two years later. Disney allows his broadly comic film to turn dark when a military man, ordered to fire on the count of ten, interrupts his commander to inform him the UFO has circled behind Congress:

COMMANDING OFFICER: Seven . . . eight . . .
MILITARY MAN: But, sir. Congress is in session. If we shoot, we may lose every single congressman!
COMMANDING OFFICER (grinning): . . . nine . . .

He relents only after learning he'll destroy a newly remodeled façade on the building.

The most telling reaction to the film came not from a cinema quarterly but *Variety*. That trade publication's reviewer noted:

Beneath the preposterous veneer lurks a comment on our time, a reflection of the plight of the average man haplessly confronted with the complexities of a jet age civilization burdened with fear, red-tape, official mumbo-jumbo and ambitious anxiety. Deeply rooted within the screenplay is a subtle protest against the detached, impersonal machinery of modern progress.[11]

Such an assessment, delivered on a tight deadline, deserves notice. Yet one might argue with a single word. Brainard is less the "average" man (that's Shelby, the conformist), more an embodiment of the last individualist, trapped in a Kafka-esque maze. Though a true man of the people, Brainard is exceptional. Still, he maintains the common touch, as when dancing at the gym with students, as no other professor will do. Ned is different, yet he doesn't make a big deal about it. He is the Disney hero, in yet another of his diverse guises, as well as the filmmaker's role model of what we all should aspire to be: self-determining, committed to community in all respects save only the surrendering of his highly individualized worldview. Most significant, he remains free from the myriad constraints of a conformist society that threaten to suffocate true, if eccentric, genius.

Though the sequel rates as a more conventional sitcom, there are moments of strong satire as well as an ongoing autobiographical subtext. In the opening, Brainard again descends on Washington, expecting to be treated with respect now that his invention's worth has finally been recognized. Instead, he receives a profound shock that tests his patriotism. At the Pentagon, Ned is denied the small advance needed to keep endangered Medfield College in operation. Though he is assured that "the money is as good as in the bank," his claim remains hopelessly tied up in red tape. "Remember," one official reminds him, "you're in Washington. Stop trying to be reasonable."

Meanwhile, the Internal Revenue Service insists that he immediately pay taxes on his estimated income. Our government's ability to all but destroy an offbeat American's loyalty had been a burr under Disney's personal saddle since 1941. Like other producers, he had eagerly volunteered his services for the war cause, producing training films for use within the military, including *High-Level Professional Bombing* and *The New Spirit*. The latter, filmed at the behest of the Treasury Department, encouraged citizens to financially support our efforts in Europe and in the Pacific. Then, in the person of Treasury Secretary Henry Morgenthau, the government whined about the choice of Donald Duck rather than Mickey Mouse for the lead. Congress refused to make the necessary appropriation for Disney to be paid the $80,000 he had spent making the film, threatening the studio with bankruptcy.[12] Though he chose not to cause a major scene, Disney finally found, more than two decades later, an artistic outlet for any residue of bitterness.

Raw capitalism threatens to corrupt even Betsy, at least momentarily. She falls under the spell of a fast-talking New York huckster (Ken Murray) who woos her with mink coats and strings of pearls. To receive such items, Betsy must convince her husband to turn over his latest invention to a Madison Avenue firm, for commercial exploitation. "Just once, couldn't we think about *ourselves?*" she sadly asks. However much Ned loves Betsy, he can't do it, though they are presently too destitute to pay the newspaper delivery boy. Though the Disneys always remained scrupulously private about their relationship, one wonders if at some rough time Lillian might have asked that very question of Walt. The temptation in the film (and, perhaps, real life) proves only temporary. When the chips are down, Betsy—echoing the wife of Dr. Thomas Stockman in Ibsen's *Enemy of the People*—stands by Ned and his ideals.

That hardly makes the situation easier for the eccentric genius. At one point, Ned—like numerous other Disney characters—grows so hungry that, despite status and reputation, he's reduced to stealing food, in this case from a neighborhood Halloween party.

SCENES FROM THE CLASS STRUGGLE IN BEVERLY HILLS

IN SEARCH OF THE CASTAWAYS (1962)

In Search of the Castaways inverts the male/female roles from *Lady and the Tramp*'s class struggle. This film might have been subtitled *The Gentleman and the Street Urchin*. The sincere pauper is Mary Grant (Hayley Mills), destitute daughter of a ship's captain lost at sea, circa 1858. The rich youth is John (Michael Anderson, Jr.), whose wealthy father, Lord Glenarvan (Wilfred Hyde-White), owned the missing boat. The device that brings them together is a rescue note, found in a bottle by Gallic geographer Paganel (Maurice Chevalier). Believing it hails from a still-living Captain Grant, Paganel gathers up Grant's "orphans," Mary and her little brother Robert (Keith Hamshire). The three journey to Glasgow, hoping to persuade Lord Glenarvan to search for their father (Jack Gwillim).

Though based on a Jules Verne fantasy, the film's opening recalls Dickens's vivid images of starving children. The shabbily dressed trio arrive at Glenarvan's yacht at evening time, only to find an elaborate party in full progress. They are restrained from entering by a guard (Ronald Fraser), himself lower-class Cockney, now in the employ of the rich. Corrupted by his weekly paycheck, he's grown insensitive to members of his own class and is far ruder to the paupers than any of the aristocrats are. Once the trio slip aboard, all thoughts of Captain Grant momentarily dissolve at the sight of a lavish buffet. The children crawl under a table, desperately reaching up for food; old Paganel loses control, eating everything in sight. Consistently, hunger underlines works in the Disney oeuvre, even as it does the novels of Hugo.

Eventually, Lord Glenarvan is convinced to embark on the mission by his son John, who is attracted to Mary. This film chronicles their difficult transformation into a couple, despite all class barriers that threaten to keep them separate. As for Glenarvan, he proves the most questionable of the film's heroes. A capitalist, he can reveal a greedy streak, complaining about how much the search costs. As a member of the Anglo upper class, he unintentionally condescends to friendly natives encountered along the way, whereas his pauper-companions treat such people with respect. While we laugh *with* the others, we often laugh *at* Glenarvan. As always, though, Disney is too evenhanded to suggest that such aristocrats are all bad. So we encounter Glenarvan's foil: Thomas Ayerton (George Sanders), the corrupt faux gentleman. Though he offers to help, Ayerton is actually the pirate who stranded Grant. Not surprisingly, Mary—Earth Mother in embryo, her very name suggesting spirituality—senses Ayerton's insincerity at first sight.

BACK TO THE BASICS

SUMMER MAGIC (1963)

For his highly personal adaptation of the Kate Douglas Wiggins timeworn chestnut *Mother Carey's Chickens,* Disney returned to his beloved turn-of-the-century setting. This film begins in despised Boston, where residents happily dance to the ragtime beat. Soon, though, their glee comes to seem superficial, for all such celebrants are oblivious to neighbors who have just lost everything. Following her husband's death, Margaret Carey (Dorothy McGuire) realizes she and her "chicks" must abandon their luxurious home, selling every object of value. A trusted family friend—one more corrupt capitalist, motivated by self-interest—sold the late father a portfolio of worthless mining stocks. Mrs. Carey descends in a single day from reigning queen of her *demi-monde* to its lowliest pauper in a swift, even tragic, fall from worldly grace. Out of sheer desperation, the family heads for a small Maine village, Beulah, which shortly will prove a biblical land of salvation. Financial concerns are not important here. Osh Popham (Burl Ives), local postmaster and county executive, fudges official records so the Careys can rent a large old vacant house. Though what he does is technically illegal, Disney's context suggests that it is the right—"good"—thing.

THE FIRST HIPPIE COMMUNE. Predating Arlo Guthrie and "Alice's Restaurant" by half a decade, Disney presented the first onscreen image of a "We Are Family"–style makeshift community, living close to nature, in *Summer Magic* (1963); an Old Left folksinger (Burl Ives, second from right) and a young British "bird" (Hayley Mills, far right) teach the joys of sweet soul guitar playing to various refugees from the big city.

Osh does the needed repairs, insisting:

You can forget all about the money. When we're all done, we can work that out.

All he wants is to be part of their rapidly expanding community of family and friends. Soon, everyone contributes what he has to the common good, supporting each other spiritually and financially.

They eventually constitute a working commune, of the type Arlo Guthrie would five years later immortalize in his "Alice's Restaurant" recording, brought to the screen by Arthur Penn in a 1969 film. Margaret is Disney's Alice, an Earth Mother who, with her hippie-ish (and incongruously British-accented) daughter Nancy (Hayley Mills), encourages others to leave cynical civilization and move back to the basics. Not that Disney offers an idealized pastoral. Everyone works here, and works hard, as if living out the Marxist/Leninist vision of true happiness. Margaret's younger son, Peter (Jimmy Mathers), complains about not having a job of his own, then goes out and finds one. Nor are all country people necessarily free of corruption. For foils, Osh has a nosey, money-coveting wife (Una Merkel) and a lazy son (Michael J. Pollard, who would become a hippie-era icon as C. W. Moss in *Bonnie and Clyde*). He dreams of moving to the city, hoping for a larger paycheck with less work.

Once again, however, money is not necessarily portrayed as the root of evil. Young millionaire Tom Hamilton (Peter Brown), a world traveler (and true sophisticate), returns to town, attending one of the Careys' impromptu outdoor parties (a "happening," in sixties jargon). He's smitten with Nancy, as much owing to her protohippie-ish ways as her beauty. Under Nancy's natural influence, Tom uses his money for "good" purposes: sharing its practical value with the less fortunate, establishing him as one of Disney's enlightened rich.

A PARADIGM FOR THE SIXTIES

A TIGER WALKS (1964)

Tiger is a prediction of changes that would shortly tear through the fabric of society. As such, the film serves as Disney's paradigm for mainstream America's transition from conventional morality to countercultural values. No wonder, then, that one critic described this as "a very strange film, not the least because it paints a fantastically ugly portrait of small-town American life."[13] *Tiger* appears less "strange," however, when compared to the similar vision more subtly conveyed in earlier films. As Ward Kimball noted, after hearing someone crack that his boss's films had turned saccharine, Disney movies actually reveal "an indictment of mankind."[14]

This film opened in theaters the same week that the Beatles first appeared on *The Ed Sullivan Show*. The phenomenon that would come to be called the British Invasion is here presaged by Julie (Pamela Franklin), yet another child-woman, presumably American yet once again blessed with an incongruous English accent. She's accompanied by another long-haired youth played by Kevin Corcoran, here called Tom Hadley, suggesting a cross between Twain's Tom and Huck. They inhabit a crossroads village in the Pacific Northwest, employed as Disney's microcosm for America itself. The title creature arrives with Ram Singh (Sabu), a turbaned visitor from India. Ram embodies the Eastern spiritualism that would shortly influence the Woodstock generation, Maharishi Mahesh Yogi serving as guru to celebrities ranging from the Beatles to Mia Farrow.

The circus tiger escapes from its truck when Ram's coworker, Josef Pietz (Theodore Marcuse), stops to change tires. Baldpated Josef, who enjoys torturing big cats, serves as a forerunner to skinheads, emerging even as longhairs, along with their peace-and-love mentality, disappeared from the American scene. The townsfolk, seemingly incorruptible small-town types, prove to be incipient raw capitalists of the worst sort. Though they never before revealed a propensity for greed, that owed less to purity than lack of opportunity. Bob Evans (Doodles Weaver), local newspaperman, views the situation as his shot at getting a byline in the national press; hotel owner Mrs. Watkins (Una Merkel) raises the price of rooms upon realizing that media people will swarm in. In a sly bit of self-referencing, director Norman Tokar (with Walt's full backing) has this nasty woman gleefully hum "Zippa-dee-doo-da" with such regularity that the song becomes, in context, an ironic chorus. Her emphasis on "What a wonderful day!" (originally sung, on a more serious and less greedy note, by Uncle Remus in *Song of the South* as he enjoys the natural beauty around him) occurs whenever Mrs. Watkins makes money off some person's fear of being mauled by the frightened beast, itself a terrified creature that is likely to be shot dead at any moment.

Some townsmen, forming a posse, transform into a twentieth-century variation on the American community-at-large as depicted in the most liberal (and implicitly anti-American) postwar westerns. Initially, the group is as mindlessly self-righteous as the vigilantes in *The Ox-Bow Incident* (1943). Having found Josef's corpse, they panic, deserting sheriff Pete Williams (Brian Keith), thereafter becoming rugged individualists in the worst sense, like the townsfolk in *High Noon* (1952). Pete, Disney's combination of Henry Fonda in the former and Gary Cooper in the latter, faces a crisis of conscience. Adoring his daughter and his wife, Dorothy (Vera Miles), who deeply care for all animals, Pete hopes to find a way to bring the tiger back alive. Still, as a public servant up for reelection, he must survive in society. His (all-male) advisory committee insists that killing the tiger would endear Pete to the redneck populace, thus cinching his victory at the polls.

The film's ideology ripples, Capra-like, to the heart of darkness in American politics. The unnamed state's governor (Edward Andrews), oiliest of political animals, cares nothing about the safety of his citizens, much less the poor beast. He makes all decisions, particularly as to how involved he will become, by considering the polls and possible impact on his image. Nor do the media escape Disney's wrath. TV reporters purposefully misrepresent the situation, making the tiger seem more dan-

Copyright Walt Disney Productions; courtesy Buena Vista Releasing.

THE CHILDREN'S CRUSADE. In the late 1960s, young people from middle-class suburban communities would loudly protest in front of institutions that represented "the Old Politics," chanting against gun violence and in favor of animal rights; the 1964 Disney film *A Tiger Walks* was the prototype for all such future action and, perhaps, actually inspired it.

gerous than he is, beefing up the story to increase ratings. Shortly, the country's populace is glued to their TV sets, following with fascination the ongoing events in this out-of-the-way community. The situation recalls Billy Wilder's classic study in cynicism, *The Big Carnival/Ace in the Hole* (1951), as the locals here tremble behind locked doors less owing to any real threat than to a McLuhan-age media-created myth.

However inadvertently, though, the media also initiate the greening of America by inspiring a children's crusade. Disney provides a foreshadowing of the manner in which saturation coverage of the Vietnam War formed a global village, youth turning away from traditional politics to support peace candidate Eugene McCarthy. Eager to create instant celebrities, the film's reporters drag Julie before the cameras for a Warholian fifteen minutes. She speaks out in favor of animal rights, a cause unknown to the general public in 1964, now a lasting legacy of the sixties. Across the country, children mail in their change, hoping to help save the tiger. Many arrive at the governor's mansion (modeled on the

White House), marching up and down the street. Images of youth protesting against political leaders provide an uncanny glimpse of the shape of things to come within two years of this film's release. The reactionary governor, peering out the window at a growing army of radicalized kids, notes sneeringly that they're mostly under twenty-one.

"At least none of 'em are old enough to vote," one sleazy assistant (the governor is surrounded by forerunners of H. R. Haldeman, John Erlichman, and John Dean) notes. Hoping to appeal to his older constituency, the governor calls in the National Guard. This presents an even more frightening premonition. On the field, they panic and fire wildly, hitting an innocent bystander; this, six years before the deaths of four students, none particularly radical, at Kent State. No wonder Leonard Maltin notes that "much of this is pretty potent, not just for a Disney film, but on anyone's terms." [15] His praise once again is muted by a misconception revealed in the unfortunate use of that phrase "not just for a Disney film."

Disney's guarded optimism dominates the third act, when Pete must make his moral choice: Play to the lowest common denominator of American politics by killing the confused creature, or become truly enlightened in a way that would be championed by the hippies. Flanked by Julie, Tom, and Ram, Pete thumbs his nose at the authorities. The film ends as Pete, Julie, Tom, Ram, and Dorothy create, for the tiger and his family, something then innovative, if today considered (happily) the norm: a prototype of the modern zoo without bars or cages.

LONDON BRIDGE IS FALLING DOWN

101 DALMATIANS (1961)

MARY POPPINS (1964)

A pair of films—one animated, the other combining animation and live action—employed Old London town, a favorite Disney setting here serving as an objective-correlative for ideas emerging in 1960s America. Early in the decade, with *101 Dalmatians*, Disney forsook the heavier style of the full-length fairy-tale films for the lighter, more contemporary animation—brightly colored, purposefully sketchy in style—that had proven popular with modern audiences in *Lady and the Tramp*. Here, though, the human heroes (and dog owners) are, in comparison to Lady's well-to-do master and mistress, virtually destitute. Roger and Anita Radcliff live in a small if cozy home just off Regents Park. Though without sufficient funds, at least for the time being, they are anything but extreme anticapitalists. Roger wouldn't mind it at all if someday he did become rich, though only if he could accomplish this by doing what he loves best, composing songs. Once again, an onscreen character represents Disney himself, perfectly willing to accept big profits, though only if such funds come to him naturally—as a result of his creative output. As always, the character's Lillian-like wife stands by her man's idealist values about his popular art.

His foil is the piece's villainess, Cruella de Ville, a femme fatale in the flamboyant Tallulah Bankhead style, referring to everyone as "Dahling!" while waving a cigarette extended from an impossibly long holder in the air. (The role models in this and other Disney films do not smoke, suggesting an anti-tobacco message at a time when other moviemakers still glorified smoking; though Pecos Bill does smoke in *Melody Time*, we realize by film's end that he's actually a loser to be pitied, not a hero to be emulated.) More than merely a high-camp incarnation of evil, Cruella is Walt's most extreme caricature of the raw capitalist he clearly despises. In a stretch limo employed as a touring car, she arrives at the humble Radcliff home, bedecked in expensive furs that appear grotesque on her too-slender frame.

Dalmatians also rates, despite the seemingly escapist entertainment tone, as the first anti-fur film. This is evident from the initial confrontation between the two female characters:

ANITA: Isn't that a new fur coat?
CRUELLA: My *only* true love, dah-ling! I *live* for furs!

The villainess dismisses the Radcliffs' love nest:

This *little* house is your dream castle?

The "little" house is, of course, presented to us as the essence of a true marriage of equals. Clean and decent, it exists in comparison to the hard, cold de Ville mansion we eventually view as Cruella's own castle, in the worst sense of the term: a walled-in fortress where she lives alone.

When the puppies are born, Cruella immediately attempts to buy them.

I'll take them all. Just *name your price!* You can't afford to keep them. You can barely feed *yourselves!*

Though this happens to be entirely true, Anita and Roger, like the Brainards before them, do not have a price, cannot be bought. As was the case with Disney himself, money is meaningless unless it comes as the result of hard work at something one loves to do, particularly a creative endeavor.

Adversity, as always in Disney, pays off for those who meet it gracefully and survive life without corrupting themselves in the process. Roger is inspired by Cruella's evil to write a little ditty about her. The song hits radio airwaves even as Cruella's cronies kidnap the puppies she's been unable to buy. At movie's end, she has crashed her car and is left with nothing. The Radcliffs are becoming rich thanks to Roger's artistic rendering of their enemy's evil. Now, as Anita puts it, "We have more money than we ever dreamed of!" Best of all, they have made the money on their own terms, without selling out their ideals to do so.

Nor are they now corrupted by its presence. Rather than spend the money on a big, fancy house, they will use it to feed not only their returned pups but also nearly a hundred other orphaned dogs rounded up along with their own missing pets, the whole crew now lounging all over the much-loved little house. Simply, the raw capitalist has been defeated, while the enlightened capitalist is rewarded.

One of the many elements in the more complex, ambitious film *Mary Poppins* is the arcing of a raw capitalist into an enlightened one. In an earlier conception of London (1910), Mr. Banks (David Tomlinson) is the man of the moment: The Edwardian citizen incarnate, pleased to be an Englishman of the early twentieth century, with the emphasis on *man*. Glib, colorless, proper, and resolutely unemotional, he represents a slightly less caricatured version of Mr. Darling from *Peter Pan*—unable to enjoy his children as anything other than unformed clay whom he sees himself as duty-bound to mold into identical variations on himself.

And that he would, if it were not for the intervention of that hippie-ish heroine, Mary Poppins (Julie Andrews). She celebrates the concept of feelin' groovy more than a half century before that term would become (however temporarily) part of the popular lexicon. Conversely, Mr. Banks, like members of the Silent Majority, inwardly suffers constant little rebellions on the part of his incorrigible children. His wife (Glynis Johns), a volunteer suffragette, serves as a stand-in for the suburban women of the sixties and early seventies who—having read Betty Friedan's *The Feminine Mystique*—outraged superstraight husbands by rushing off to campaign for women's rights.

While each parent is off in the social world, Poppins whisks the children away to pastoral adventures. "Life's a bloomin' holiday with Mary," as one song insists. A few years later, rock group Chicago would echo this sentiment:

Does anyone really know
What time it is?
Does anybody really care?

Aiding Mary in creating exciting holidays is Bert (Dick Van Dyke), a lower-class "busker" who employs colored chalks to create vivid images on the sidewalks just outside Hyde Park. Bert is yet another stand-in for Disney himself. Intriguingly, though, Van Dyke was cast in the film's symbolic roles as polar opposites, common man Bert and the film's representation of a person who has surrendered his soul to the money culture.

This is Mr. Dawes, Sr., head of the bank where appropriately named Mr. Banks is employed. An aged fellow who can barely hear, Dawes Sr., can't be cited as an example of ageism in Disney, as the film contains other, positive older people who are not enfeebled caricatures. There's Admirable Boom (Reginald Owen), forever young owing to the pleasure he takes in overseeing the city from atop his home, designed as a child's playroom version of a sailing ship. And there's the Bird Woman (Jane Darwell), who sits on the bank steps and, with Mary, calls out for people to invest in nature, rather than stick funds away in a dank cell, by feeding the birds. "Tuppence a day" is all it costs.

The children find themselves trapped between Mary and the Bird Woman, appealing to the idealism of youth, and their father and Mr. Dawes, who hope to crush that very spirit. This reaches a crisis when Mr. Banks brings his son Michael (Matthew Garber) and daughter Jane (Karen Dotrice) to the bank. The impressionable boy is expected to be inspired by the immense, off-putting artifices of power surrounding him and invest his humble tuppence in a savings account. Instead, he hysterically grabs the coin out of Mr. Dawes's fumbling hand, rushing outside to feed the birds. This inadvertently causes a run on the bank, which threatens to ruin the entire financial structure of London, Great Britain, perhaps even the Western World.

Work—other than the white-collar banking and business professions—Disney, as always, heartily approves of. This is particularly true for those working-class fellows who live in communal solidarity with one another. Not surprisingly, then, the children—after running away and becoming lost—are rescued by chimney sweep Bert. Though he

THE BIRD WOMAN. Jane Darwell, Academy Award–winning Best Supporting Actress for her role as populist heroine Ma Joad in John Ford's 1940 film of John Steinbeck's *The Grapes of Wrath*, played the poor old woman of the streets who feeds the birds, sole symbol of nature in what otherwise has become an asphalt jungle; her reminder that it costs only "tuppence a day" to do the same implies one more of Disney's harsh critiques of raw capitalism.

and his fellow workers are covered with soot, the children find them delightful, enjoying the experience of dancing with them. Like the dwarfs who whistled while they worked, this little community turns chores into pleasure owing to a positive attitude toward a hard job, well done.

The little boy's act has, however, caused Mr. Banks to be summarily fired from his position. Instead of falling into a depression, he feels liberated. Like the hero portrayed by Robert Redford in a popular Neil Simon play of the mid-sixties—another seeming light entertainment that portrayed the arc of a superstraight into an incipient hippie—Mr. Banks removes his shoes and runs barefoot in the park. The following day, he embraces life, becoming an overage hippie, insisting the family must hurry off to Hyde Park, the one spot of nature in their overly civilized world, and fly a kite. The world, which was too much with him, now seems a silly thing. The children respond by embracing him even as they forget their beloved Poppins.

However much this saddens her inwardly, she is one of Disney's beloved stoics and will not show an emotion that she deeply feels. Her job was to initiate Mr. Banks's metamorphosis, and, having achieved that, this merry prankster leaves to do the same for someone else who needs to recapture that element of childhood which does not necessarily have to pass. In the tradition of Mary's final flight, Eliot, the title character in the post-Walt film *Pete's Dragon* (1977), will likewise fly away as soon as he normalizes relations between a lonely little boy and his father.

DISNEY'S LOST HORIZON

FOLLOW ME, BOYS! (1966)

Once again, Disney began an exploration of Middle American values with the image of an agent from the outside world arriving in a typical heartland community. This recurring dramatic device had earlier been employed in such diverse films as *So Dear to My Heart* and *Pollyanna*. Hickory, circa 1930, seems at first glance to be a second cousin to Shangri-La in Capra's 1937 version of James Hilton's *Lost Horizon*, the remote village having changed remarkably little since the turn of the century. Elsewhere in America, the Depression ravages society's very structures. In this isolated valley, even the bank seems invulnerable, the previous year's stock market crash barely alluded to. Yet there's something poisonous beneath that serene surface, the town so inbred that a catharsis is needed. That will be provided by Lemuel Siddons (Fred MacMurray), a young maverick whose very name appears to be an acronym for LSD.

Though clearly a variation on a recurring device in Disney films, the opening proves innovative in one respect. For this tale begins not in the small town but aboard the vehicle carrying radical change to a stagnating society. A member of Melody Murphy's (Ken Murray) traveling band, Lem is Thoreau's true individualist, even among these notably different drummers. He studies a lawbook, hoping to practice someday. Perceived as a bohemian when situated in straight society (as he shortly will be), a superstraight while surrounded by a bohemian crowd (as he currently is), Lem is so unique (if uniquely American) that he can't be tagged liberal or conservative, mainstream or countercultural, except in contrast to others.

Alone among the vagabonds, Lem senses the time has come to put down roots. When they make a pit stop in Hickory, Lem innocently catches a ball tossed about by teens. All at once, his primal sympathy is touched. Lem offers the boys his last dollar so they can buy candy from a store owned by John Everett Hughes (Charlie Ruggles). This does not go unnoticed by Vida Downey (Vera Miles), Lem's converse and the yin to his yang. He's been living a Romantic existence, while unknowingly harboring untapped traditional values; she's a traditionalist who, unbeknownst even to herself, has deeply Romantic leanings. One of Disney's protofeminist heroines, Vida is more enamored of Lem's generous soul than his good looks, though they are hardly lost on her.

Vida's current beau is her boss at the bank, Ralph Hastings (Elliott Reid, in a period-piece rendering of his conventional type from *The Absent Minded Professor*). Vida must make a moral choice, between this greed-motivated snob and the gangly, genial rebel.

Providing a foil for Ralph is his aunt, Hetty Seibert (Lillian Gish). The first time we see Hetty, she (owner of the bank) instructs Ralph not to foreclose on a destitute woman. Her nephew scoffs at Hetty's eccentric ways; Lem, on the other hand, immediately adores Hetty, as she does him. Not that he's squeaky clean. When Lem decides to stay in Hickory, working for John and pursuing Vida, he doesn't become a simple, holier-than-thou member of the pompously respectable (like Ralph) or join local lowlifes, embodied by alcoholic plumber Ed White (Sean McClory). Lem evenly divides his time between the pool parlor and the Methodist church — the latter attended less for religious reasons than because he can encounter beautiful Vida there. Neither extreme is healthy in and of itself; always, the Disney hero balances serious spirituality with the pleasure principle and, more often than not, fuses the two seeming opposites, as Lem does here.

The narrative revolves around Lem's decision to form a Boy Scout troop, offering to serve as scoutmaster when no one else wants the job. He volunteers less out of idealism than self-interest, if of a nonmonetary sort. Having learned that Vida supports such activities, he hopes to impress her, and does. Once married, Lem and Vida prove to be enlightened enough to treat each other as equals. Unable to conceive a child, they adopt a lost boy, Whitey (Kurt Russell, assuming the distinct type of role previously played by Kevin Corcoran), after Whitey's father dies in an alcoholic stupor.

Family values are key to Disney. Unlike Dan Quayle's narrow conception of that term, though, Disney's family can be makeshift, much as Sister Sledge would declare:

We are family!
I got my brothers
And sisters with me!

The group referred to in the song is not composed of biological siblings, nor is the notion of family necessarily the conventional one in Disney, for this is a fully extended family.

Lem and Vida also stand by Hetty, when Ralph attempts to have the elderly woman declared unfit. Hetty plans to contribute a stretch of lakefront property to the Scouts for a permanent campsite. Ralph opposes this:

> RALPH: Lem, do you know how much this lake property is *worth?*
> LEM: Honestly, Ralph. I never thought of it in terms of *money!*

Over the years, Lem has given up all hope of practicing law. Disney allows for Lem to have a transcendent moment, his personal American Dream—which, significantly, has nothing to do with money, but rather self-fulfillment that also benefits the greater good—momentarily incarnated as reality. In court, Ralph proves Hetty's sanity and lucidity. For Disney, as for Father Flanagan, there is no such thing as a bad boy, implying Disney's progressive politics.

For, generally speaking, liberals firmly believe that "antisocial behavior is largely the result of poverty, prejudice, lack of education, and low social status rather than human nature," while conservatives view character as "largely inborn and genetically inherited."[16] Whitey moves on to excel in life rather than be dragged down, by biological determinants, to the level of his alcoholic father. As an adult (played by Donald May), Whitey becomes a doctor, marrying a fine (and, like Vida, highly independent) young woman (Luanna Patten). Near the end of his career, Disney—whom many viewed as growing ever more reactionary—clung to his essentially liberal belief that a good (moral/educational) environment will and can win out over heredity.

DISNEY'S NEW DEAL

MONKEYS, GO HOME! (1967)

It's one thing to criticize raw capitalism while presenting admiring portraits of a socialist ideal, quite another to offer a working model by which people might achieve a happy compromise. But that serves as the serious subtext for this seemingly innocuous bit of escapism. As the film opens,

Hank Dussard (Dean Jones), halfway between Graham Greene's quiet American and William Lederer, Jr.'s ugly one, arrives in provincial France. He has inherited an olive farm, though Hank's initial hope of making big money is swiftly dimmed by Father Sylvain (Maurice Chevalier), who explains that a single man can't make an economic go of it. Extended families are necessary to gather up olives after winds blow them from the trees; to hire laborers would cost more than the owner could recoup. The undaunted American capitalist par excellence, Hank comes up with a quirky idea: Import four monkeys to do the job.

"Money and work," Gallic beauty Maria (Yvette Mimieux) complains, "Is that all you think about?" In truth, it's all Hank has considered since arriving, making him a potential villain, the raw capitalist so despised in Disney. It takes a woman—Earth Mother, protofeminist, sexually liberated—to make a man see the error of his ways. Thanks to Maria, Hank transforms into an enlightened capitalist, though not before facing a major conflict. A local socialist, Cartucci (Bernard Woringer), comes to see Hank's plan as an example of American imperialism, exploiting the European economy at the expense of locals. Shortly, villagers are massed before the villa. The signs they wave—"Monkeys, Go Home!"—evoke the anti-American-commercialism sloganeering so prevalent throughout Europe during the mid-sixties.

Hank has only one solid supporter: the priest, a virulent anti-communist who howls that the protesters are "Godless revolutionaries." Then the priest finally explains to Hank:

I'm sorry, Monsieur, but you cannot buck the system. Sell out and go back to America.

Hank flatly refuses. What appear irreconcilable differences turn out to be anything but. The real villain, we learn, is Emile Paraulis (Clement Harari), a local (and truly raw) capitalist who incited the villagers to revolt, pretending to share their socialist views. He hoped to buy up both the property and the monkeys once Hank was driven away, afterward ignoring his neighbors while amassing profits—the profits that should have gone, if to any one person, to Hank.

Upon learning this, the villagers realize Hank can be dealt with. The socialist leader reaches a compromise with the capitalist boss, working out a deal by which all will share. Hank becomes an alter ego for Walt himself, his capitalist undertaking adjusted to accommodate the best of communal thinking.

THE NEW FRONTIER

THE HAPPIEST MILLIONAIRE (1967)

Like Lillian Gish's Hetty, Aunt Mary (Gladys Cooper) drives an electric car. As this is Philadelphia, circa 1916, such vehicles are slipping out of fashion. Still, she prefers her air clean, even if this causes Mary to be derided as outré. She serves as yet another depiction of the social traditionalist as philosophic liberal: Impossibly old-fashioned, at least to the pseudosophisticated mainstream, Mary presages the progressive value system of the 1960s, as environmental issues became essential to the Woodstock generation.

Cars will figure in this film in a more prominent manner. The juvenile lead, Angie Duke (John Davidson), dreams of moving to Detroit and joining the emerging automobile industry. This would qualify him as a twentieth-century pioneer, exploring the New West much as previous Disney heroes—Daniel Boone (Dewey Martin), Davy Crockett (Fess Parker)—entered unknown areas of Kentucky, Tennessee, and Texas. There will always be pioneers, Disney implies, for there will forever be new frontiers opening for us to explore. In the film's context, Detroit serves as Disney's much-desired dual symbol: the past (a final frontier) and our future (practical science) happily combined.

Typical of Disney's heroes, Angie suffers a crisis of conscience. His dominating mother (Geraldine Page), reigning over New York's social elite, represents everything Disney hates. She prefers that Angie take a more conventional job, closer to home, an entry-level position at some money-oriented firm. Mrs. Duke would snuff out Angie's creativity were it not for another of Walt's hippie-ish heroines, Cordelia Drexel Biddle (Lesley Ann Warren). As always, the worship of money, not cash itself, qualifies Angie's mother as a villain. Cordelia is also rich, the daughter of iconoclastic millionaire Anthony J. Drexel Biddle (Fred MacMurray), who employs his riches for positive purposes.

Biddle is *Pollyanna*'s Pendergast, transformed from supporting role to title character. He is *Summer Magic*'s Tom Hamilton, grown older but not corrupted, thanks in large part to a perceptive and instinctual wife (Greer Garson). Situated in the city's center, their mansion has a deceptively civilized façade, while the interior provides a home to all things natural. Twelve alligators crawl about the corridors, nibbling at guests and servants until only the most bravely eccentric remain, the weak weeded out. This millionaire is "happiest" because, though possessing wealth, he has no interest in money-as-power.

Mr. Biddle (an enlightened capitalist and Disney's final autobiographical figure) and his wife open wide their doors to all classes of society. Their friends are not the Anglo bluebloods of the Dukes' mansion, but Irish working-class immigrants. Biddle's roguish butler, John Lawless (Tommy Steele), is treated more as family member than servant. When he first arrives, looking more than a little like Beatle John Lennon, the intriguingly named Lawless carries with him the exuberant free spirits (as expressed in song and dance) of the British Invasion.

Suitors for Cordelia's hand are invited to enter a boxing ring with her father. Biddle discerns their mettle through natural selection at its most brutal and most democratic. Any man who can stand up against him is admired, however humble his social standing. Angie wins Biddle's admiration by defeating him through knowledge of jiujitsu, another fascination of the emerging youth culture that Walt uncannily presages. The sequence serves as forerunner to Tom Laughlin's *Billy Jack* (1970), Bruce Lee in *Enter the Dragon* (1973), and David Carradine in TV's *Kung Fu* (1973).

Initially, this seems to be shaping up as Disney's *King Lear*. Biddle considers dividing his empire between two sons (Paul Peterson and Eddie Hodges) and the aptly named Cordelia. Despite the obvious potential for full-blown tragedy, Disney effectively alters his approach in mid-movie. When the aging social magician eventually closes his own books, Biddle represents Disney as much as *The Tempest*'s Prospero did Shakespeare. The film transforms into an up-cry epitaph for an oeuvre geared to the stuff that modern American dreams are made on.

The key theme is established in the opening shot: an old-fashioned milk delivery truck receding into the distance, as a shiny new automobile approaches. Disney refuses to cinematically suggest that one element is positive, the other negative. Rather, Disney—as always, bittersweet in tone—mourns the loss of an appealing past while embracing the potential of an exciting future. Shortly, John Lawless sings of "Fortuosity," Disney's final term for his concept of life's complex workings—a heady combination of fate and free will. This is something Biddle, laudable yet flawed, must himself learn.

Surprisingly, Cordelia wants to attend a stuffy girls' academy. Fearing such an experience might turn her into a conformist, Biddle initially refuses. He relents at the urging of his intelligent wife, who senses Cordelia must determine her own life's journey. Ensconced at the school, Cordelia asks her social-climbing roommate Rosemary (Joyce Bulifant) to teach her how to flirt—that is, how to be a phoney, like other girls.

At a blueblood party, her inability to master such skills turns off the shallow boys. Only Angie finds her attractive, touched by her lack of social graces. What he falls for is not her wealth (other girls are equally well off) or good looks (others are as pretty), but her naturalness. She cannot "learn," even by "imitation" of Rosemary and the others. Angie's love at first sight (recalling Cinderella's prince) legitimizes Cordelia's sincerity. Likewise, she provides him with the moral courage to stand up to his mother.

Millionaire's final image features Angie and Cordelia heading off for Detroit, recalling Crockett and Russel departing for Texas. They, of course, died there; we have no idea whether Angie and Cordelia will flourish or fail. What matters is that they try. Modernist pioneers, they blaze a new frontier's twentieth-century trails. Before they leave, Cordelia returns home, confiding to her father that she has, after gaining experience, fully accepted her identity as nonconformist. Her evolution vindicates Disney's point of view. Eccentric individuality, when imposed by someone in authority, is as offensive as the conformity which Angie's mother would impose on him. Disney teaches through his entertainments that parents need to allow their children freedom of choice. Only then will, more likely than not, a child happily choose to follow in his or her parents' footsteps. Or, as Crosby, Stills, and Nash put it, "Teach your parents well"!

Unlike some artists, Disney practiced what he preached. Though his daughters attended traditional Sunday school, they were allowed to pick the church. As Walt wrote in a 1943 letter to his sister Ruth:

Little Diane is going to Catholic school now which she seems to enjoy very much. She is quite taken with the rituals and is studying catechism. She hasn't quite made up her mind yet whether she wants to be a Catholic or a Protestant. Some people worry about [this] but I feel differently about it. I think she is intelligent enough to know what she wants and to do and I feel that whatever her decision may be is her privilege.[17]

The values expressed in the movies were the same as those held by the person of singular intelligence who stood behind them. When little boys and girls of the late 1950s and early '60s reached their teenage years, what they had learned from Disney entertainment would be essential to creating the mind-set of a radically redefined America.

5 My Sweet Lord
Romanticism and Religion in Disney

When Murray Head's recording of "Superstar" first appeared on radio airwaves early in May 1971, the religious right reacted with expected outrage. This was perceived as the ultimate insult to traditional values; the hippies now dared to mockingly portray Jesus Christ in the guise of a rock star. A mere five months later, after the Andrew Lloyd Web-

Copyright Walt Disney Productions; courtesy Buena Vista Releasing.

SPLENDOR IN THE GRASS. In *Fun and Fancy Free* (1947), socialist author Sinclair Lewis's character Bongo the Bear answers the call of the wild, deserting the prisonlike lifestyle found in society, getting back in touch with his Wordsworthian "primal sympathy" via a return to nature, there finding free love with a flower child.

ber/Tim Rice musical *Jesus Christ, Superstar!* made its bow on Broadway (October 12, 1971), those of conservative morality reversed their position. Rather than being denounced as a burlesque of Old Time Religion, the rock opera was accepted as an effective means of making the New Testament relevant to a younger generation, expressing old ideas through the then–still relatively new medium of rock 'n' roll.

Such music, the nation's faithful had decided, was not necessarily Satanic. Rock was only an amoral conduit that could be used to convey any message, negative or (in this case, and in their minds) positive. Shortly, the concept of "Christian rock"—unthinkable ten years earlier, when all rock 'n' roll was written off as the devil's music by conservative forces—had fully emerged. As *Time* put it:

In 1966, John Lennon casually remarked that the Beatles were more popular than Jesus Christ: now the Beatles are shattered, and George Harrison is singing "My Sweet Lord." [1]

As a member in good standing of the avant-garde Plastic Ono Band, Lennon continued to sing another tune. To enact his vision of utopia, one had to first

Imagine no religion;
It isn't hard to do.

Yet Lennon was essentially a lone voice, crying out in the pop-culture wilderness. Harrison represented a new wave. Rock and pop groups of varying talent offered diverse hit singles, all with spiritual overtones and/or religious undercurrents: the Beatles ("Let It Be"), Norman Greenbaum ("Spirit in the Sky"), Dion ("Abraham, Martin, and John"), Dusty Springfield ("Son of a Preacher Man"), Stevie Wonder ("Heaven Help Us All"), Wadsworth Mansion ("Sweet Mary"), Aretha Franklin and Dionne Warwick ("I Say a Little Prayer"), Three Dog Night ("Eli's Coming," "Joy to the World"), Ocean ("Put Your Hand in the Hand"), Helen Reddy ("I Don't Know How to Love Him"), Les Crane ("Desiderata"), Simon and Garfunkel ("Bridge over Troubled Water"), Paul Simon ("Mother and Child Reunion"), Judy Collins ("Amazing Grace"), Cat Stevens ("Morning Has Broken"), and Kris Kristofferson ("Sunday Morning, Coming Down") most notable among them.

This "May-December marriage of conservative religion and the rebellious counterculture" [2] was not as unlikely as it at first seemed to those who had long perceived (incorrectly, as it turned out) the 1960s youth movement as essentially liberal in outlook. Such a misconception is belied by statements from leading members of what has been tagged the

New Left. Shortly after the takeover of Columbia University by the SDS in 1969, radical Mark Rudd announced:

Liberal politics were exposed as just so much shallow verbiage and wasted effort when compared to the power of a mass radical movement, around significant issues such as racism and imperialism.[3]

This was no misstatement offered in the heat of the moment. Rudd continued to rail against "the liberal faculty, so treacherous and yet so impotent."[4]

The reasoning behind the New Left's harsh rejection of liberalism is far too complex to adequately deal with in anything other than a full study of the subject. In a nutshell, though, student radicals, armed with their understanding of postwar policies and contemporary history, held those liberals they might have been expected to feel some kinship with, rather than conservatives who hated the young radicals, as primarily responsible for everything the sixties youth believed to be wrong with mid-1960s America. The presidency of Democrat Harry Truman (1945–1953) had initiated America's new international position as an active world player. This resulted, during the 1950s, in Third World adventuring of outright (Korea) and undercover (Indonesia) attempts to alter the futures of other cultures for what we believed to be our—thus, the world's—greater good. The Vietnam War these radicals so despised was perceived as the inexorable end result of a foreign policy that Republican conservatives, with their isolationist attitudes, had opposed. At home, meanwhile, the old liberal belief that inequities could be solved by slow, nonviolent progressivism was rejected as an embarrassingly naïve and dated solution to problems that the youth movement (or at least its most radical members) hoped to immediately end through revolutionary tactics that included direct confrontation—culminating in the Yippie standoff against Chicago police during the Democratic National Convention in early August 1968.

That, of course, was *before* the good vibes given off at Woodstock, then the bad ones from Altamont. On December 6, 1969, the countercultural dream entered its death throes. The "good trip" of the flower-power generation degenerated into the "bad trip" of the hard-drug culture. Religion offered solace to the disillusioned, a hope for redemption and salvation. In fact, though, a religious element had always been a part of the youth movement. A pair of Catholic priests, the Berrigan brothers, had been key players among the antiwar activists. Yet hippie-era religiosity was not necessarily of a traditional Judeo-Christian order; the pursuit of Eastern gurus by diverse celebrities attested to an inner search for faith, potent as any outward attempt to save the world. This quest for nirvana likewise received popular expression in song, Donovan insisting that

> First, there is a mountain;
> Then there is no mountain;
> Then, there is.

In this, the hippies recall the Romantics:

In Wordsworth's conception of nature there is a shift from something like animistic pantheism to a conception reconcilable with traditional Christianity. Nature is animated, alive, filled with God.[5]

Seemingly, Disney would qualify as an agnostic. While re-creating an idealization of his childhood—"Main Street, USA," for his original theme park—Walt self-consciously included every possible building *except* a church. In part, this owed to his lifelong dislike of organized religion; in part, the move was calculated to not offend anyone holding divergent beliefs, demonstrating what would decades later come to be called politically correct thinking as to the sensitivity of others. As one biographer noted:

Walt considered himself religious, yet he never went to church. The heavy dose of religiosity in his childhood discouraged him; he especially disliked sanctimonious preachers. But he admired and respected every religion, and his belief in God never wavered. His theology was individual.[6]

Individual, yet essentially pantheistic, this view owes to a certainty that the free world of nature, not the restrictive insides of a church, most fully reveals God to us. In his films, Disney—while all but ignoring organized religion—emphasizes the spiritual side of life. Like Blake, Disney perceives "Heaven in a wild flower." When, in *The Living Desert* (1953), rain finally appears, allowing the fauna to at last emerge from under parched ground, we are informed that we're witnessing "the *miracle* of the flowers—one of *nature's* great triumphs" (emphasis added). In *The Vanishing Prairie* (1954), a confused and terrified rabbit runs directly into a prairie fire; we are told that "by some *miracle* [it] emerges singed but safe" (emphasis added). For Disney, the work of a supreme being— a positive Force, as George Lucas would later tag it in *Star Wars* (1977) —is always in ample evidence around us. The earth serves as an emblem of that abiding power, much as the nineteenth-century Romantic—and twentieth-century pantheist—believed.

"A HOUSE SHOULD BE OF A HILL"

THE LIGHT IN THE FOREST (1958)
SNOW WHITE AND THE SEVEN DWARFS (1938)

Disney's Romantic attitude toward nature is most economically expressed in the opening sequence of a live-action historical drama, *The Light in the Forest.* The initial shots alternate between panoramic wide angles on unspoiled woods and tight close shots of the specific flora and fauna which compose this entirely natural landscape. Presented via a dissolve montage, juxtaposing such images in a languid, dreamlike manner, the technique wordlessly conveys the notion that this is indeed what painter Edward Hicks would have called "a peaceable kingdom." Animals of various types dart about busily, each off and running on its own agenda, harmless to one another. The bright lighting in which they are bathed and soft sounds surrounding them suggest a beatific tranquility that transcends the here and now.

Then, in a split second, the onscreen image darkens as loud noises encroach. Animals panic, dart about, try to escape from some dangerous force. In time, we are allowed to view the menace: An army of men, an extension of civilization, self-importantly tramping on its way to some dire meeting. Oblivious to the beauty, these conformists (dressed in identical uniforms) unwittingly destroy, with heavy boot steps, everything in their path. They, incredibly, are the *heroes* of the piece, not our villains, as we might initially guess from their being negatively caricatured on first appearance. People—at least, Anglo men—can't help but menace the good garden. It is the way they have been taught to behave. The only exception is a frontier scout, Del Hardy (Fess Parker), different because he has lived with Native Americans, adopting their less civilized, more enlightened view. This allows for a harmony with nature. Del's fringed jacket makes clear that he has more in common with the Indians than the suited colonials.

Others have learned the ways of civilization by copying their elders. "We learn by imitation," Wordsworth complained. Yet the best among them still retain the long-dormant spirit of nature deep inside, waiting to be rekindled. Nearly twenty years earlier, in *Snow White*, the huntsman was a man of the forest, thus the least civilized person on view. He had been assigned to kill the title character but could not, though he had obviously operated as the queen's executioner many times before. The Grimms' incarnation of the huntsman was, by today's standards, a male chauvinist, moved to spare Snow White solely owing to her extreme beauty. Disney's primitive, in contrast, responds to this radical innocent by coming to grips with a "primal sympathy" long dormant within him, but which, as Wordsworth wrote, "having been, must ever be." This occurs, not surprisingly, while they are in the woods. Far from the castle (civilization/evil), he—here in the midst of nature/goodness—hesitates to strike after noting that she sings to (is at one with) the doves and picks wildflowers. *Inner* beauty, her affinity with the abundant goodness around her and oneness with it, is what touches him. Nothing can ever "bring back" his own earlier state of absolute childhood innocence—his own moment of enjoying, as Snow White does now, "splendor in the grass, glory in the flower." Still, he can find the strength necessary to spare her life and accept the consequences by momentarily reestablishing contact with the remaining element of that good force still latent within him. Observing her in contact with nature, the huntsman is able to come back into touch with half-forgotten

> . . . soothing thoughts that spring
> Out of human suffering;
> In the faith that looks through death,
> In years that bring the philosophic mind.
> —"Ode, Intimations on Immortality"

Upon learning of his original intent, Snow White rushes off in horror to the deepest, darkest part of the wood. Identical for the moment at least to the Grimms' Snow White, Disney's child-woman "felt full of terror, even of the very leaves on the trees." The brothers Grimm leave off their fearful description here, though the brothers Disney add a scene expressing their own notably different point of view. Yes, there is much to fear in nature, if we choose to see it in a certain way. Grotesque dead trees do briefly appear to be menacing monsters. But it isn't nature's context that makes them monstrous, or at least seem so, rather the limits of human perception. Misshaped branches, she (and we) realize, are gruesome only when perceived as such by the modern mind, which carries into nature the baggage of civilization. As dawn breaks and light filters through the leaves, she grasps that those huge eyes penetrating the darkness belonged not to deadly forces but to rabbits and other gentle creatures.

Nothing, Shakespeare wrote, is either good or bad; thinking makes it so. The horrors were not inherent in the raw forces of nature, but in (to borrow from Prof. Morbius in MGM's 1956 sci-fi classic *Forbidden Planet*) "monsters from the Id." Frightening (mis)conceptions arise from man's collective unconscious, then are projected onto a natural world that in actuality is benign. Perception is reality; Snow White, still perceiving as a civilized person, saw evil everywhere. As fear recedes, though, she realizes there is no threat, only an escape route from the danger posed by civilization. Then she embraces the animals, as unafraid as the title figure in Henri Rousseau's *The Sleeping Gypsy* (1897). They, at one with her, lead the natural woman to the dwarfs' cottage.

Our first image of the house, cozily nestled among trees rather than haphazardly imposed on the terrain, brings to mind Frank Lloyd Wright: "A house should not be on a hill, but of the hill."[7] In Disney animation, as in Wright's architecture, the "best men" achieve a oneness with nature; the dwarfs' cottage appears to have organically emerged from its natural context. To a degree, the dwarfs represent natural man, insofar as they live free from the hypocrisies of society. But they are, at least on first meeting, far from full enlightenment. Petty and mean, they need help in completing their oneness with the natural world. This justifies a plot device in which the animals (though sensing the dwarfs' innate goodness) flee every time the little men appear in the film's early scenes.

Snow White, predecessor to the flower children, provides a bridge between these partial converts to nature and the pure beasts. An illustration of the Romantic principle, the two groups are finally at one with each other when Snow White is again endangered by civilization's evil queen. In conquering and killing her, the dwarfs recognize the beast within, while the beasts achieve the righteous moral outrage of humankind.

THE CONCERT IN THE THICKET

BAMBI (1942)

ADVENTURES IN MUSIC: MELODY (1953)

In the words of one literary critic, Romantic poets feel duty-bound to present a "sense of the mystery of the universe, and the perception of its beauty."[8] As, in his time, Disney did. Combining soft-focus photography with gentle pastels, he created a visual equivalent for such poetic lyricism. *Bambi*'s opening sequence is a case in point. An extended pan shot, the camera lyrically gliding across a forest, rendered so as to provide an in-depth sensation, allowed for a full three-dimensional effect without the need for special glasses. We note diverse locations within the wood, each of equal if notably unique beauty. The technique visually parallels a Romantic ode. Shelley confessed his ability to discover the sign of God (more likely than not a pagan deity) even in the cold gusts of a harsh west wind in autumn:

Angels of rain and lightning; there are spread
On the blue surface of thine aery surge,
Like the bright hair uplifted from the head
Of some fierce Maenad . . .

Likewise, *Bambi*'s opening is cinematically equivalent to the Romantic poet's "dreamlike unreality" and "sense of the mystery." This sets into motion the film's overall Romantic tone. Specific details of flora and fauna are rendered with remarkable accuracy. Disney had filled the studio with a virtual zoo so that his artists could make every movement of each animal appear strikingly true to life.[9]

Such efforts were hardly rewarded with praise. The *New York Times* critic complained that Walt's "painted forest is hardly to be distinguished from the real thing."[10] The comment, if partly true, reveals a journeyman reviewer's failure to grasp Disney's larger and grander ambition, then analyze the degree to which the artist succeeded or failed in terms of realizing his own unique aims. Instead, the reviewer falsely judged the effect by comparing Disney's achievement to the reviewer's misconception of what the artist's ambition ought to have been: "Mr. Disney has come perilously close to tossing away his whole world of cartoon fantasy."[11] That, in fact, is a perfect description of what Disney set out to achieve. Going against the grain of conventional thinking, he implicitly raised the question, Why must animation *always* present us with an alternative universe? Simply because that's what everyone had previously done is not an acceptable answer, at least not for an authentic innovator, as well as pioneer, within his medium of choice.

And not for any critic who understands the art of animation. As Leonard Maltin has noted, far from a minor subgenre of motion pictures (which it's often wrongly considered), animation is the form to which all filmmaking aspires.[12] Here alone, the filmmaker exerts total control over his subject matter. And this is something that artists working in earlier media—painting, literature, etc.—would have taken for granted. What kept film (in the tradition of its predecessor, still photography) from being accepted as a legitimate art form for so long was an abiding misconception. The camera, as theorist Andre Bazin long ago believed, is essentially an objective recording device; as such, it cannot lie. If one accepts this notion, then neither can the camera be used to express the subjective vision of an individual artist.[13]

To pick one obvious example that evidences the falseness of such thinking, the nature photography of Ansel Adams does not simply share mountains and rivers that he came across. Rather, the images—singly (New Criticism) and collectively (Auteurism)—convey a unique point of view, a philosophy expressed in visions rather than words. What Adams achieved is notably different from what any other photographer, arriving on the same scene with a camera and shooting film there, would have rendered. Any Adams work is immediately identifiable as "his," even as, say, a painting by Van Gogh or Gauguin was clearly created by either of those highly disparate sensibilities, including canvases from the period during which the two geniuses—their approaches similar in some respects, differing in others—painted side by side.

Likewise, Shelley and Wordsworth would describe the same natural scene in similar yet not identical ways. While sharing key Romantic values, each also boasted his own unique vision within the larger school. Like them, like the impressionists, like Adams (who is, as Walt Disney, an artist inhabiting the machine age), Disney discovers in nature a confirmation of his own inner beliefs. Adams and Disney offer images that paradoxically convey subjective attitudes via the representation of a seemingly objective scene. "In trying to achieve a real-life naturalism," the *Times*'s reviewer continued, "why have cartoons at all?"[14] Seemingly a commonsense observation about the inherent fallacy in Walt's work, the statement actually makes clear how misunderstood Disney has been. The answer: Because Disney (at this point in his career) believed it would be impossible to convey his double vision—respect for the authenticity of the natural scene coupled with an artist's need to endow it with his own attitudes toward natural phenomena—via a camera that photographed such scenes in their natural locations. When his confidence eventually increased, Disney would then create the *True-Life Adventures* series.

Properly understood, Disney's camera visually approximates a technique that Wordsworth, Coleridge, Shelley, and Keats (among others) considered essential: Reintroducing (in their case, through words) jaded, city-oriented pseudosophisticates to the magical world of nature. This is achieved by establishing, as literary critic Rene Wellek noted, "a vivid sense of the almost dreamlike unreality of the [real] world."[15] Romantic odes have been widely hailed as verbal "hymns," suggesting that in nature's benevolence, we can, if our experience reaches the point of transcendence, discover a secret source of spirituality. Likewise, *Bambi*'s opening is set to an orchestration notable for its religious feeling. Sight and sound combine to transform, for the viewing audience, this cinematic rendering of nature's basic goodness into a metaphysical experience.

Shortly, the film's score (by Frank Churchill and Edward H. Plumb) will subtly merge with forest sounds. The two conjoin to create what, for Disney, is the perfect symphony for our time: half natural creation, half human-made. This signifies that we the viewers—people in general, like the artist in particular—can, indeed should, aspire to live in just such harmony with nature. Such an approach is consistent throughout. When lightning strikes, it is nature's kettle drum; as two dueling male deer lock horns, they appear onscreen as nature's cymbals crashing together. Ultimately, what we recall, as in the best Romantic poetry, is nature's positive side. A bird in Bambi's forest, gaily singing in early spring, seems far more inspired by Keats's "Ode to a Nightingale" than anything in author Felix Salten's novel, on which the film was based.

Many of England's Romantic poets were better known in their own time by a more specific term applied to their outlook. "The Lake School"[16] implied a verbal lyricism with the delicate beauty of Renoir's paintings of water lilies. Disney, properly understood, emerges as their cinematic counterpart. His particular love for the subtle beauties of calm waters is always contained within his more generalized devotion to the greater glory of the all-encompassing natural world. In *Bambi*, Disney concentrates on water in the opening sequences, particularly a waterfall emptying into a river, which then snakes its way through the forest. At first, this seems merely another aspect of the abundant beauty. As the film progresses, it becomes clear that Disney's camera eye seeks out the forest's water whenever possible, employing water as a storytelling device and ongoing motif. What in Salten qualified only as a charming detail here becomes a mute metaphor.

Bambi comes to terms with himself while studying his reflection in a pond. He first sees Faline when her reflection appears beside his own. Most major events in the film—the sudden storm, the forest fire—are not depicted directly, with Disney's camera trained on them. Instead, we experience them indirectly, reflected in a body of water. During the wintertime sequence, the key action takes place on that same lake, now frozen, as Bambi and his rabbit companion, Thumper, slide and play. When Bambi matures, his courtship of Faline concludes on a natural bridge above the lake; what we see is the reflection of them nuzzling as their loving act is visually doubled down below.

Copyright Walt Disney Productions; courtesy Buena Vista Releasing.

GLORY IN THE FLOWER. Working in the once controversial, radical, and essentially anti-Judeo-Christian tradition of Romantic poetry, painting, and philosophy, Disney posits a vision in which nature is not—as conventional Anglo thought insists—a deadly jungle, but a peaceable kingdom; in *Bambi* (1942), animals from different species are seen not as natural enemies but as potential friends, in this benevolent garden.

Other key elements, presented realistically in the novel, take on a symbolic dimension in the film. Chief among them is the changing of seasons. This and all other cycles are perceived—here, and in Disney's canon—as a positive thing, even though such cycles contain potential for considerable suffering. As the film's first song puts it:

> Love is a song that never ends;
> One single theme, repeating.
> Like the voice of a heavenly choir,
> Love's sweet music goes on.

This continues an agenda that Disney had begun in his earliest animated experiments. A quartet of cartoons—*Springtime* (1928), *Summer* (1930), *Autumn* (1930), and *Winter* (1930)—celebrated the distinct joys of each season. *Bambi* collapses these individual conceptions into a single animated epic.

The spiritual-religious element that Disney discovers in nature has a major impact on the way Bambi's story here unfolds. There are storms as well as bright sun in this all-encompassing vision. We see Bambi and his fellow deer on the edge of starvation during winter's worst hours. Hardly sentimental, Disney will not idealize nature as some sort of utopia for his youthful audience. Instead, he chooses to include images of striking violence (Bambi and another male deer, mortally locked in combat over Faline), death (Bambi's mother at mid-movie, his father, by implication, in the final shot), and destruction (a lightning storm, the forest fire). A single year in the life of one deer—including good and bad, leading to the survival of his species—becomes emblematic of life itself. The forest emerges as Disney's microcosm, reflecting the often dark but ultimately benign universe.

Not surprisingly, he—like the Romantic poets who preceded him and the Woodstock generation to follow—finds harmony in what might strike the Classicist's eye as chaotic diversity. At the birth of Bambi, prince of the forest, animals congregate to observe this natural phenomenon, a miracle if one chooses to see it that way. Birds and beasts momentarily enjoy a sense of community. No sooner are the festivities over than each species goes about its own business, resuming individual roles in the grand scheme of things.

What proves a problem for some leads to the best of all possible worlds for others. The rainstorm that sends most animals scurrying for cover brings the ducks out of hiding and onto the water's surface. Only man, the intruder, takes on a totally negative quality within Disney's vision. The camera assumes an unseen hunter's point of view as he approaches the grazing deer. The viewing experience here is unpleasant enough to make a child resent being forced into such a relationship, however temporary, with the character—a human, and the only true predator. We preferred our earlier identification with the deer.

This theme is furthered in varied films and programs that would appear from their titles to have other things on their mind. One striking example occurs in the featurette *Adventures in Music: Melody*, which ostensibly exists to teach children some basic facts about the art form indicated by its title. Yet Disney furthers the Romantic notion that we can learn from nature, quite literally in this case. Professor Owl holds his classroom high in a treetop. "Let us fly to nature," the eccentric, even hippie-ish professor tells his flock, "and lend an ear to the multitude of musical sounds in her." That final word, incidentally, lends an essentially feminist sensibility to Walt's work. All that appears beneficent in his world is associated with what, in modern terminology, we refer to as the female principle—the Great Goddess in the vocabulary of pre-Christian myth and pagan religion.

Crickets, rubbing their legs together, soon join in the natural orchestra, at least to the sensitive (i.e., Romantic) ear. The title of the theme song indicates an underlying harmony to be found in the seeming discord of nature's diversity: "The Bird and the Cricket and the Willow Tree." As all sing:

> You don't need a ticket
> For the concert in the thicket.

What Professor Owl's bird-students (and the young people watching) are educated about is life as nature's art form. This is God's multicolored canvas on earth. From birth, through education, on to mating and parenthood, finally concluding in old age and death, this song serves as Disney's equivalent to Shakespeare's "Seven Ages of Man" speech, if rendered with considerably less bitterness than Jacques implied in *As You Like It*.

This theme would be developed further in the *True-Life Adventures* series. In *The Living Desert*, for example, Disney juxtaposed image with sound to create "the symphony of the mud pots."

DISNEY AND DARWIN

FANTASIA (1940)

FUN AND FANCY FREE ("BONGO") (1947)

Romantic thinking had, following the publication of Rousseau's theories in France and their enthusiastic acceptance by England's own anti-Classicist counterculture in the early 1800s, advanced a total rejection of all that had for years been uncritically accepted as true within the Judeo-Christian culture. During those years following the publication of Wordsworth's poetry but before the popularization of Darwin's theories, Romanticism encouraged occidental culture to accept anything natural as good, anything civilized (previously lauded by the Classic sensibility) as, conversely, false, pretentious, evil. Sophistication did not make us better people, as had been generally believed by the citizenry of Western civilization since the birth of Classical thought in ancient Greece. Instead, this cut man off from what was best (if, for numerous centuries, unduly repressed) within him: The primitive, the pagan, the pure.

Yet as Marx would eventually inform us, every force creates its equal but opposing counterforce. Such a dialectic is unending. Following the onset of the twentieth century, with its scientific rationalizations, Romantic thinking would in turn be challenged. What a few decades earlier had been accepted as a liberating revolution suddenly seemed sentimental, even silly, to a scientific, logical, modernist mindset. Following wide press and radio coverage of the Scopes monkey trial in 1925, a prosecution undertaken by the precursor to today's religious right to (ironically, as things would turn out) silence the scientific voice, the public at large became too aware of Darwin's views to continue clinging to a know-nothing stance. Could one go on believing in the Romantics' lyrical vision of nature once society at large grasped the notion of survival of the fittest?

Swiftly, the pastoral poetry of Wordsworth, Shelley, Keats, and Coleridge gave way to harsh, unsparing, purposefully nonornamental prose by Upton Sinclair, Theodore Dreiser, and Frank Norris. As always, the popular arts drew inspiration from contemporary thought; Romanticism gave way to the naturalist school in art and ideology. Nature and the city, once polar opposites in symbolic thinking, become emblematic of one another. How else explain the term "the asphalt jungle"? In Norris's *McTeague* (1899) and its cinematic counterpart, Eric von Stroheim's *Greed* (1923), civilization still appears as corrupt as in any Romantic work. Now, though, artists no longer posit nature as its attractive counterpart but as a twisted mirror image. Apelike McTeague—modern man reimagined as Darwin's missing link—flees his San Francisco sty only to find himself lost amid the horrors of Death Valley, the hideous reminder of our primordial past.

The old dichotomy of Classicism and Romanticism threatened to give way to a new, darker philosophy. Neither nature nor civilization could any longer be pegged as positive or negative; both simply existed amorally. God, viewed either as Classicism's logical instigator of a perfectly ordered machine (most often symbolized by a watch in literature and the arts) or Romanticism's originator of a spontaneously growing organism (symbolized by the tree), was replaced by the notion of a world existing without rhyme or reason. Man no longer debated whether a sense of purpose in the universe existed from the moment of its inception (Classicism) or is better understood as what an ever-emerging world aspires to (Romanticism).

As William Butler Yeats, the first great modern poet, put it in 1919 in "The Second Coming":

Things fall apart;
The center cannot hold;
Mere anarchy is loosed on the world.

Yeats may have been read only by intellectuals, but his worldview trickled down, in time, to the common folk. Writing for the popular theater, Kurt Weill wondered whether we were all "lost in the stars." The notion of a centerless world constituted a dark zeitgeist that, in time, threatened to lead man past the Existentialist's pit of doubt and confusion into the deep, dark bog of Nihilism. Nothing means anything, everything is nothing, life (as Hemingway put it) is only a dirty biological trick.

Growing in prevalence as the century wore on, this view can hardly be conducive to any kind of satisfying life. Needed, if life were to retain or regain a sense of meaning, was a popular philosophy able to reconcile the disturbing ideas raised by Darwin with the positive principles of Romantic thinking. This would require a much-needed yet seemingly unattainable fusion of polar opposites—the nineteenth-century vision of nature as beautiful somehow joined with twentieth-century science's conception of nature as brute force. Just such a balanced view would be achieved and communicated to the public in the Disney films. *Fantasia* marked the great endeavor's starting point.

Generally recalled as an ambitious project that failed both critically and commercially at its initial release, *Fantasia* over the decades gradually won admiration as the greatest animated film of all time, if only for sheer technical audacity—forever altering animation's state of the art. Also, though, *Fantasia* was a movie of ideas, not all of them about music and its relationship to motion pictures.

To convey the full revolutionary fervor that greeted the first performance of Igor Stravinsky's *Rite of Spring* in 1913, Disney had to find an equally radical visual subject for the segment. He chose the then-emerging scientific version of the earth's creation. Onscreen, an immense cosmos exists for what appears to be billions of years. Then, a big bang creates yet another speck, this one gradually taking form, over eons, as our planet. Volcanoes explode, sending lava up and out, over the earth's surface; seas gradually form, and in them emerge microbes that, in time, evolve into more complex forms. Some of these eventually crawl up and out of the ocean, onto the surface. A dissolve carries us several million years further in time, and we see varied forms of dinosaurs roaming the earth.

However visually spectacular the sequence remains today, it hardly seems like something that could have ever engendered controversy. Coming as it did in 1940, though, Disney's artistically rendered validation of science seemed a slap in the face to the era's equivalent of the religious right, fighting to keep such subjects out of public classrooms, which they largely managed to do until the mid-fifties. Then, science became our obsession. For the conquest of space now emerged as a future reality, though we would have to hurry if we hoped to catch up after the Russians launched the space probe *Sputnik* in mid-autumn 1957. Disney had already spurred us in that direction. His *Disneyland* TV series, then two years old, included annual broadcasts of *Man in Space*. A trilogy of *Tomorrowland* shows, these installments combined elements of entertainment and education, making the scientific concepts of space travel accessible to the general public.

Likewise, *Our Friend the Atom* (January 23, 1957) attempted to appease some of the then-prevalent fears about nuclear war by presenting the positive possibilities for atomic power. That program's very title has, ever since, been employed to damn Disney as an apologist for the power structure. But if the term "liberal" implies a forward-looking view that eagerly accepts change, particularly technological, then Walt was, as he once put it, "the *true* liberal." [17] And if an interest in such things seems strangely at odds with a Romantic sensibility, we ought to recall that, after poesy, Shelley's great love was science, a point driven home by his wife, Mary, in her novel *Frankenstein* (1818).

Even if audiences did not flock to *Fantasia*, vast numbers of them did see various sequences, including this one. The film was broken down into its components, each individual sequence fitted into various Disney TV programs. Though the official debate may have continued in the public arena as to whether God had indeed created the world in six days, the public at large came to accept science as a result of their exposure to the Disney version of creation, vividly modernist in approach.

Not that Disney ever negates the precepts of religion. He does, after all, conclude *Fantasia* with a most reverent rendering of "Ave Maria." As the dark monster of the previous sequence—Tchernobog in Modest Mussorgsky's *Night on Bald Mountain* (1886)—is defeated by the first light of day, the morning sun bathes forest *and* city with a benign warmth. Borrowing one of the most essentially Christian hymns,

Disney juxtaposes the music with visuals to reveal not a patriarchal vision of God, but a pantheistic notion that true religion is found in the natural world around us.

It's worth recalling, in this context, that Disney chose to reimagine Beethoven's *Symphonie Pastorale* (1808–1809) as a visual ode to paganism. Nymphs, satyrs, and centaurs all engage in an ancient orgy. They wallow in wine and sensuality, presented without any of the moral outrage that a truly simplistic Old Hollywood reactionary like Cecil B. De-Mille had in store for such "sinners" whenever a similar sequence appeared in one of his films (*Sign of the Cross*, 1932; *Samson and Delilah*, 1949; *The Ten Commandments*, 1956). Disney's attitude, expressed in the sequence's tone, is clearly a joyous acceptance of such practices, difficult as that was to pass by censors in Production Code days.

Disney also educated the public as to Darwin's survival-of-the-fittest theory. Initially, the dinosaurs appear relatively benign, so long as the camera focuses on such vegetarian species as the brontosaur and stegosaur. Despite lumbering size, they form a peaceable kingdom as much as the bunnies and fawns in Disney's modern forests. Only when the giant carnivore Tyrannosaurus rex appears does such gentle grazing end. Significantly, Disney chose to depict the plant-eaters as existing in groups, the T. rex as a single, isolated beast. The audience is asked to side with creatures who understand the need for community and oppose those who practice rugged individualism at its most fascistically self-serving.

A battle, lengthy and memorable, then follows between the T. rex and a sad-faced triceratops. If Disney were indeed the sentimentalist he's so often characterized as, the benign beast would survive and the predator would be vanquished. That's not what occurs. The triceratops is defeated and eaten by the T. rex. That, Disney informs us, is nature's way; that is also, of course, what Darwin was trying to tell us.

This may initially appear to belie Walt's Romantic view of nature as a benign garden. Yet it's important to recall that long before the publication of Darwin's thesis, Keats suggested there might be such a thing as an "optimistic evolution," including the necessary disappearance of species:

We fall by course of Nature's laws,
Not force . . .
. . . for 'tis the eternal law
That first in beauty should be
first in might.

DEMYSTIFYING DARWIN. The 1925 Scopes monkey trial had made the public familiar with Darwin's concepts of evolution, though most Americans remained skeptical; the "Rite of Spring" segment in *Fantasia* (1940) so convincingly portrayed the scientific notion of creation that, despite continuing protest by the Christian Right, this became the accepted view.

Such thinking was not confined to the single poem "Hyperion" (1820). Indeed, "All romantic poets conceived of nature as an organic whole, on the analogue of man rather than a concourse of atoms—a nature that is not divorced from aesthetic values, which are just as real (or rather more real) than the abstractions of science."[18] That is, nature as a monist conceives it: The good and the bad that happen all necessarily intermingle, as part of an intelligence which, forsaking the Classicist's master plan of a logical God, nonetheless serves an ongoing struggle toward the perhaps impossible dream of eventual perfection.

When the sequence concludes, we are left with the overall feeling that, if this is indeed the way things are, it is not the way they ought to be. That is apparently how Disney wanted to part with his viewer, as the upsetting ending to his artistic sequence serves as a spur for us to, in the future, do things differently. By vividly depicting a survival-of-the-fittest element in nature, Disney makes his case *against* Social Darwinism—Herbert Spencer's inherently conservative notion that, if our own society is merely a state-of-the-art extension of nature's ongoing way, then we should not trouble ourselves too much about the loss of various species, including subraces of man, and overall biological diversity. Disney rejects all such thinking; children watching the sequence sense that what happened may once have been the way of things, but that doesn't make it right.

Such a situation can, indeed must, be corrected by an evolving human society. Thus, we can accept what is best in nature while also rejecting the worst of what we find there. In many regards, the fullest projection of Disney's attitudes on this subject is found in "Bongo," the first half of *Fun and Fancy Free*. The featurette is based on a story by Sinclair Lewis, the favorite author of many early-twentieth-century socialists, including Walt's father, Elias. "Bongo" opens on a miniature bear, ever-smiling star of a traveling circus who rides a unicycle high on a tightrope and then dives down onto a wet sponge. Everyone in the crowd—mass society, in search of diversion—assumes Bongo will be treated with respect and affection once the show is over. Disney slips us backstage to witness the abuse of such performing animals, commonplace in that beloved American institution, the circus, a fact that is nowhere, save by Disney, depicted in a Hollywood film of that era.

Nightly chained and caged by his "civilized" owners, Bongo—like numerous other Disney characters—survives only by creating a fantasy life that becomes more real to him than the insufferable world he daily lives in. A Romantic idealist, Bongo peers out of the circus train's window, noticing nature—where, he senses, a bear ought to be—dreaming of someday becoming a part of the great outdoors. "The call of the wild," our narrator—drawing on another socialist writer, Jack London—informs us, continued to "ring in his ears" day after day. Eventually, Bongo escapes from the train as it passes a particularly beautiful stretch of woods. As always employing animal characters as emblematic of the human world, Disney has Bongo's flight represent the back-to-nature movement America's intellectual elite had called for ever since Thoreau first slipped off to Walden Pond in 1845, yet which did not become a major mainstream preoccupation until the 1960s.

Bongo is at once lost in the beauty of nature. It seems, for a brief moment, that the dream has become real, his ideal now his everyday life. Bongo spies a distant mountain, reflected in a placid lake. Surrendering to the serenity, he swiftly becomes one with it, the onscreen image serving as Disney's visual equivalent of Shelley's "Mont Blanc" (1816):

> The everlasting universe of things
> Flows through the mind, and rolls its rapid waves . . .
> Now lending splendor, where from secret springs
> The source of human thought its tribute brings . . .

As a post-Darwinist, though, Disney must also acknowledge the precepts of naturalism. Bongo, as it turns out, has been too thoroughly civilized for so easy a transition to full harmony with natural beauty. Stumbling over wild roots, unable to climb trees, he is threatened with starvation after trying and failing to catch fish in the stream. What initially seems a perfect pastoral ("play around the lazy countryside") gives way to a grim image of nature as potential destroyer of this less-than-fit subject.

Bongo curls up in fallen leaves, attempting to sleep. Any hope for such a peaceful interlude is disturbed by nature's nightlife, including grotesque bugs feasting on the plentiful vegetation. Then, moths emerge from cocoons, mosquitoes wildly flock about, rain and lightning appear to be directed specifically at vulnerable Bongo. The Romantic aspect of Disney's worldview early on offered us a vision of nature's brightness and its beautiful element. Now, the modernist side of Disney's sensibility allows for the achievement of a greater honesty by countering the Romantic "ideal" with the Darwinist's "real."

While Disney's inclusive view forces him to admit nature's dark side, his essential sense of optimism (however guarded) ultimately engenders a return to brightness. The ritual return of daylight brings with it a sense of hope. Bongo meets and is smitten with Lulabelle, a pretty girl-bear initially glimpsed as only the Romantic mind could perceive her, bathing in a forest pool. She appears a charming caricature of Venus emerging from the eternal ocean on a half shell, less a potential mate than Bongo's true inamorata. The two briefly share bliss, wilderness giving way to garden as they surrender to the sensuality of their surroundings.

But if sex is half the natural dichotomy, violence is its counterpart. A big, bullying bear named Lockjaw tears through the woods, intent on claiming Lulabelle by eliminating Bongo. Ironically, though, Bongo's exposure to civilized activity causes him to "survive" after emerging as "the fittest." Employing tricks learned in the circus, Bongo runs rings around Lockjaw. A smaller creature's brains, as is so often the case in Disney, allow him to defeat a larger opponent relying strictly on brawn. As one twentieth-century literary critic, defending Romantic poetry with its optimistic view of a benevolent nature in spite of the difficult demands of post-Darwinist thinking, put it:

As for survival, it has not usually been the lone wolves, the savage, the predatory, who have been most successful; but rather the adaptable, the responsive, the cooperative, and those who have developed enough imagination and intelligence to learn by experience.[19]

He might have been describing Disney's "Bongo," for Lockjaw is sent floating downriver, presumably to die. As Bongo and Lulabelle again embrace, harsh wilderness transforms once more into gorgeous garden. Romanticism and Darwinism are not, Disney's moral fable illustrates, incompatible ideas. The harsh process of natural selection—dark, difficult, deadly—must be endured before the peaceful garden can (and, he insists, will) be achieved.

THAT OLD-TIME RELIGION

POLLYANNA (1960)

Reverend Ford (Karl Malden) has unwittingly sold out his own youthful dream of being a good shepherd to a flock by allowing himself and his pulpit to be co-opted by raw capitalism in the genteel guise of Aunt Polly (Jane Wyman). This, against the better judgment and warnings of a truly moral wife (Leora Dana) who, like Disney's other instinctual women, knows better. Ford takes the cues for his Sunday sermons directly from Aunt Polly. She emphasizes "the perishability of our mortal bodies," an attitude Disney—consistently a celebrator of life's natural side—satirizes.

As foils, all positive characters offer variations on Rousseau's natural man. Pollyanna and her partner in juvenile mischief, Jimmy Bean (Kevin Corcoran), hurry off to the woods whenever possible, dirtying their clothes, a seeming travesty to Aunt Polly. She is unappreciative of the soil's rough goodness. Cleanliness clearly is not next to godliness in Disney's context, only a form of sterility. Dr. Edmund Chilton (Richard Egan) spends his Sundays far from church, off in the woods fly-fishing, Hemingway style, in a magical river that, as Norman Maclean would write, runs through it.

Older than anyone but the mayor, Pendergast (Adolphe Menjou), the area's resident iconoclast, lives far from the center of town and its focal point, the church. His is a decaying mansion, worthy of Dickens's Miss Haversham, invisible to the passerby owing to vegetation that has, over the years, all but swallowed the building. To the Classicist mind—Joseph Conrad in *Heart of Darkness* (1902), James Dickey in *Deliverance* (1970)—such a situation would symbolize the character's negative surrender to a regressive jungle. To a Romantic like Disney, it rather suggests positive possibilities for a man who appreciates a natural garden. While Pendergast initially seems frightful, we sense he will soon emerge as one of the film's positive characters.

POSITING PANTHEISM FOR THE GENERAL PUBLIC. No film ever dramatized the view that God is to be found in nature more effectively than *Pollyanna* (1960); despite its reputation as cornball nostalgia for small-town America, the movie savagely satirizes the fire-and-brimstone reverend (Karl Malden) who sold out to a big-money matriarch (Jane Wyman) and her Hoover-Coolidge attitudes. When the reverend comes to his senses, he leads his flock into nature, where they experience a bliss and transcendence they never knew inside the stultifying church.

Pendergast has less trouble getting back in touch with his primal sympathy, under the tutelage of this child as swain, than more conformist adults such as Aunt Polly. Like Polly, he is wealthy. All similarity ends there, between both the people and the homes that signify their values. On his property grows the town's best tree for climbing, trees in Disney symbolizing the absolute center of nature's goodness. Walt's vision is akin to that of Ross Lockridge, Jr., in *Raintree County* (1948); it was not for nothing that Disney brought Joyce Kilmer's poem "Trees" (1916) to the screen in *Melody Time*, emphasizing the relationship of nature to spirituality ("Only God can make a tree").

Earlier, Pollyanna first discovered Jimmy Bean in church. She survives the reverend's dull, didactic sermon by secretly engaging in antisocial behavior, playing pranks on more conventional girls. A little later,

Pollyanna rediscovers him happily crawling about in the branches of a tree, like the free little monkey he in fact is. Pollyanna (who, owing to Aunt Polly's stern influence, still suffers from a few confining attitudes) suggests Jimmy may be a little too wild for his own good.

JIMMY: Don't you believe in God?
POLLYANNA: Of course, I do!
JIMMY (indicating the tree): Well, *He* put it there.

Pollyanna herself soon learns to climb. It is while climbing a tree that she falls, suffering the accident that paralyzes her, perhaps for life. If that appears self-contradictory in terms of the symbolism, we must recall Pollyanna was, in context, abusing the tree by using it to crawl into Aunt Polly's house, countersymbol of conformity and capitalism.

Disney's equivalent of Shakespeare's rude mechanicals, the working-class women and men employed by Aunt Polly, know better and understand more than she, despite their lack of formal education. At one point, parlor maid Angelica (Grace Canfield), a sour-pussed yet savvy commentator on the action, sadly notes that Sundays have become a despised ritual owing to the reverend's fire and brimstone sermons. "Death comes unexpectedly," Ford repeats over and over. He is the Bible thumper incarnate, at one point actually doing just that. Clearly, he was drawn from the despised ministers Walt suffered in his youth. So we should not be surprised that little Jimmy Bean—Disney's re-creation of his own self as a mischievous child—ignores the whole thing. Jimmy entertains himself by slipping a frog into the bonnet of a prim girl. The good mayor (Donald Crisp), meanwhile, dozes off. At the height of the reverend's diatribe against sexual activity, the likable young people Nancy (Nancy Olsen) and George (James Drury) exchange provocative glances, planning to meet secretly later.

Disney, like the moral center of his film—Pollyanna herself—adores such innocent rebellion, so he portrays it with considerable relish. Condemned, on the other hand, is the reverend's stiff insistence that all present must be "born again" if they wish to avoid the everlasting fires of damnation. It's worth noting that *Pollyanna* was released concurrently with Richard Brooks's film of Sinclair Lewis's *Elmer Gantry*. Critics heaped (deserved) praise on that "adult" movie for daring to attack the hypocrisies of organized religion in America. In retrospect, though, Disney's film ought to be considered the more courageous of the two. The religious element satirized in *Gantry* was the fringe evangelical movement, a relatively easy target, whereas Disney went for the jugular, striking at a respectable small-town church of the type his supposed target audience attended weekly.

All pagan (Celtic, Druid, etc.) worship of nature deities took place outdoors, and the Christian concept of group prayer within church walls (civilization) can be viewed as a direct reaction to this earlier form of religious practice. Reaching back to ancient tradition while looking ahead to New Age attitudes, Disney has Reverend Ford dramatically arc. He reverses his earlier attitudes once he truly "sees the light" (i.e., rejects all the Puritan values he for so long steadfastly preached). Reverend Ford insists that his flock abandon the sterile white building, instead worshiping outdoors, even insisting that this is the only proper place to discover God. Shortly, a joyous congregation is engaged in a notably pagan celebration of nature, wildly dancing around trees.

BLOWING IN THE WIND

THE SCARECROW OF ROMNEY MARSH (1964)

If Ford represents, before his conversion to pantheism, Disney's notion of a man of the cloth at his worst, the ideal was presented in this TV miniseries. Based on a book by Russell Thorndike and William Buchanan, this is in many ways a throwback to *Robin Hood* and *Rob Roy*, the period-piece British epics in which Walt aggrandized rebels fighting against an unfair Establishment. This time, however, the hero of the common people is (like Don Diego in *Zorro*) a highly educated aristocrat, who nonetheless bleeds inwardly when the simple folk do so in actuality. Beyond that, he is a preacher. Christopher Syn (Patrick McGoohan) serves as the vicar of Dymchurch, a seaside community on Britain's southern coast, circa 1775. At night, he assumes an alter ego. As the Scarecrow, Syn—who, his name notwithstanding, is Disney's hero, despite the fact that he does sin in the eyes of the status quo—rides out at night to defy King George's excessive taxation. The Scarecrow leads a group of smugglers. More political outlaws than self-serving pirates, they employ their gains to pay the taxes of poor but honest country folk.

"There's a new idea blowing in the wind," Dr. Syn informs one of his confederates, mirroring a Bob Dylan song that hit the pop charts all but simultaneously. Rebellion, violent and even deadly if necessary, is enacted to correct a system that has forgotten its democratic values. Terry Gilkyson's ballad insists that this man of the cloth, by becoming the Scarecrow, "rides from the jaws of Hell" while uttering a "devilish laugh." As the names of the vicarage (Dymchurch) and the vicar himself both imply, one man's devil is another's savior. The best man of the cloth, in Disney, is the radical priest. Here, he is a period-piece fictional character who, like the real-life Berrigan brothers of the antiwar movement, dared—in the tradition of the initiator of all such action, Satan himself—to rebel.

6   Gotta Get Back to the Garden
Disney and the Environmental Movement

MY OWN, MY HUMAN MIND . . .
HOLDING AN UNREMITTING INTERCHANGE
WITH THE CLEAR UNIVERSE OF THINGS AROUND.
—Percy Bysshe Shelley, 1816

WE GOT TO GET OURSELVES BACK TO THE GARDEN . . .
—Crosby, Stills, and Nash, 1969

As a contemporary issue, environmentalism—always present in American thought, particularly after the Theodore Roosevelt administration created our national park system—rose in the public consciousness following World War II. An age of scientific "enlightenment" led to ever more ambitious biological engineering applied—if not for the first time,

AN INSPIRATION FOR GREENPEACE. The radical environmental movement born in the 1960s, which refused to rule out violence as a means of saving our oceans, derived its paradigm for operation from Disney's *20,000 Leagues under the Sea*; whereas the Captain Nemo of Jules Verne's imagination had been a misguided madman, Disney reinvented him (in the person of James Mason) as a tragic hero and highly sympathetic idealist.

then with a new seriousness of intent—to agriculture, through the use of DDT and other pesticides. Outraged by potential dangers, Rachel Carson, a former marine biologist with the U.S. Fish and Wildlife Service, set to work in 1958 on a series of revealing articles. Popular magazines, with the exception only of the *New Yorker*, crumbled under pressure from chemical-industry advertisers, declining to publish findings that they knew to be true.

Carson persisted. In 1962, her book *Silent Spring* belatedly brought "the basic irresponsibility of an [ever more] industrialized technological society toward the natural world" to the public's attention.[1] Hardly by coincidence, President Kennedy responded by creating a special panel of his Science Advisory Committee to study long-term problems created by uncontrolled chemical spraying, setting ecology into place as a significant sixties issue. Carson was hardly the only person hammering home such ideas; similar concepts were advanced by social critic Paul Goodman, German philosopher Herbert Marcuse, and anarchist-ecologist Murray Bookchin (aka Lewis Herber), among others. All proceeded from a single concept, considered radical at the time: "The history of life on earth has been a history of interaction between living things and their surroundings," a natural balance now endangered by human meddling.[2]

However extremist this sounded in 1962, the theory had already been advanced and popularized by Disney. *Bambi*—rereleased every seven years, the case with each Disney animated classic before the home video era—offered an ecology-oriented, anti-hunting statement to one set of young people after another. They would eventually emerge as a more environmentally oriented generation than had ever existed in mainstream America. Precisely how much Disney influenced sixties youth is impossible to say. No question, though, that they did experience the movies, the most basic element making up our popular culture, at an extremely impressionable age. The same would be true of Disney's upcoming nature films, containing, like *Bambi*, a vividly rendered and "prescient message with their warnings about the environmental dangers of human invasion of the natural world."[3] Disney's own statements reveal his firm belief that a new generation, weaned on his films, could avoid the mistakes of its elders as to nature, as well as the betrayal of the previous generation's own primal sympathy:

An adult has lost the sense of play he once had. He's the victim of civilization. The spontaneity of animals? You find it in children, but it's gradually trained out of them.[4]

The *True-Life Adventures*, beginning in 1950, proceed from a slightly different perspective than *Bambi*, since the first modern ecologists had begun their work. Disney's self-ordained if unstated mission was to take such radical findings, previously directed to the country's minuscule intellectualized reading audience, and popularize them by incorporating such concepts into crowd-pleasing entertainments. In this manner, Disney could educate the mass audience without its ever even realizing that a propagandizing process was taking place. More than one nature film ends with narrator Winston Hibler explaining that enlightened individuals among us had begun approaching nature as a helpful partner rather than a dangerous adversary. Though he lived out most of his life during the twentieth century's first half, Disney rejected the abiding conventional wisdom of his time. In its place he offered a sensibility that would not come to fruition until the late 1960s, at least partly as a result of his harnessing commercial entertainment to radicalize his all but captive audience.

THE VITALITY OF NATURE

SEAL ISLAND (1950)

BEAVER VALLEY (1950)

Having matured as a filmmaker, Disney came to realize he could exert the necessary artistic control over his subject matter—the natural world—without needing to employ animation. Such technical elements as the careful pruning of raw footage had, years earlier, led the Russians to conclude that "editing is the foundation of all film art."[5] Likewise, the musical sound track and spoken narration allowed for further manipulation of seemingly objective imagery for a political purpose. So the *True-Life Adventures* series was initiated. This, incidentally, freed Walt's work in the animation field, no longer shackled by a need to offer intensely accurate renderings of the world. Not coincidentally, the cartoons became ever more stylized and surreal, from *The Three Caballeros* (1945) through *Melody Time* (1948) to *Alice in Wonderland* (1951).

The first *True-Life Adventures*, created in the tradition initiated by Robert Flaherty with *Nanook of the North* (1922), showed primitive pockets of life, observed for what they can by implication tell us about ourselves. To achieve this, Disney had instructed documentarians Alfred and Elma Milotte that, when they arrived in Alaska, they should "not show any indication of man's presence."[6] This allowed Walt to create a continuity with those early *Silly Symphonies*, focusing on each of the seasons. The new film emphasized "the life cycle of the seals," in particular the two great motifs in all Disney movies: sex and death.[7] This resulted in an early recognition of what, in the upcoming decades, would be tagged the Generation Gap: Presented as entirely natural—i.e., positive—is the challenge by young male seals to the old for dominance over their society, particularly over females of child-bearing age. A violent fight erupts, in which the young vanquish the old. We see, in this normal occurrence, seemingly removed from human society and universalized in a natural arena, a paradigm for America in the following decades.

The remainder of the film, however, concentrates on more positive elements of the seals' lifestyle, as the community migrates into the Pacific Ocean for the coming winter. Here, Disney again follows a pattern set by the Romantic poets, whose work accords

great significance [to] the abundant manifestations of mutual helpfulness, or symbiosis, in flora and fauna; [there] is a vast system of beneficent interrelationships.[8]

In the following film, *Beaver Valley*, Disney chose the title animal for his focus after research indicated that the beaver was a "leading citizen" amid the myriad life-forms found in river-wood areas.[9] Above all, though, the positive relationship of this species to the other fauna and flora was emphasized. As to Disney's high opinion of the beaver, that reflected his ongoing political attitudes. This is amply illustrated throughout the featurette as beavers put into practice Walt's beloved work ethic, each on his or her own contributing uniquely to the overall good of the group.

As did Shelley in his poetry, Disney concerns himself with "the vitality of nature, its continuity with man, and its emblematic language,"[10] which allow the understanding heart and the knowing mind to grasp God's presence on earth. Clearly, though,

nature did not really appear here on its own terms. Instead, it was a kind of canvas upon which Disney and the American audience painted an array of [contemporary] concerns . . . an implicitly American ethos of competition, adaptation, individual initiative, and [community-oriented] industriousness.[11]

ADVENTURES IN THE EVERYDAY

NATURE'S HALF ACRE (1951)

Though his nature films would eventually cover the entire world, one aspect of Disney's ambition for the early works was akin to that of Wordsworth, who believed that enlightenment, like charity, ought to begin at home. Analyzing man in relationship to nature, the poet insisted that the terms "imagination" and "creative" must always be employed together. Thus fused, our symbiotic "creative-imagination" provides us with a means of perceiving any stretch of nature, however humble, as a microcosm. Close study of the "ordinary" and "specific" would provide, for a now enlightened observer, a fuller understanding of the universe's great secrets. A poet who embarks on such adventures into the everyday "sees into the life of things," at which point "Imagination is thus an organ of knowledge which transforms objects, sees through them, even if they are only 'the meanest flower.'" [12]

Disney's twentieth-century equivalent to the ancient art of "poesy" is the motion picture medium. *Nature's Half Acre* studied those elements of the wild still existing in the life native to the single vacant lot in any modern suburban neighborhood, with particular emphasis in this case on the insect kingdom, as portrayed (by director James Algar and cinematographer Murl Deusing) via state-of-the-art time-lapse photography. As to Romantic parallels, the first two films had approximated Coleridge; for him, poetry's great appeal resided in its ability to make the unknown comprehensible to the average person. This 1951 short veered closer to Wordsworth, who called on the poet to reveal elements of the unknown in what, to casual eyes, appears ordinary.

For Disney, as for the Romantics before him and the hippies to come, nature constituted "imagination itself." The goal for all three: a higher consciousness allowing the sensitized person

> To see a world in a grain of sand;
> and Heaven in a Wild Flower,
> Hold infinity in the palm of your hand
> And Eternity in an hour.

This Wordsworthian approach was not lost on film critics of the time. One actually claimed that such films demonstrated "the Creator has a plan for all, no matter how mighty or humble"; [13] another insisted that "God's master plan for the existence of this planet is dramatically enacted every second of the day" [14] and that this concept is illustrated in the Disney nature films. Though the *Christian Herald* had in the past always selected films with a notably religious theme as its "Pictures of the Year," the editors included two Disney nature movies in 1955, owing to what they perceived as an "adherence to Christian concepts of morality." [15]

The irony is that though the films are all extremely spiritual, the theology being advanced is anything but traditionally Christian. Walt argues in favor of pantheistic principles, the Romantic's creative imagination constituting an organic force that allows an open human mind to gain "insight into reality, read nature as a symbol of something behind or within nature not ordinarily perceived."[16] That is, monism, which adds to the pantheist's notion of nature as earthly evidence of God's existence a further belief in a single intelligence behind the myriad facets we see. Such a summarizing of the monist's credo perfectly describes the ambition of all *True-Life Adventures* to follow.

GOING FLAHERTY ONE BETTER

THE LIVING DESERT (1953)

THE VANISHING PRAIRIE (1954)

THE AFRICAN LION (1955)

SECRETS OF LIFE (1956)

JUNGLE CAT (1960)

Despite any implication contained within the series title, each film begins in animation, not live-action photography. A cartoon paintbrush draws a relief map of the area to be scrutinized. Gradually, the painting gives way to documentary footage, if only after Disney has visually implied that what will follow has been filtered through his unique vision. In some of the films, notably *Secrets of Life*, additional transitions in time and place are also provided by the paintbrush, animated sequences intruding on what we've been watching as "true-life." In this manner, Disney deconstructs the viewing experience. He reminds us, meanwhile, that while this may be drawn from reality, all of it is reality interpreted for a specific moral purpose.

No concept is more essential to this series than the notion of cycles. This is most evident in *White Wilderness*, with its emphasis on the migratory aspect of many arctic animals. Also, *Living Desert*'s closing commentary could serve for any and all other entries in the series: "In this fantastical world, there are no endings or beginnings. After every night, the new dawn. And so it will be till the end of time." Such words articulate one aspect of Woodstock thinking, as embodied by the anthem "Turn, Turn, Turn," itself a modernized Ecclesiastes:

To everything,
Turn, turn, turn;

There is a season,
Turn, turn, turn,
And a time to every purpose
Under heaven.

The song, written by Old Left folksinger Pete Seeger, was revived in the late 1960s for the folk-rock audience by the Byrds. The words echo early Disney cartoons, which celebrate the four seasons via animation.

For a sense of perspective that would make his material comprehensible, Disney began *The Vanishing Prairie* in the present. Gradually, though, the narrative voice draws us back in time to pioneers crossing the plains, then to the Indians preceding them, finally moving further back to Disney's true interest: the *original* prairie, vanishing owing to civilization, as it existed before the first appearance of man. This approach invites further comparison between Disney and Flaherty. *Nanook* and all of Flaherty's subsequent films focused on the rare remaining examples of primitive man, living in harmony with natural settings as civilized people fail to do. Like Disney, Flaherty was an artist of Romantic temperament. Disney would provide much the same thing in his later *People and Places* series. Initially, though, he went Flaherty one better, attempting to recapture for viewers a vision of nature *before* man's intrusion, even that of primitive man—a time when "nature alone held domain," as narrator Winston Hibler informs us.

Always for Disney, the balance of nature is emphasized, while a master plan including seemingly random negative actions is revealed. Though *Jungle Cat* describes the leopard as "executioner of the plain," we immediately learn his function: "to weed any other groups of their weaklings," ensuring survival of the species in a way that man's pleasure-hunting practices do not accomplish. Without the seemingly worthless devastation of a volcano's lava flow, Hibler informs us in *Secrets of Life*, the earth's crust could not replenish itself, allowing life to continue. "What is famine for one is often feast for another," we learn in *African Lion*. When locusts devour the grass, gazelles starve; yet hungry storks joyously feast on the locusts. This particular film proceeds from the notion that the title animal "is one among many on the plains, and all have a part to play in nature's pageant." The very choice of that intriguing term—"pageant"—suggests an event, either preplanned or organically emerging. Either way, it is based on cosmic order and, accordingly, implies something other than chaos.

Disney takes a consistent approach toward Darwin's survival-of-the-fittest theory. Widely misunderstood, Darwin's thesis seems to suggest that cruel predators will always conquer weaker prey. Yet in *Jungle Cat*, two dangerous predators are matched, jaguar versus alligator. The jaguar emerges victorious owing to effective strategy as compared to the alligator's brute strength. Intelligence, coupled with that other quality so admired by Disney, courage, will prevail: "Again, the jaguars conquer," Hibler intones, "because they know no fear." Perhaps not at this point. Fear, however, is precisely what causes the jaguar to later fail, while pursuing a seemingly defenseless sloth. The pathetic creature, through courage and cleverness, uses its "one great gift"—an ability to climb—to escape, extending itself high onto a branch that intimidates the vertigo-prone jaguar, which swiftly retreats.

"The predator suffers a failure of nerve," Hibler explains. "Thus do the meek survive." And, biblically speaking, inherit the earth. The jungle is not, we learn from Disney, a nihilistic bog favoring the cruelest predator, but an ordered cosmos where the values that we learn from religion —*any* of the world's great religions—are in full evidence. The sloth, by understanding its environment, lives to face another day. A silly marmoset, however, lacks common sense, daring to play foolish games with a nearby boa. Shortly, the snake wraps around the creature, crushing it to death. That act is depicted here with surprising vividness, though hardly to exploit the ugly sight, *Mondo Cane*–style. Rather, Disney includes the ugly incident for the purpose of moral instruction: "Foolhardiness must pay its price," Hibler sighs. Still, following an admission of nature's dark (Darwinistic) side, Disney always moves on to its positive (Wordsworthian) counterpart.

So an extended sequence in *Vanishing Prairie* depicts a mother cougar pursuing a young deer into the brush. Though we are spared the frightful moment of truth (death takes place offscreen), we witness her dragging the carcass back to the lair. How easy it would have been, particularly in a film designed to appeal largely to children, to make the cougar a villain, the deer her poor victim, thereby encouraging audience members to cheer for the deer to escape. How much more demanding Disney's complex vision is; after all, the cougar cubs must eat. As *Living Desert*'s narrator insists: "In her desert drama, nature knows neither hero nor villain; she's impartial to all."

Predators are portrayed as equal in morality to prey, since—as we are constantly reminded—such animals kill for survival, not (like man) for sport. The death of a deer resembling Bambi's mother is not here a source for mourning, as in that animated film. Disney's prescient dismay at the ways of man does not extend to the animal kingdom, where we are

SURVIVAL OF THE FITTEST. All the Disney *True-Life Adventures*, including (clockwise from top left) *Secrets of Life* (1956), *The Vanishing Prairie* (1954), *The African Lion* (1955), and *The Living Desert* (1953), vividly portray the grim realities of nature, yet the Disney oeuvre attacks the notion of Social Darwinism, arguing that as human beings, we ought to strive for a higher level of existence.

told "creatures kill only for food, to survive." Such violence is functional, therefore acceptable. So a rattlesnake's battle with a cute prairie mouse in *Living Desert* isn't presented as evil attacking good. Not even an adorable mouse, so significant a creature in the Disney iconography, is favored. Later in *Living Desert*, we witness a duel to the death between hawk and rattlesnake. When the hawk wins, there are no cheers, no hisses, from an audience held spellbound—without the filmmakers ever resorting to the cheap, obvious involvement tactic of taking sides.

Such elements as music, narration, and film editing, all of which can easily be employed to manipulate the audience's response, here are used to create a sense of balance. As *Vanishing Prairie*'s cougar closes in on that gentle deer, any building emotional response on our part is curtailed by a crosscut to the cougar's cubs, hungrily waiting at home. "Nature labels no creature good or bad," we are told. "All are equal, and must be given an equal chance to survive." Moreover, Disney consistently corrects prejudices against creatures that are, in our eyes, ugly, and as a result maligned by popular mythology. This explains why, in *Living Desert*, a close-up of a hideous bat is undercut by a surprising revelation: This species "lives entirely on insects and helps keep the pest population under control." Understandably, then, a Gila monster is not the simplistic villain of the piece, except in the mind of those adorable ground squirrels he menaces. Disney will not allow his audience—even little children—to take the cuter creature's side: "Nature's theme," we are reminded at the moment of truth, for both hungry Gila monster and frightened squirrel, "is always the preservation of the species."

Unaccountably, Richard Schickel charges that Disney "explains away the necessary, endlessly entrancing mystery [of nature] far too easily."[17] In fact, essential to the series is the notion that some things should never be explained. In *Living Desert*, we witness "the riddle of the rocks that move," far-reaching paths in the sand providing proof of huge boulders passing from one location to another. How could this phenomenon occur? The film will not tell us, partly because no one knows but also because the magic of any secret can continue only if we are left to consider its wonders in the context of our individual imagination.

No aspect of the nature films has been more heatedly criticized than Disney's tendency to humanize animals. In *Jungle Cat*, an otter's playing on a branch is likened to "a trapeze routine." *African Lion* treats us to the spectacle of a long-legged bird eating parasites off the hippo's back, stopping to snack on its eyebrows: "a bird beautician, as it were." *Living Desert*'s setting is grim, yet the roadrunner provides this natural theater's "comedy relief," while "at the residence of Mrs. Tarantula, it's always open house"—a darkly ironic comment, seeing as the guests provide themselves as dinner. *Living Desert* included the most highly humanized character in all of the *True-Life Adventures:* Skinny, a kangaroo rat. Like most Disney heroes—human, animated, or "natural"—he is a misfit-individualist, who after much travail earns his place in the society.

Again revealing his implicitly leftish leanings, Disney displayed in all the nature films an abiding admiration for those species that operate as groups: kangaroo rats in *The Living Desert*, prairie dogs in *The Vanishing Prairie*, elephants in *The African Lion*, etc. Though the camera does pick out particular individuals in each setting, such a character's loyalty to the group (Skinny risks his life to save the community-at-large) qualifies it as a Disney hero. Though his movies are indeed "implicitly American"—as are those of Ford, Hawks, Capra, and (truth be told) even longtime expatriate Welles—they are inclusive. Each contains a mixture of the best of liberal and conservative attitudes, in Disney's case owing to his signature "blending of instinctive individualism with community obligation."[18]

As had been the case with animated work reaching back to Oswald Rabbit, anthropomorphism was the basis for Walt's approach. Animals take on the qualities of people, their misadventures serving as moral cautionary fables for the viewer. This sets Disney squarely within a tradition of folk art that can be traced back to Aesop, whose ancient fables supplied Disney with plentiful material for *Silly Symphonies*. Yet many critics approached *Living Desert* from a false, naïve assumption: What they were about to see would be literally and objectively rendered, which, of course, is quite impossible from anyone possessing a unique artistic sensibility. As one literary critic long ago put it:

Such is the power of creative imagination, a seeing, reconciling, combining force that seizes the old, penetrates beneath its surface, disengages the truth slumbering there, and, building afresh, bodes forth anew a reconstructed universe in fair forms of artistic power and beauty.[19]

Yet when Disney opted for a natural continuation of his already established approach, now extended into live-action filming, he was confronted by hostile critical reaction. In *Time*'s review of *Living Desert*, the writer complained: "Disney seems afraid to trust the strength of his material. He primps it with cute comment and dabs it with flashy cosmetic touches of music."[20] More outraged still was Bosley Crowther, then influential film reviewer for the *New York Times*. Crowther was incensed at the "playful disposition to edit and arrange . . . so that it appears the wildlife . . . is behaving in human and civilized ways."[21] Such comments, mistaken at the time for common sense, are naïve at best, ignorant at worst. External reality, captured on celluloid, was of negligible value until, in the editing room, the artist could reach "beneath the surface chaos of the external world in order to reveal its infrastructure" to the audience.[22]

England's John Grierson, credited with coining the term "documentary," always insisted that objectivity had no place in fact-based films, at least not if they were to be anything of lasting significance—that is, moving beyond a merely journalistic rendering of detail. Years later, American documentarian Albert Maysles insisted:

We can see two kinds of truth here. One is the raw material which is the footage . . . no one has tampered with. Then there's the other kind of truth that comes in extracting and juxtaposing the raw material into a more meaningful and coherent storytelling form which finally can be said to be more than just raw data.[23]

What it can be "said to be" is art, the documentary film as, in the words of early filmmaker/theorist Hans Richter, an original (i.e., unique) art form.[24]

As Keats put it a century and a half earlier: "What the Imagination seizes as Beauty must be Truth whether it existed before or not." The poet's words serve to answer those who sniffed at the sight of a scorpion mating ritual in *Living Desert* transformed, through bravura editing and reverse-motion photography, into a square dance, complete with western swing music and a country caller: "Stingers up for the stingaree, but watch out, gal, you don't sting me!" Disney's imagination seized on the beauty inherent in this idea, which emerges as a truth onscreen, though it didn't necessarily exist in raw footage presented by Paul Kenworthy, Jr. The true poet, as Shelley wrote in *A Defence of Poetry*, "participates in the eternal, the infinite, and the one" by lifting a dark veil to reveal the "hidden beauty of the world, and makes familiar objects be as if they were not familiar."[25] The poet's imagination is "an instrument of knowledge of the real," allowing us to understand the world—its inner meaning, not the surface data—more fully.[26]

This is what Disney achieved. *Living Desert* and its follow-ups were conceived and executed by an artist desiring to express "the romantic deification of nature" while proving that man and nature are "not only continuous, but emblematic of each other."[27] Or, as Blake put it,

Each grain of Sand,
Every stone on the Land . . .
Cloud, Meteor, and Star
Are Man Seen Afar.

Thus seen, the depictions that most provoked criticism are not merely defensible but necessary. A burrowing snake's movements captured in slow motion to suggest a ballet, or mating movements of tarantulas transformed into a tarantella are not facile gags—mere desperate attempts to make mundane material fun for the public. All, rather, are essential to Disney's vision, his discovering universal truths for mankind in specifics of the natural world. In actuality, the tarantella was created as a human rendering of the spider's stratagem; art, as Aristotle put it, an imitation of life, in this case man's art an imitation of natural life. Humankind's imitation of existence in the wild implies a cognition, however unconscious, of our ongoing connection to that primordial world.

Always, Disney remains the guarded optimist. So while much has been made in *Vanishing Prairie* of humankind's destructive influence,

Disney (being Disney) can only conclude: "Mankind *is* beginning to understand nature's pattern, helping to replenish and rebuild, so that the vanishing pageant of the present may become the enduring pageant of the future." Like Carson and her colleagues, Disney believes that we must make the effort to reintegrate ourselves into the natural world. In the late 1960s, that effort would become a major social movement—initiated by those who had seen Disney's films in the late 1950s and early '60s.

TOWARD A NEW ART FORM

PERRI (1957)
NIKKI, WILD DOG OF THE NORTH (1961)
THE LEGEND OF LOBO (1962)
THE INCREDIBLE JOURNEY (1963)

Up to this point in his career, Disney had attempted to break down all preexisting barriers between animation and live action. Shortly, he would embark on a series of films that went the *True-Life Adventures* one better, purposefully destroying the invisible wall between fact and fiction, always a tenuous distinction at best. *Perri* opened with a natural panorama that, in terms of beauty, surpassed anything the studio had done, even the visual exploration of a forest that opened *Bambi*. In that animated classic, all such visual effects were achieved through the cartooning process. In the opening sequence of *Vanishing Prairie*, however, all corresponding images had been achieved with an on-location camera. Part of the significance of *Perri* is that for the first time, Disney combined animation and documentary footage in a revolutionary manner. It's literally impossible to tell where the one leaves off and the other begins.

This blending is what, in films as different from *Perri* as *Mary Poppins* (1964), the Disney sensibility is *about*. Visually, he informs us that our supposed "fantasies" and "realities" are as inseparable as Freud insisted our dreams and everyday experiences are. Advance publicity insisted that *Perri* was not another of the *True-Life Adventures*, but the first of a new series, the *True-Life Fantasies*. Closely following a novel by *Bambi*'s author, *Perri* conveyed with the camera what the Disney artists had, on that earlier project, managed with paint and brush.

The squirrel's winter dream sequence is one of the great examples of the antirealistic cinema initiated by Luis Buñuel and Salvador Dali with their avant-garde groundbreaker, *Un Chien Andalou* (1929), and eventu-

THE FIRST (AND ONLY) "TRUE-LIFE FANTASY." Disney collapsed the previously sacrosanct genres of animated fantasy and true-life adventure in 1957 with *Perri*, based on a novel by *Bambi* author Felix Salten; sadly, narrow-minded critics complained about the mixing of such disparate elements, though this was always essential to Disney's genius: combining P. B. Shelley's notion of making the ordinary appear extraordinary in art and S. T. Coleridge's concept of making the outlandish seem everyday.

ally served up to America's adult audience by Dali and Alfred Hitchcock in *Spellbound* (1946). Disney extended this popularization of the avant-garde principles to children, allowing them their first significant taste of the outright surreal. This blurring of fact and fiction, causing *Perri* to be roundly attacked as a "bastardization,"[28] was, properly understood, one of the first attempts in Hollywood to achieve what Soviet theorist/director Sergei Eisenstein had been praised for in such films as *Ten Days That Shook the World* (1929). Seemingly a documentation of the revolution that had occurred a decade earlier, the film was shot on actual locations for a sense of total surface authenticity, yet included endless dramatic inventions. Eisenstein's ongoing reputation as a pioneer/genius of the movie medium is in large part based on experimentation with the fusing of fact and fantasy. Ironically, many reviewers who earlier lambasted Disney for doing much the same thing later lauded Woodstock-era filmmakers when they revolutionized the commercial cinema by following Walt's example, as in Peter Watkins's *The War Games* (1966), Gino Pontecorvo's *The Battle of Algiers* (1967), and Haskell Wexler's *Medium Cool* (1969).

Disney, as always, was the key transitional artist who bridged the gap between earlier experimenters and those to follow. In *Nikki*, Disney adapted a cinema verité technique, developed only a few years earlier by practitioners of the French nouvelle vague, their handheld newsreel cameras employed to lend a fiction film a factual semblance. When such "groundbreaking" directors as Arthur Penn (*Bonnie and Clyde*, 1967), Dennis Hopper (*Easy Rider*, 1969), and Martin Scorsese (*Mean Streets*, 1973) opted for such an approach, they were hailed for daring to break down barriers between an overly staid commercial cinema and the off-beat experiments of European auteurs, something Disney had done a generation earlier. Essential to *Nikki* was a complex view in which no species, including humans, is utterly dismissed. The film includes a hor-rifyingly realistic sequence in which a corrupt man of civilization, LeBeau (Emile Genest), attempts to turn Nikki into a killer for brutal dog fights by teaching him to hate. He is countered by Coutu (Andre Dupas), the good man of the woods who previously befriended Nikki, offering him love. Humans are not necessarily good or bad, any more than any species; for Disney, it's the individual that counts. Finally, Coutu returns Nikki to the wilds, where they, along with their third friend, a bear, all live (like ebony, ivory, and jade in a popular Wood-stock-era song) in perfect harmony—balancing their makeshift com-munity in nature with an understanding of the need of each to maintain his own territorial imperatives.

A similar approach informs *The Incredible Journey*. Three house pets—a bull terrier, a Siamese cat, and a Labrador retriever—together make their way across 250 miles of Canadian woodlands to rejoin their human family. The approach of allowing each a distinct personality en-raged those already embittered by that technique in *Living Desert*. Yet by making his youthful audience vividly identify with individual animals as well as their unlikely but functional community, Disney furthered the already growing ecological movement, which could not have rippled into the vast mainstream without instigating a newfound respect there for animal life.

If the humans are notably nice in *Journey*, they are consistently un-pleasant in *Legend of Lobo*. Then again, Disney here purposefully set for himself a difficult ambition: Make a lone wolf, long considered the out-law animal of the American West, as likable and sympathetic as any cute deer or squirrel. The title character passes through all the life cycles so basic to earlier films, as birth and loss of his mother force Lobo to sur-vive on his own. As always, in Disney's unique combining of Republican and Democratic values, rugged individualism must be tempered by community involvement. The loner joins a pack by first proving his worth—working his way up to leader via superior skills, eventually mating and bringing a new generation into the world. By film's end, the wolf has been so thoroughly transformed into a typical Disney hero that all the age-old stigmas about the supposedly "big bad wolf" (including Disney's own!) have been removed. Not surprisingly, the posthippie generation would treat the wolf far more fairly than had ever been the case before; Robert Redford's Sundance Institute reveals great sympathy for the much-maligned animal.

Shelley wrote in his *Defence of Poetry* that the artistic imagination, properly employed, proceeds from the "principle of synthesis," without which poetry—verbal in his time, cinematic today—cannot feature an "expression of the imagination."[29] Likewise, Disney does not go to nature to report without intrusion, any more than Flaherty did. Nature, for all three artists, exists as a possible source of content—waiting for one of creative temperament to structure it, while expanding the possibilities of his chosen medium, into a work of personal expression—a process resulting in art.

LAUNCHING GREENPEACE

20,000 LEAGUES UNDER THE SEA (1954)

One result of widespread environmental consciousness-raising was the creation of ecology-oriented organizations. Few proved more visible or controversial in "ecoteur" (economic sabotage) action than Greenpeace. Formed in Canada in 1971, originally Vancouver-based, Greenpeace swiftly transformed into a multinational group, combining two key 1960s causes, ecology activism and antiwar protest. Early leaders, including Robert Hunter, Paul Watson, and David McTaggart, made it clear that Greenpeace would not (like traditional reform-minded environmental groups such as the Audubon Society and the Sierra Club) settle for speeches and sit-ins. Rather, Greenpeace would operate on the principle of "direct action," particularly on the high seas. The group first attracted attention by sailing its vessels directly into a nuclear testing zone off the Aleutian island of Amchitka, located in the north Pacific. As a result, Greenpeace—despite its avowed intention to stop the despoiling of our oceans *and* achieve world peace—came to be perceived as potentially dangerous by numerous governments, as "each of the expeditions sought to make visible an identifiable 'evil'" through media publicity.[30] Again, the question begs to be asked: Where did the founding fathers of radical environmentalism get such ideas?

In 1954, the children who would grow into the young adults who formed Greenpeace were presented with a virtual blueprint for their course of action. The most ambitious of all Disney live-action films, Walt's adaptation of Jules Verne's *20,000 Leagues under the Sea* brought environmental-activist ideas to the public's attention, even as Rachel Carson's first book, *The Sea around Us*, remained a subject of fervent discussion among the nation's intellectual elite. Disney's choice of this fantasy adventure and his unique approach to the material allowed him to present a convincing defense of a radical environmentalist who insists that violence, including murder, is necessary to make his point, without ever losing an audience's sympathy.

That character is Captain Nemo (James Mason), Verne's fictional "mad genius." In 1868, Nemo has, on his secret island Vulcania, managed to split the atom, harnessing its energy, to be used for peaceful or destructive purposes, even as modern scientists had done in the years immediately before Disney made this movie. Such perfect timing hardly seems coincidental. Few subjects were more heatedly debated during the 1950s than whether atomic energy would, in time, prove our salvation or our demise. Disney's take on the Verne classic allowed him to present his audience with a perfect paradigm for that problem, safely contained (to ward off possible censorship) within a period-piece setting.

At movie's end, Nemo's atomic submarine, the *Nautilus*, disappears under the Pacific's waves, while a mushroom cloud circles his island, Vulcania. Nemo himself has set the charge. Gradually, he has been convinced by a brilliant, enlightened scientist, Professor Arronax (Paul Lukas), to cease violently radical raids on military bases. Instead, Nemo hopes to share his wonderful secrets, finally won over to Arronax's guardedly optimistic belief that humans will be willing and able to use the split atom for our greater good. Returning to Vulcania with such a positive purpose in mind, Nemo instead discovers his island overtaken by a shoot-first, ask-questions-later international military force, summoned (through messages in bottles) by captured seaman Ned Land (Kirk Douglas) and Arronax's secretary, Conseil (Peter Lorre).

As the three escape and witness the island's destruction, including all occupying soldiers, earlier words from Nemo (presented as a voice-over) close out Disney's film:

There *is* hope for the future. When the world is ready for a new and better life, all this will someday come to pass. In *God's* good time!

Such words express Disney more than the original author. The book's greatest appeal—its science-fiction premise, vividly envisioning what another pioneer of the genre, H. G. Wells, chose to call the shape of things to come—was no longer viable. Even as Disney produced his movie, the Department of the Navy readied its first nuclear sub, appropriately named the *Nautilus* in homage to both Verne and Disney. In addition to recalling with awe Verne's remarkable powers of prediction, Disney's film necessarily served as an objective correlative for the world of today. In the Disney version, the narrative voice within the old story admits that, a hundred years ago, humankind proved itself unworthy of a Nemo. The film allows for both hind- and foresight: The Nemo of Disney's imagination utters, in 1868, his dying words, looking forward nearly a century to the 1950s. Through that speech—again, marbled with a characteristic guarded optimism—Disney expresses his own ongoing hopeful belief. In the present, man has evolved to the point where an incredible power for good or evil may be harnessed for the good.

There is, of course, no proof that the outcome will be positive. In the spirit of a true crusading liberal, Disney passes his message on to the audience, knowing that they—we!—will have the final word. The intent is to spur us on to do the right thing—to become the peaceniks Nemo would have surrendered to, not the violent militarists who indiscriminately fire on him. Not that Disney made the mistake of overt didacticism. Despite telegraphing his message at movie's end, every effort was made to maintain a balance between the substance of what Walt had to say and the appealing style the public had paid to see. This can (and has) been rudely dismissed as "Disneyfication," resulting in the trivialization of a profound theme through comedy relief. A cute Disney animal has been added, in the form of a scene-stealing seal named Esmeralda; Conseil, Verne's quiet secretary, is transformed into a source of broad physical humor; Land, Verne's unassuming sailor, a strutting, womanizing macho man, even performs an elaborate song-and-dance routine ("Whale of a Tale").

Despite critical brickbats, Disney instinctively understood a concept that, in time, he allowed Mary Poppins to articulate: A spoonful of sugar helps the medicine go down. Here, his "medicine"—Walt asks a middlebrow audience to sympathize with Nemo as he blows up sailing ships, killing the innocent along with the guilty—would have been impossible to accept were the bitter pill not sugar-coated with ample entertainment. Nemo's words about protecting the natural world were echoed, twenty years later, by author-activist Edward Abbey:

When someone invades your home, you don't respond objectively and reasonably. You strike back with emotion, with rage.[31]

True, Disney would have made a more "pure" film had he forsaken such frivolous additions. Then again, he would have made a movie without mass appeal, one that would have played art houses where works containing such statements preach to the converted. Instead, he set into motion a mind-set that would in time change the world. Once more, a classic was drawn upon as a source, then entirely rethought, becoming part of a unique moral consciousness—a mind-set presented to the public through individual works that, like colorful fragments of a jigsaw puzzle slowly being assembled, gradually reveal a full, rich vision.

GOD IS AN ARTIST

TEN WHO DARED (1960)

Even before Theodore Roosevelt made an interest in environmentalism a serious aspect of American politics, John Muir founded the California-based Sierra Club. Beginning in 1892, this organization advanced his notions of "preservation" and the "right use" of wilderness.[32] But as champions of our rich forests and deep waters, both men had been preceded by Major John Wesley Powell, hailed in retrospect as "the west's first great resource analyst."[33] In 1869 Powell fully explored the Colorado River, making maps and bringing back fossils that allowed geology to move light-years ahead. Yet that landmark journey had never been the subject of a film from Hollywood. Since the main party never entered into conflict with hostile Indians, the story was ignored as uncommercial; Powell himself, a physically disabled (one-armed) intellectual, hardly seemed potent material for a rousing western.

Not surprisingly, the very elements that had discouraged other producers attracted Disney. The opening credits of *Ten Who Dared* suggest that this project may well have been intended as an apotheosis of Disney's previous nature, historical, and western films. Like a *True-Life Adventure*, the movie opens with a montage, displaying the natural wonders of the American West. As in a historical film, we view a map of the area in which the adventure will occur; as in the dramatic movies, a book (Powell's autobiography) magically opens, allowing us to enter.

Significantly, though, an antiheroic attitude pervades the piece, setting the pace for nouveaux westerns of the 1960s by such filmmakers as Sam Peckinpah (*Ride the High Country*, 1962; *The Wild Bunch*, 1969). The tone here is a far cry from that of *Davy Crockett*, with its glorious approach to frontier adventures, a mere five years earlier. The "ten who dared" ironically turn out to be a shiftless lot, composed of alcoholics, thieves, and other lowlife types—a *Dirty Dozen* minus two, filmed in the grim style of that characteristically antiheroic epic of the mid-sixties. Powell's own younger brother, Walter (James Drury)—psychologically scarred by experiences in Andersonville prison camp—brutally attacks the group's only Southerner (Ben Johnson). The portrait of the group's scout, Bill Dunn (Brian Keith), is anything but a celebration of the mountain man. Greedy, scurrilous, less knowledgeable about the ways of the West than he lets on, this is the screen's first anti-Romantic image of such a frontiersman.

Likewise, there is no attempt to transform quiet, introspective Powell into a traditional movie hero. As portrayed by John Beal, he's insecure in the world of men, happy only when alone with the beloved fossils he's collected. The only person in the movie who in any way recalls a typical hero is Jim Bridger (Roy Barcroft), unaccountably referred to here as "Jim Baker." The ten encounter this real-life figure while camping near Echo Cliff. Bridger and his Indian wife (Dawn Little Sky) offer them sage advice, she—in Disney's protofeminist tradition—proving far more helpful than her famous husband.

As in the *Crockett* shows, based on Davy's own diary, there is a strong suggestion of historicity. Words spoken by Beal on a voice-over are drawn directly from Powell's journals. Yet this is Disney entertainment, so a boy-and-his-dog story was added. The youngest member of Powell's group, Andy Hall (David Stollery), smuggles a pup aboard one of the four boats on which they navigate the always beautiful, often treacherous Colorado River. Such a touch is hardly decorative. Disney employs this to include such recurring themes as death and the work ethic. Initially, Powell insists the animal must be shot, assigning Andy to kill his own pet, as it might prove a nuisance. Powell rescinds that order, which would have portrayed man imposing himself on a natural creature (always bad in Disney) rather than nature taking its course (always good, even when deadly). Powell sighs, hoping the dog may yet prove useful; at the end, he does. When Major Powell becomes trapped on a cliff, the dog sniffs him out, finally finding practical work to do. However acceptable survival of the fittest may be when found in nature in the raw, man must, Walt insists, aspire to a higher level.

Likewise, the recurring issue of capitalism is raised. Howland (R. G. Armstrong) and several other team members came along only because they believed Powell was, despite his stated intent, looking for precious metals. "I can't be bothered," Powell insists, "hunting for gold." They assume he's either lying or crazy. At one point, raw capitalism gets the best of them; even Dunn joins the crazed men as they insist that Powell open his treasure pouch, only to stare in disbelief at artifacts of the Paleolithic Age. The scout asks if such objects as prehistoric insects, fossilized in rock, can bring them money upon return to the East. Powell tells Dunn:

These are too precious to sell. You give them away, to museums.

These are the words of a true Disney hero, a species quite unlike any other Hollywood screen protagonist of the twentieth century's first half. Also, the film's incarnation of Powell proves to be one more of Walt's pantheists, seeing in nature the hand of God—not only God the Creator, but God the Artist. He muses, while gazing at the beauty of natural stone formations:

The giant hand that created these monuments from sand and rock used only the wind and water for his paint and brushes.

We recall, in retrospect, the animated paintbrush, splashing color onto a map of America in the opening sequences of *Living Desert* and *Vanishing Prairie*, at last comprehending its full significance. Powell also sets the pace for Indiana Jones in the trilogy of films produced and directed by George Lucas and Steven Spielberg, the two contemporary filmmakers most indebted to Disney. In each film, Indiana is first seen as a practical and realistic man. The key distinction between him and the mercenaries who compete with him for lost artifacts is that he wants to give them to a museum, whereas they want to profit from a sale. In time, he learns the true spirituality that endows the ark of the covenant or the Holy Grail with its greater significance.

ACHIEVING A DELICATE BALANCE

THE GNOME-MOBILE (1967)

Early in the twentieth century, a budding conservation movement was attacked by capitalists, in particular those involved in the cutting of timber, as "an anticorporate social movement."[34] This situation escalated when Republicanism shifted from TR's Rough Rider style to the later belief that the best possible president was himself a businessman. During the Hoover and Coolidge administrations, ecologists were written off as Reds; by the 1930s, with another Roosevelt (this one a Democrat, though no less progressive than his predecessor on ecology) in the White House, lumber businessmen were persuaded to go with the con-

Copyright Walt Disney Productions; courtesy Buena Vista Releasing.

INTRODUCING THE ENVIRONMENTAL MOVEMENT. Despite its lighthearted tone and seemingly escapist approach, *The Gnome-Mobile* (1967) was the first feature from a major Hollywood studio to convey the "radical" environmentalist themes that members of the counterculture were then proffering; an old, enlightened millionaire (Walter Brennan) and his flower-power grandchildren (Matthew Garber and Karen Dotrice) rebel against the commercial values of middle-age, middle-class, middlebrow adults and set out to create a natural refuge for an endangered species of leprechaun-like creatures.

servationist flow, putting aside raw capitalism for a more enlightened form. Then,

the language of conservationism was increasingly appropriated by the resource-based industries and other industrial interests attracted to the concepts of efficiency, management, and the application of science in industrial organization.[35]

This real-life solution could have been scripted by Disney, for it actualizes his positive progressive view that things can change, and for the better, though only through conscious, concerted, constant effort.

His final live-action fantasy film fully expresses Walt's belief that a delicate balance between business and environmentalism—i.e., capitalism with a conscience—could be achieved. Lumber tycoon D. J. Mulrooney (Walter Brennan) takes his grandchildren Rodney (Matthew

Garber) and Elizabeth (Karen Dotrice) on a forest picnic. He teaches them to enjoy the lasting beauty of the giant redwoods, even as he explains that his company now carefully plants and harvests other trees so these can be left to live. Elizabeth comes across Jasper (Tom Lowell), a two-foot gnome, who enlists their help. Knobby (also played by Brennan), Jasper's 943-year-old grandfather, is dying. He's convinced the wee forest folk are about to become extinct, having lost the will to live. Jasper requests that local gnomes be relocated in another part of the forest, where man has not yet penetrated, to find others of their kind, whose presence will thus inspire the discouraged gnomes' continued existence.

Old D.J. (first name beginning with "D," perhaps standing for "Disney"; he's played by an actor whose name also happens to be "Walt") is happy to oblige. He redesigns his elegant 1930s Rolls-Royce into a makeshift hippie van. The old man and his young wards (old and young always enjoy a special connection in Disney) embark on their own little odyssey to oppose the death of a species, a full dramatization of the artist's own anti–Social Darwinist viewpoint. Man can, should, *must* "do something."

Middle-class, middle-aged people prove considerably less enlightened. Ralph Yarby (Richard Deacon), vice president of the lumber company, at one point has D.J. committed to a home for the insane. Other awful people kidnap the gnomes and put them in a freak show. In time, though, the two gnomes are reunited with others of their kind. A bevy of beautiful female gnomes compete to see who will mate with Jasper; having won all such contests (proving herself "fittest" in the happiest sense), Shy Violet (Cami Sebring) enjoys that honor. Social Darwinism does not claim America's gnome population thanks to their natural attitude toward sex.

This could not occur without the blessing of D.J., who as an enlightened capitalist sets up a sanctuary, including 50,000 acres of redwood forest that humankind is forbidden to invade. In many respects, *The Gnome-Mobile* is Disney's equivalent to the far better-known *Finian's Rainbow*, only with a strong environmentalist theme, which that more adult-oriented musical failed to properly emphasize. The film offers Walt's final paradigm of how all businesspeople ought to proceed if we are to create a better world.

7 "Hell, No! We Won't Go!"
Disney and the Radicalization of Youth

CAST YOUR WHOLE VOTE, NOT A STRIP OF PAPER MERELY.
—Henry David Thoreau, 1846

THE ONLY VALID FORM OF WAR IS THE REVOLUTION.
—V. I. Lenin, 1916

From its opening hours, the decade of the 1960s was marked by "the growing desire among students to make a difference in the world."[1] Equally important was the oft-overlooked fact that "the student move-

Copyright Walt Disney Productions; courtesy Buena Vista Releasing.

THE RIGHTEOUS WAR. If Disney often conveyed pacifist ideas, they were limited and guarded by his belief in a righteous war, fought for defense rather than imperialistic reasons—particularly when such combat set decent citizens against a true force of evil like the Nazis; a Wiccan woman saves the British empire from invaders in *Bedknobs and Broomsticks* (1971), the final film that Walt personally initiated before his death in 1966.

ments of the 1960s were, in one way, simply the reappearance of an age-old phenomenon. The difference was in the precise issues now raised, and in the size and intensity of the response."[2] As to that "size and intensity," they naturally grew from the suddenly burgeoning number of young people now attending college, youth exposed in ever greater numbers to controversial ideas.

Such a situation could not help but create a distinct and disorienting sense of irony. For nimble young minds noticed a sharp distinction between the ideal world, as espoused in their classes, and the actual corrupted world of which, as became ever more obvious, their own colleges were a part. After all, ROTC trained young people on the campus itself to fight in future wars. Dow and other chemical companies co-opted the universities through grants guaranteeing research that might be used in the creation of chemical warfare weapons, as well as defoliants that would further diminish the ecological balance at home. As one early-sixties student put it:

The University is a vast public utility which turns out future workers in today's vineyard, the military-industrial complex. They've got to be processed in the most efficient way to see to it that they have the fewest dissenting opinions, that they have just those characteristics which are wholly incompatible with being an intellectual. . . . People have to suppress the very questions which reading books raises.[3]

Such statements, dismissed by the right as vaguely anti-American, were deeply embedded in the original American mind-set. As Jefferson insisted early on in the creation of our Republic, endless "little rebellions" would be necessary to ensure that our government did not over the years stagnate—did not, as Jefferson feared, become that very hated thing which the first *true* Americans—i.e., the first true *rebels*—had reacted against.

Our social rebels, over the centuries, thus "serve generally a useful purpose in a watch-dog capacity, exposing the corrupt and awakening the conscience of a busy and practical country."[4] Or, as critic/historian Kenneth Rexroth noted in 1960, "Certainly ours is the only great culture which, throughout its life, has been accompanied by a creative minority which rejected all its values and claims."[5] We must expect radical manifestos in such a democracy to regularly appear.

Many of us were early converted to a belief in the possibilities of a regenerated social order, and to a passionate desire to *do something* in aid of that regeneration. The appeal is not only to our sympathy for the weak and exploited, but also to our delight in a healthy, free social life, to an artistic longing for a society where the treasures of civilization may be open to all.[6] (emphasis added)

Perhaps surprisingly, the words do not hail from Tom Hayden and the SDS, but from an equally radical (if less remembered) spokesman for such causes in 1913, Randolph S. Bourne.

As to the antimilitary mentality that would dominate the sixties, organized student protests had begun shortly after the end of World War II. Then, boycotts of ROTC were staged on numerous campuses. Yet if the press bothered to report such pacifist protests at all during the fifties, it did so in minor ways. And, perhaps more significant still, it did so only to negatively link such activities with the Red paranoia prevalent at the time. Until, that is, the mid-sixties, when the long-running (if heretofore tightly contained) Vietnam War was swiftly escalated by recently elected president Lyndon Johnson.

This stimulated "a world-wide upheaval of disgust" on the part of young people at the disastrous mess their elders had made of things.[7] Or, as Emerson noted more than a century earlier,

Things are in the saddle
And ride mankind.

As always, Disney films, standing out from conventional Hollywood fare, fervently expressed the need for Jefferson's "little rebellions" by Rexroth's "creative minority."

MAKE LOVE, NOT WAR!

DONALD'S SNOWBALL FIGHT (1942)

America's internal conflict over Vietnam was still forming when Walt passed away on December 15, 1966. He did not, then, personally supervise any films released by Buena Vista during the height of this conflict and the antiwar protest against it. Nonetheless, those young people who, in ever greater number, turned against Vietnam had been raised on Disney movies. And as far back as 1942, at the height of a popular war, a Disney cartoon implied a pacifist attitude within the context of obvious anti-Hitler propaganda. *Donald's Snowball Fight* opens with an image of the Duck, skiing down a hill. He spots his three nephews, peacefully building a snowman. Donald transforms into a fascist bully, purposefully plowing into the comrades, destroying their collaborative creative endeavor. In response, these diminutive allies build another snowman, this time with a large stone hidden inside, causing Donald harm when he repeats his action.

Anger then escalates, much as it does in the classic Laurel and

Hardy short *Big Business* (1926), until what began as a silly game of one-upmanship transforms into full-scale Armageddon. At the end, the imperialist attacker has been devastated by the community, which gained great strength and the upper hand through solidarity. The common enemy defeated, they return to peaceful, artistic endeavors. The meek do inherit the earth, if only after waging a righteous and, in a sense, revolutionary war (youth standing against their corrupt elders). Their fight was undertaken against those who invade the boundaries of their existence while denying them a right to peaceful activity.

They are, in Disney's view, right in defending themselves, just as Donald was wrong in initiating his attack. Here, Disney crystallizes his views on war, best described as "limited pacifism." Though Walt didn't make public announcements about this or other aspects of his politics, his work effectively speaks for him. His views, which precisely anticipate the attitudes of most 1960s antiwar activists, were well articulated some years earlier by Major General Smedley Butler, a two-time Congressional Medal of Honor winner. In 1933, Butler grew bitter about having been sent adventuring all over Central America and the Caribbean (during the century's first half, the equivalent of Southeast Asia in the second) on behalf of United Fruit and varied big oil interests. Delivering a speech at the height of the Great Depression, Butler eloquently stated a radical point of view:

War is just a racket. A racket is best described, I believe, as something that is not what it seems to the majority of people. Only a small inside group knows what it is about. It is conducted for the benefit of the very few at the expense of the masses.[8]

Nothing really changes, only the specifics at any moment. What in 1933 Butler noted in our southern hemisphere answers the question posed by Norman Mailer in his 1969 novel, *Why Are We in Vietnam?* And, as one close observer of the current political scene recently put it: "Regrettably, little has changed except the places we send the Marines. Instead of Guatemala, they now range to Iraq and beyond."[9]

As Butler's medals make clear, he was anything but a coward or a pacifist. The general continued:

If a nation comes here to fight, then we'll fight. The trouble with America is that when the dollar earns only 6 per cent over here, then it gets restless and goes overseas to get 100 per cent. Then the flag follows the dollar and the soldiers follow the flag. I wouldn't go to war again as I have done to protect some lousy investment of the bankers. There are only two things we should fight for. One is the defense of our homes and the other is the Bill of Rights.[10]

We already know what Disney thought of the bankers. The phrase coined by anti-Vietnam activists and repeated endlessly was: "I will not fight an *immoral* war in Vietnam!" (emphasis added). The implication is that the majority of war resisters were not necessarily outright pacifists, opposed to all war. Their opposition was to what they considered the immoral aspects of our involvement. For a vivid if brief illustration of such a viewpoint, we have *Donald's Snowball Fight*, depicting Disney's moral war, precisely the same as Butler's.

Disney would develop that theme in a series of films. First, though, there was the necessity of depicting the coming-of-age process by which youth learn to understand, and on some level accept, the presence of evil in a world that, during their tender years, they had been protected from by well-intentioned parents.

DISNEY AND THE DEATH OF INNOCENCE

TREASURE ISLAND (1950)
KIDNAPPED (1960)

The first of the live-action films, *Treasure Island*, was shot on location in England, with an all-British cast, excepting only Bobby Driscoll as cabin boy Jim Hawkins. The film is drenched in death, which constantly challenges the youth's initial innocence. Also, the film contains graphic violence, which in 1950 appeared as groundbreaking as *Psycho*'s shower sequence a decade later. Not surprisingly, the movie struck some observers as "less Disneyesque than any other up to this point."[11]

In particular, the image of pirate Israel Hand (Geoffrey Keen) shot between the eyes by the child hero proved so upsetting to concerned parents that it was eventually removed from rerelease prints. This, along with the focus on a young person whose father has just died (the passing of a parent is the most consistent device to open a story in the Disney oeuvre), establishes *Treasure Island* as a true Disney film, serving as the necessary male correlative to the female-oriented coming-of-age fairy tales.

The Jim Hawkins of Robert Louis Stevenson's 1883 novel is, despite the story's being set a full hundred years earlier, a typical Victorian-era child. Like any normal boy, he harbors a romanticized notion of pirates, falling under the spell of charming rogue Long John Silver (Robert Newton in Walt's film). In Disney's more psychological retelling, Jim has learned, early and from hard experience, an unpleasant truth. He and his (unseen) mother have been harboring a fugitive pirate, Captain

OF INNOCENCE AND EVIL. As in the best classic (*Shadow of a Doubt*, Alfred Hitchcock, 1943) and contemporary (*Silence of the Lambs*, Jonathan Demme, 1991) films, Disney offers in *Treasure Island* (1950) a vision of youthful innocence (Bobby Driscoll as Jim Hawkins) falling under the spell of seductive evil (Robert Newton as Long John Silver); the dark denouement makes vividly clear that it's naïve to think the two can be kept entirely separate in the real world.

Billy Bones (Finlay Currie), in their humble inn, this figure presented as anything but a romanticization. When a bloodthirsty buccaneer, Black Dog (Francis de Wolff), shows up in search of a treasure map, Jim is loyal to the old man less because he believes Bones is a "good" pirate than because of ancient biblical rules of hospitality mixed with raw capitalism: Bones is a paying customer in his family's establishment.

Serving as audience surrogate, Jim must accept loss through death (beginning with Bones) and move on. Shootings, knifings, and bludgeonings occur owing to the presence of one man: Silver, sometimes tavern cook and occasional pirate, hired by well-meaning but naïve Squire Trelawney (Walter Fitzgerald) to oversee the *Hispanolia*'s mess. Before the journey can begin, Silver slips his scurvy mates aboard, arranging to kill the honest seamen. One instance stands out: the murder of Mister Arrow (David Davies), trusted aide to Captain Smollett (Basil Sidney), by playing on Arrow's only weakness, alcohol. Significantly, Silver makes Jim as complicit in this as the hero of a Hitchcock film becomes in the villain's plans, most notably with Farley Granger and Robert Walker in *Strangers on a Train* (1951). As yet unaware that the genial cook plans a mutiny, the cabin boy is persuaded to steal a bottle of rum, doing so for a man he believes to be his special friend. Silver waits for a stormy night, then laces Arrow's meal with alcohol. The following morning, everyone mourns a sailor lost at sea.

Later, Jim crawls deep inside the ship's symbolic womb, a fruit barrel, having heard of a superstition that once the last apple is gone, land will be sighted. Here, Jim overhears Silver and his cohorts (unaware of the boy's presence) plan their mutiny. Visually signifying the death of Jim's innocence, Silver nearly kills the boy with a knife as he tries to spear an apple. Now fully aware that Silver is a villain and has violated the morality of their supposed friendship, Jim might be expected to reject this false father figure, particularly with so decent a man as Dr. Livesey (Denis O'Dea) present. That never happens, though Silver appears ready to kill the boy if it will further his purposes. Likewise, Jim makes clear he will shoot Silver for the good cause, if need be. We know, from his point-blank killing of Israel Hand (no other producer of family films would have dared present such a nightmare-inspiring image, particularly in the early fifties), that Jim is up to the task.

Regardless, a strange form of love develops between the still relatively innocent lad and this incarnation of evil. Perhaps this is because

Long John is a very magnetic character; a completely unscrupulous man who remains in his most wicked moments totally beguiling, to Jim as well as to us. His sense of humor and irony almost never desert him, and it is the knowledge that his façade is not entirely phony that makes him so irresistible.[12]

Disney scuttled Stevenson's original (and, truth be told, pat) conclusion, in which Long John escapes by his own efforts. In contrast, the film dramatizes an innocent's acceptance of death as a part of life, as well as his own inner capacity for evil, as his rite of passage and, in Emerson's words, a necessary journey into adult life.

Here, Long John escapes in a small craft, holding a gun on Jim, forcing the boy to row down a narrow channel toward the sea. Initially, Jim does as he is told. Then he courageously beaches the boat, leaving one-legged Long John stranded, unable to push off. Jim could hurry away, but chooses instead to stand nearby, watching as the pirate struggles in vain. Long John raises his pistol, threatening to shoot if the boy doesn't help. Jim braces for the blast he believes will come, standing in for every child viewer. But Long John can't shoot; however evil, there's something fine in his feelings for the lad. Realizing this, Jim reacts to something deep (and dark) within his own otherwise decent psyche. Operating not out of an instinct for self-preservation but a far more complex emotion, he leaps forward, pushing the craft out to sea. No sooner is Long John's escape assured than Jim's conscious mind regrets his instinctual action, owing to rules stuffed into his (our) superego by society.

Tortured eyes reveal a pang of conscience; knowing full well the wickedness and death Long John will continue to loose upon the world, Jim cannot grasp how he could have facilitated such a thing. Momentarily, Jim is joined by Trelawney and Livesey, unaware of his deed. Jim appears ready, like so many Hitchcock heroes, to make full confession; like them, his desire is blocked. Reasonable, responsible Livesey, having heard Trelawney suggest what the sharks may yet do to Silver, admits: "God help me, but I'm half-inclined to hope he makes it!" Surprised to hear such words from the most moral of men, Jim smiles with relief, secretively waving good-bye, and Silver returns the gesture. In the world according to Walt, much like the universe of Sir Alfred Hitchcock, the opposing poles of innocence and evil intersect in the best and worst of us. We are all strangers on the train of life; always, there remains the shadow of a doubt.

Disney, however, managed what no other Hollywood filmmaker, not even Hitch, had been allowed to portray during Production Code days: A murderer gets away scot-free, without retribution. Still, some purists carped that Disney had taken too many liberties with Stevenson. As if to rectify that, he presented a decade later a remarkably faithful version of the same author's *Kidnapped* (1886), continuing to develop the loss-of-innocence theme. The second work is more anecdotal in approach, its episodic plot at times seeming nothing more than a loose thread, tying together an exhausting string of deaths.

The opening shot is of a tombstone, belonging to Alexander Balfour, recently deceased teacher in a small English village. Young David (James

MacArthur) has only one legacy, a letter instructing the teenager to head for mountainous country and find his wealthy uncle. On the way, an old crone, Jennet Clouston (Eileen Way), warns him in witchlike manner that the Balfour property is bathed in blood. As it turns out, she's right. Upon David's arrival, Uncle Ebenezer (John Laurie) points a blunderbuss in the boy's face. Thereafter, Ebenezer sends David marching up a winding staircase in the dark. The lad realizes at the last possible moment that he's reached the end of a precipice and might have died had he followed his uncle's instructions. Once again, the Generation Gap is present as the corrupt older order attempts to kill off this idealistic young turk.

In fact, the land and house should have been Alexander's, not Ebenezer's. When David discovers this, his uncle arranges to have him kidnapped by Captain Hoseason (Bernard Lee). Aboard the ship, the young cabin boy (John Pike) is brutally murdered by Shaun (Niall MacGinnis), a cruel first mate. Fortunately for David, Alan Breck Stewart (Peter Finch), a charismatic rogue, shortly joins the crew. Aware that the cutthroats plan to murder Stewart, David aids the adventurer in killing them first. In a notably gory sequence, David fires point-blank at an attacking sailor and brings the man down in an image that recalls Jim's shooting of Israel Hand, suggesting Disney remained unapologetic for his earlier employment of graphic violence.

Though this act fills David with remorse, Stewart casually dismisses what happened:

Oh, upset cause you killed a man? I 'member it m'self; the first time, that is.

A highlander, Stewart is on a mission to murder an old enemy. Essentially, Stewart is a more presentable version of Long John. The moral high ground is taken by David, clinging to his old values despite the appeal of a dark mentor. As David warns Stewart, "Christianity forbids revenge." Such high-minded words hardly dissuade Stewart. When David encounters the much-despised Colin Roy Campbell (Andrew Cruickshank), the latter is shot down by an unseen assassin. Stewart swears he didn't do it, yet there's a wink in his eye. Apparently, he's lying, since no one else was around.

The film politicizes death in a way *Treasure Island* did not. This is fitting for a Disney English epic of the 1960s, that decade when America's apathetic young became highly politicized. Initially, David himself is (at least when first encountered) an apolitical character, as perfect an audience surrogate for a Woodstock-age audience as Jim had been for *Treasure Island*'s Eisenhower-era child-viewer. As in the previous film, the young protagonist is the only Brit character played by an American. Brought up as a Whig, David has never questioned his conventional values.

When David meets Stewart, everything changes and radicalization begins. Disdainful of the British occupation of Scotland, Stewart is a rebel. Campbell is assassinated in the Disney version less owing to lingering clan grudges than for having accepted the Brits and for wearing a red jacket. Though the British consider Stewart a terrorist, the Scots view him as a freedom fighter, a theme Disney had earlier explored in *Rob Roy*. Cementing an apparently intended connection between the two films, the son of that outlaw hero, Robin Oig MacGregor (Peter O'Toole), shows up to help Stewart escape pursuers.

In light of Disney's own father and his leftish leanings, William Empson's tongue-in-cheek analysis helps explain Stewart's view:

> The Communists . . . disapprove of death
> Except when practical.[13]

Though David never completely accepts Stewart's belief that violence is necessary for social change, he does learn to tolerate killing as an idealist's last resort. In the finale, the two part company, recalling the earlier image of Long John heading one way, Jim another. On his way to the mansion he now finally owns, David glances back over his shoulder at his departing comrade, a notable hint of sadness in his eyes now that this part of his life is over. Disney's viewpoint is not that different from how Jack Kerouac views his dangerous onetime best friend in *On the Road:*

> A western kinsman of the sun. . . . Although my aunt warned me that he would get me in trouble, I could hear a new call and see a new horizon, and believe it at my young age; and a little bit of trouble . . . what did it matter? I was . . . young . . . and I wanted to take off.[14]

Stewart will, like Long John Silver and Dean Moriarty, make more mischief, in Stewart's case involving the death of political adversaries. David, now a wealthy member of the Establishment, steps away from not only a man but a way of life he briefly flirted with. Yet he will never forget Stewart. They have stood together, fought together, *killed* together; they are brothers in the blood of righteous rebellion, and that bond lasts forever.

MAKE LOVE, NOT WAR

*THE STORY OF ROBIN HOOD
AND HIS MERRIE MEN* (1952)
DAVY CROCKETT, KING OF THE WILD FRONTIER (1954)
DAVY CROCKETT AND THE RIVER PIRATES (1955)

In the live-action version of *Robin Hood*, as King Richard and his loyal followers leave England for the Third Crusade, Disney slips in a hint of the limited pacifism that would characterize many sixties radicals. He (the opposite of Shakespeare) favors a civil war at home while condemning all imperialist action abroad, even if the motivation for that action is ostensibly righteous. As the Archbishop of Canterbury blesses Richard's troops before their departure, Disney's director, Ken Annakin, tilts the camera downward. The more conventional approach would have been to allow an audience to look up at a hallowed moment; the downward camera implies a negative response toward whatever is being filmed.[15] Though the ceremony itself is objectively (and accurately) staged, the choice of camera angle conveys Disney's subjective philosophy. This, he implies, is a mistake.

The Disney westerns and other tales of American folklore were filled with action, often of the most violent nature. Yet they were among the few films that deromanticized combat at every turn, creating among the youth who watched them a belief in the sort of limited pacifism that would be the hallmark of the Woodstock era. The initial *Crockett* installment (December 15, 1954) opened with an artist's rendering of the historic Fort Mims massacre. An immense animated arrow demolishes the stockade, all its inhabitants killed. As a stanza of the George Bruns–Tom Blackburn ballad informs us:

> In 1813, the Creeks uprose,
> Addin' Injin arrows to
> The country's woes.
> Old Andy Jackson, as
> Everyone knows, is the
> General they sent,
> To fight the foes.

The sequence in which Crockett (Fess Parker) leaves his family to volunteer for service (deleted for the sake of time from the condensed theatrical-release version) reveals Disney's attitudes about war. Polly (Helene Stanley), the female peace-principle incarnate, begs Davy not to go. He in turn reminds her of Mims, then departs not to achieve personal glory or serve some national cause—only out of the fear that if such an action is not met with immediate response, there will be repetitions, eventually threatening their own community.

The narrative that follows contains none of the glorification of combat that audiences witnessed in the era's more "mature" westerns. During his initial skirmish with Creek warriors, Davy shoots several in the back, all but inconceivable within the context of family entertainment. This ultrarealistic approach is continued in a large-scale battle, in which Crockett's volunteers join with General Jackson's (Basil Ruysdael) regular army to destroy a Choctaw village. The fighting, shocking and horrific rather than conventionally exciting, offers an image of genocide. Indian women and children are killed along with Creek warriors, serving as a foreshadowing of the My Lai massacre some fifteen years later. Crockett himself is nearly killed when he encounters face-to-face the Indian leader Red Stick (Pat Hogan), who defeats him. This constituted another first; never before had the hero of a theatrical or televised western lost such a personal duel. Throughout the battle sequence and after, Davy's eyes—while observing the combat itself or the piles of bodies heaped high in its aftermath—register the disgust of our role model at war's waste.

If this is a hero who hates to make war, he is also one who loves to make love. Unlike the typical hero of juvenile-oriented westerns, famed for kissing his horse and riding away whenever a woman shows interest, Davy was married before the story even began. And there are plenty of children around as a result of their union. In every sequence featuring Davy and Polly, it's made abundantly clear they cannot keep their hands off one another. The Crockett children are clearly aware of this, as Disney's camera cuts to their reactions whenever Davy and Polly embrace, the kids laughing happily at such "natural" behavior. Also, the physicality of their love is unique in another respect. Ordinarily, an intense man-woman relationship (one recalls the famed beach scene between Burt Lancaster and Deborah Kerr in *From Here to Eternity* one year earlier) occurred between illicit lovers. Disney stood more or less alone in depicting the heads of a big, happy, functional family who are strongly attracted to one another.

That openness about sex may, incredibly, include George Russel (Buddy Ebsen), Davy's best friend. During the Creek Indian War, Russel saves Davy's life. Instead of thanking his friend, Davy suggests that Polly may, upon hearing of Russel's brave action, reward Georgie with sexual favors. Upon their arrival back home, Georgie immediately announces: "Guess I'll collect what's coming to me." He then grabs Polly and kisses her. When Polly, embarrassed, turns to catch Davy's reaction, he explains the situation. At this point, Polly—one more of Disney's highly sexed heroines—replies, "Well, in *that* case," and (all this occurring in front of gleeful Crockett children) begins groping Georgie.

If Crockett is taken aback, it's not at the sight of his wife in another man's arms, only that Georgie is so clearly out of his league. "You'll never get a woman *that* way," Davy scornfully tells his friend. "Here, lemme learn y' how!" Crockett then pulls Polly away, overpowering her with his kiss. Georgie, an eager student, nods his head. The three then proceed into the Crockett cabin, arm in arm, to continue inside; tactfully, they leave the children outside. Fifteen years later, at the height of the hippie era, William Goldman's screenplay for *Butch Cassidy and the Sundance Kid* would be considered mildly shocking for daring to suggest a ménage à trois among the title characters (Paul Newman and Robert Redford) and their female companion, Etta Place (Katharine Ross). Yet all such scenes pale in comparison to Disney's earlier movie.

Despite "Indian Fighter" being the subtitle of the first TV installment, the story's thrust is in fact Davy's attempt to create a lasting peace between these two American peoples, Anglo and Native. After several fierce combats, he enters the Creek camp alone, making it clear that all men are, under the skin, brothers:

CROCKETT: I ain't a soldier. I'm a settler, a hunter, *just like you.*
RED STICK: Hunter? You hunt Indians.
CROCKETT: Only because you make war on us. Your [other] chiefs have found out that *war's no good.*
RED STICK: White man talk. War no good because soldiers all die.
CROCKETT: How many Creek warriors have died? How many women are crying for their men? How many young-uns ain't got no father?
RED STICK: You talk like *woman!*
CROCKETT: I'm talking sense, and you know it . . . you're a bad chief.
RED STICK: Because I take many white scalps?
CROCKETT: No. Because we could all go home in *peace* if you'd listen to reason.

Davy's words would be echoed in one of the most memorable of 1960s antiwar anthems, an Edwin Starr hit single:

War!
What is it good for?
Absolutely *nothin'.*

Following a brief scuffle, Red Stick comes to see the rightness of Davy's attitude. The two shake hands and exchange warm smiles; blessed are the peacemakers.

In the third episode, the theme of a righteous war's morality, and the redemption of one's death in the service of Lenin's ongoing social revolution, returns. *Davy Crockett at the Alamo* (February 23, 1955) defends Crockett's decision to become involved in the battle, as expressed through Disney's interpretation of the Texas-Mexican conflict (1835–1836). Viewed (as revisionist historians often do today) as an act of Anglo aggression against Mexicans then in power throughout the Southwest, the Alamo must be dismissed as an immoral, racist, and imperialist action. In contrast, Disney chooses to interpret the incident as an act of political defiance, jointly initiated by Anglos (Texicans) and Spanish (Tejanos) against an authoritarian government. That this, and not the Spanish element, is being opposed Walt makes clear by never once identifying Santa Anna's oncoming army as Mexican, while focusing attention whenever possible on the Hispanics among the defenders. Thus, the death of Crockett and his multicultural companions is portrayed as positive, a last stand by common men of all colors, united in opposition to tyranny. Even in such a context, though, Disney refuses to romanticize combat. Thimblerig (Hans Conried), a gambler who has arrived with Crockett's company, mutters: "They say war is the most exalting experience a man can endure. For me, it's the most miserable form of suicide." Here, as in other films to come, Disney made clear his preference for peace.

In the prequel, the mission of Davy, whose reputation as a fighting man takes a backseat to his limited-pacifist leanings, is to end a potential war between Anglos and Indians before it can begin. In *Davy Crockett's Keelboat Race* (November 16, 1955) and *Davy Crockett and the River Pirates* (December 14, 1955), the hero never once fights Indians—only wicked whites attempting to rob Native Americans of their inalienable right to a peaceful existence.

BLESSED ARE THE PEACEMAKERS

THE GREAT LOCOMOTIVE CHASE (1956)

The following year, Disney featured his new western star in an even more blatantly antiwar message movie. *The Great Locomotive Chase* covers the same historic incident previously depicted by Buster Keaton in his silent masterpiece *The General* (1925). Union spy James J. Andrews (Parker) brings a group of raiders (pretending to be loyal Kentuckians) into the South, stealing a train, with plans of devastating the communications lines there. The Disney version opens after the action has concluded. Surviving raiders, including storyteller William Pittinger (John Lupton), have been summoned to Washington, D.C., where they are to be the first recipients of the newly created Congressional Medal of Honor.[16] Pittinger recalls those members of their group who did not survive, including Andrews and William Campbell (Jeff York).

The central conflict in Keaton's comedic version was between Andrews (renamed "Anderson" in the 1925 film) and the bold Southerner (Keaton as "Johnny Gray") who ultimately captures the raiding party. Though Disney does include the dogged pursuit by Jeff Fuller (Jeffrey Hunter) as a subplot, his retelling deemphasizes the element of romantic adventure as *The General* is pursued by *The Texas*. Instead, Walt's film focuses on the conflict within Andrews's group, most notably between its civilian (and closet pacifist) leader Andrews and the battle-prone Campbell. Campbell loudly accuses Andrews of being a coward owing to the leader's refusal to stop along the way and fight the pursuing Southerners.

One by one, other members of the group are won over to Campbell's position. When the intellectual Pittinger finally joins Campbell, their leader realizes the impossibility of continued opposition. No sooner have they halted and taken defensive positions than they are overwhelmed. Andrews, it turns out, was right when he insisted a conventional battle, involving death, is the least effective way to wage a war.

Later, the imprisoned raiders attempt a daring break, crawling up and over stockade walls. Campbell, about to leap to safety, glances back and is stunned to notice Andrews courageously sacrificing himself by single-handedly holding off Confederate guards. Realizing all at once that Andrews was never a coward, but is in fact the most heroic figure among them, Campbell makes his moral decision—lowering himself back down and joining Andrews, both men recaptured after buying precious time that allows Pittinger and several others to slip away. Along with Campbell, the impressionable child audience of 1956 was taught a lesson they would recall more than a decade later, at the height of Vietnam: There is nothing cowardly about passive resistance. This is, rather, the truest form of heroism, for it takes the greatest (and wisest) type of courage to avoid violence, except as a last resort. Campbell—never able

THE PACIFIST AS A NEW AMERICAN HERO. Even in such an action-oriented TV program as *Davy Crockett, Indian Fighter* (1954), the character (played by Fess Parker) preferred to make love rather than war; in *The Great Locomotive Chase* (1956), Disney took that concept a giant step further, casting Parker—who certainly looked like a conventional action hero—as James J. Andrews, the Yankee spy whose main interest is in ending the Civil War quickly, while avoiding violence—and the loss of human life—at all cost, causing him to be mistaken by more conventional types for a coward.

to achieve full enlightenment by moving beyond his redneck-macho attitude—at least expresses his newfound respect for Andrews shortly before they are executed as spies. In response, Andrews voices Disney's Hamlet-like notion that the readiness (for death) is indeed all:

> CAMPBELL: Well, we sure showed 'em we know how to fight!
> ANDREWS: Yeah. Now, we've got to show them that we know how to die.

SO YOU SAY YOU WANT A REVOLUTION?

THE LIGHT IN THE FOREST (1958)

TONKA (1958)

Disney's heroes, like so many key figures in American literature and American life since the Republic's inception, "may be viewed as social rebels rather than revolutionists; they are members of a society that is ever changing, that, in addition, has in its structure the political and social ingredients to ferment new changes."[17] The distinction is a key one, explaining why a true and total revolution never occurred in America, even during the darkest hours of the Great Depression. Instead of surrendering to socialism, America under the New Deal co-opted the best elements of such thinking, progressively accommodating them within an ongoing democratic/capitalist system. Despite its myriad faults, the country contained (as other nations did not) the mechanism by which wrongs could be righted, if slowly and painfully.

As the Beatles, perceived by many as a revolutionary force, insisted (to the surprise of many fans) at the height of the Vietnam War:

> Say you want a revolution?
> Well, we all want to
> Change the world.
> But when you start talkin
> 'bout Chairman Mao,
> Don't you know that's when
> You can count me *out!*
> Don't you know it's gonna be
> *Alright!*

Fervently opposed to the war, as the on-campus rebels were, the Beatles, within the context of their complex worldview, on occasion implied an antirevolutionary position. Their attitude, and the guarded optimism that the American system will always (if with difficulty) right itself, are the very essence of Disney.

The theme song for *The Light in the Forest*, appearing over the opening credits, drastically alters the literary conception of Conrad Richter to predict the peace-and-love generation that would reach fruition precisely one decade later:

> Look for the light
> In the forest,
> For truth is the light
> Shining there.
> The light in the forest
> Is *peace;*
> The light in the forest
> Is *love.*

Though peace is to be desired, Disney never offers any sentimental notion that such a hoped-for state can be achieved without violence. In *Light in the Forest,* Myra (Jessica Tandy), a key symbol for the positive peace-principle as embodied by women, reads out loud from the Bible to her son (James MacArthur): "Blessed are the peacemakers." Her words, spoken softly yet with an undercurrent of strength, are immediately followed by a loud rifle shot. Gazing outside, Johnny notices the community's bullyboys, firing at a target mocked up to look like one of Johnny's beloved Indian friends. Before peace can be achieved, he must enter into a fistfight with Uncle Wilsey (Wendell Corey), leader of the redneck racists. That this youthful revolution against an unenlightened male element of the adult population is, in Disney's view, "righteous" is made clear when Shenandoe (Carol Lynley), Johnny's girlfriend and another key representative of the peace-principle, puts such values aside to cheer Johnny on.

Even when dealing with as potent a theme as the antiwar sensibility, Disney refuses to simplify. In *Tonka*, the peacenik message is effectively conveyed despite both of the film's heroes—Native American and Anglo—being dedicated warriors. White Bull (Sal Mineo) speaks of a desire to take cavalrymen's scalps and count coup; Myles Keogh (Philip Carey) literally licks his lips in anticipation of violent action against the Indians. At the Battle of Little Big Horn, each eagerly enters into combat, enthusiastically killing members of the other side. This they do because neither knows any other members of the "enemy" on a personal level. But they have come to know, like, and respect each other, owing to the device of the title character: the horse White Bull calls Tonka, and which Keogh (riding the steed into battle) has named Comanche.[18] Spotting each other across the field, neither can fire. Death in war is, for Disney's heroes of various races, impossible once one knows an adversary as an individual human being.

The film's overriding antiwar sensibility is then conveyed through an effective use of camera. Our point of view pulls back to a far range, revealing the insanity of the carnage from an oblique angle. This device determines both the film's and the audience's attitude toward the concept of friends killing one another. We literally see at this point what the leading characters know but cannot express: that war is madness, both heroes falling victim to the wild firing. Adding to the growing sense of absurdity is White Bull being hit not by a cavalryman's bullet but by an arrow fired by one of his fellow Lakota.

WAR! WHAT IS IT GOOD FOR?
ABSOLUTELY NOTHIN'!

THE MIRACLE OF THE WHITE STALLIONS (1963)

Despite the Vietnam debacle looming on our collective horizon, producers of most major motion pictures continued to glorify war. Whether a specific film revealed moviemaking craftsmanship at its best (*The Longest Day*, 1962) or worst (*The Battle of the Bulge*, 1965), a gung-ho mentality not much advanced beyond that of films turned out during the World War II years pervaded such blockbusters. In sharp contrast stands Disney's only live-action, relatively realistic film with a World War II backdrop, its very title also revealing both Disney's animal-rights activism and his Capra-esque concern for finding evidence of divine intervention in seemingly everyday activities.

Miracle is based on the true story of Colonel Podhajsky (Robert Taylor), head of Vienna's riding school, where the famed Lippizan stallions were bred. A Schindler of the equestrian world, he in 1945 dedicated himself to getting as many of the horses out of the war-torn area as possible, before regular bombings of the city by the Allies literally put an end to their breed. Disney's decision to depict Podhajsky's difficult but ultimately successful mission adds an important footnote to earlier works in which Walt came to grips with Darwinism in general, Social Darwinism in particular.

Podhajsky's achievement attests to Disney's belief that races of animals (or, as his continuing anthropomorphism implies, men) can and should be saved, and will be if mankind grasps its duty to do precisely that. Recall in this context the very title of *The Vanishing Prairie*, and that the film, after cataloguing evidence of many life-forms about to die off, finally implied that the audience, if inspired by the viewing experience, ought to turn activist and *do* something about it. In *Miracle*, just such a success story is dramatized to prove that mankind can, should turn the tide. We must provide a slap in the face to Social Darwinism, with its ruggedly individualistic attitude that, however sad such a situation may be, nothing much can be done.

A feminist element is, as always, present. Vedena (Lilli Palmer), the colonel's wife, serves as both his conscience and full partner in the positive action. Finally, there's the evenhanded depiction of the warring powers' military leaders, remarkable at a time when most American films still depicted Germans as simplistic villains. The "miracle" could

Copyright Walt Disney Productions; courtesy Buena Vista Releasing.

WAR! WHAT IS IT GOOD FOR? ABSOLUTELY NOTHIN'! The antiwar attitudes so basic to Woodstock-era rock lyrics were present in Disney's films a full five years earlier; 1963's *Miracle of the White Stallions* depicts the near-destruction of the famed Lippizan stallions by General Patton's war machine.

not be carried off without the cooperation of, in turn, German General Tellheim (Curt Jurgens) and American General Patton (John Larch). Disney even dared make Tellheim, depicted as a secret anti-Hitlerite and closet pacifist, more sympathetic than Patton, a blustery war lover.

BROTHER AGAINST BROTHER

JOHNNY SHILOH (1963)

WILLY AND THE YANK (1967)

Disney returned to the Civil War for several television miniseries appearing at precisely the time when our involvement in Vietnam was escalating. *Johnny Shiloh* (January 20 and 27, 1963) features Kevin Corcoran in the title role, a boy who serves as drummer for the Union forces. Any glorious aspect to battle that Johnny might have hoped for must be swiftly set aside. Action sequences reveal war as unrelentingly brutal, Johnny's early romantic dream of combat swiftly dismissed. Significantly, he serves as audience surrogate for young people who shortly would face the prospect of a very real and modern war.

The title notwithstanding, the dramatic focus shifts in the second installment to a young Southern soldier who captures Johnny, yet cannot bring himself to shoot the Union boy in the back when Johnny chooses to walk away. The Confederate well knows that Johnny will inform a Yankee officer (Brian Keith) as to the South's battle plans, causing a massive defeat for the South. Still, picking up and advancing the *Tonka* theme, the reb can't bring himself to fire a shot that would save his cause—the life of a single individual (even an ostensible enemy) now more important to him than ideals or country.

Four years later, Disney presented *Willie and the Yank*, a three-parter (January 8, 15, and 22, 1967) that further develops that relationship. Here, the central character is an underage Southern volunteer (Kurt Russell) who comes to respect a Union adversary (James MacArthur) as much as, if not more, than his fellow Southerners, including Major John Singleton Mosby (Jack Ging), the celebrated "Gray Ghost." By the series conclusion, the true bond of love and friendship is the one that has formed between the title characters, they having established what novelists Ernest Hemingway and John Knowles would tag "a separate peace." That these shows were broadcast immediately preceding the creation of an antiwar movement by young people who, more likely than not, had been exposed to them (in the sixties, a remarkable number of people watched the Disney show on Sunday evening) provides further evidence that Disney played a key part in shaping the mentality of a generation.

OF MEDIEVALS AND MINISKIRTS

THE FIGHTING PRINCE OF DONEGAL (1966)

Death had always been essential to Disney's British adventure films, particularly those starring Richard Todd as Robin Hood and Rob Roy. Each also glorifies a populist outlaw-hero who fights and kills aristocrats, planting the seed in the mind of young moviegoers that political liberation cannot be achieved without violence and death. In the sixties, Disney chose Ireland for his final swashbuckler, the theme remaining the same: Common folk rebelling against a moneyed world power that oppresses them. This was precisely how the people of North Vietnam viewed those American forces arriving, in ever larger numbers, in autumn 1966, precisely as *The Fighting Prince of Donegal* was released. The central character, Red Hugh (Peter McEnery), views himself as a freedom fighter; to the Brits, he is, like Robin Hood, Rob Roy, and Alan Stewart, a terrorist.

Typical of Disney, the film opens with the death of the hero's father, Hugh O'Donnell. Despite the title, the lead character turns out to be a peacenik in embryo. Red Hugh calls the clans together not to fight the British, but to end violence. Only when the British leader, Captain Leeds (Gordon Jackson), betrays Hugh's trust does the lad lead a brutal attack on Donegal Castle. After defeating Leeds, Red Hugh chooses not to kill the man, instead persuading him to sign a peace treaty. Though this has been dismissed as unhistorical and sentimental, it does reveal Disney's essential antiwar attitudes. Likewise, Hugh attacks Donegal Castle to rescue his beloved colleen, Kathleen McSweeney, played by Susan Hampshire. Closely associated with miniskirt roles in swinging London films, Hampshire's very presence—despite her skillful creation of a period dialect—implied a distinct contemporaneity. Set in the sixteenth century, this was implicitly a film about the mid-sixties, an era in which youth chose to make love, not war—not, unless, that war was revolutionary in nature.

As early as 1960, years before the major youth movements for civil rights and against Vietnam, *The Nation* noted:

In talking about the Revolt of Youth we should never forget that we are dealing with a new concept. For thousands of years nobody cared what youth were doing. . . . During the past couple of years, without caring about the consequences, making up their techniques as they went along, organizing spontaneously in the midst of action, young people all over the world have intervened in history.[19]

The Disney films and television shows made during that time anachronistically employ young people from the past, transforming them into predictive symbols of the New Youth that would attempt to change the world for the better. If popular entertainment can influence our behavior, these period-piece youth were key role models that provided formative viewing experiences for the impressionable young audience which absorbed them.

THE LAST GOOD WAR

BEDKNOBS AND BROOMSTICKS (1971)

Though not released until five years following Disney's death, this *Mary Poppins*–like fantasy about a genial witch was envisioned by the filmmaker during his final years as Buena Vista's creative overseer. The film's antiwar mentality can be credited to the artistic consciousness of the man who initiated it. Disney would doubtless have been proud of the opening artwork preceding the film proper: Wiccan women flying through the night sky on brooms, accompanied by joyous music inducing a young audience to, for once, *not* be afraid of such mythic figures. The musical score turns frightening only when we notice Nazi troops landing on the English shore. Evil, we sense, is not perpetrated by free-spirited women in the skies, but by imperialistic men walking among us. When we do hear incantations, they are directed against the invaders. Wiccan women, positive if peculiar forces living peaceably in the world, stand at the forefront of those opposed to the real evil.

The story is set in 1940, at the outset of what American author James Jones would, in novels like *From Here to Eternity* and *The Thin Red Line*, refer to as "the last good war": The final conflict in which Americans would feel confident that we were indeed involved in a cause as worthy as what General Eisenhower defined in retrospect as our Crusade in Europe. The film begins before American involvement, when the continuous blitzing of London by German aircraft caused concerned parents to ship their children off to rural areas, there to be quartered with locals. Carrie (Cindy O'Callaghan), Paige (Roy Smart), and Charley (Ian Weignill) are siblings who are to live in rural Pepperidge with Miss Eglantine Price (Angela Lansbury). Though she is a witch, she makes her values clear to them: "The work I'm doing is so important to the war effort!"

Despite those words, and her anti-Nazi bias, Miss Price is yet another of Disney's pacifist heroines. Her greatest hope is to personally help in bringing about world peace. To do this, she and the children must make a journey (via a "traveling spell," flying together on a highly Freudian bed). Off they go to London in search of an ancient book, *The Spells of Astoroth*, containing the magic words that will end the war and, she hopes, all war. At film's end, Miss Price transforms inanimate objects —ancient English armor—into a ghost-army that chases away Nazi invaders. Indeed, the entire tradition of British gallantry—knights, courtiers, redcoats, Beefeaters—joins in the righteous battle, enacting General Butler's notion of a *defensive* war, fought against people who want to rob helpless victims of basic human rights. Everything best about a great tradition unites, thanks to the wisdom, faith, courage, and independence of a unique woman, to defeat everything that's worst—the nihilistic evil of Nazism—in the modern world.

Miss Price echoes the words of Shakespeare's Henry V: "For England, and St. George!" The key difference between the narrative situations reveals the important distinctions between Shakespeare and Disney in their attitudes toward combat. The Bard glorified an offensive attack on a peaceful foreign community; Henry's words are spoken outside the town of Harfleur in France, which the English king has vowed to conquer, with the author's full blessing. Disney's Englishwoman wants only to defend her homeland's shores, then be left to live in peace.

8 Providence in the Fall of a Sparrow
Disney and the Denial of Death

The celebration of life that (at least in our popular mythology) characterized the mid-sixties, culminating in Woodstock's three days of peace, love, and music, appears far removed from anything so dark as death. In

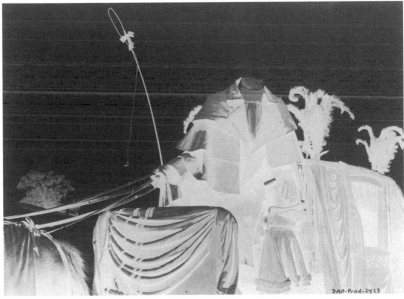

DEATH BE NOT PROUD. Every bit as horrifying as Ingmar Bergman's cape-shrouded Grim Reaper in *The Seventh Seal* (1957) are the images of death in Disney films; no single incarnation of the dark messenger in motion picture history quite compares to the translucent coach driver in *Darby O'Gill and the Little People* (1959), as the title character prepares for his entry into a Celtic vision of Hades.

fact, every element of the youth culture existed as a reaction to the ultimate event in all our lives. For essential to the 1960s social revolution was
the Vietnam War: Hippiedom coalesced as a result of collective horror
at daily body counts in a faraway land, reported by the modern Cassan-
dra, television news. A sixties syndrome of tuning in (to the war-reality),
turning on (to drugs, as temporary escape), then finally dropping out (of
a death-driven society) was motivated by a dread, at once individual and
generational, of becoming one more corpse sent home in a body bag.
No wonder, then, that amid all the sex, drugs, and rock 'n' roll at Woodstock, Country Joe (McDonald) and the Fish brought the house down
with their "I-Feel-Like-I'm-Fixin'-to-Die Rag":

> Be the first family on your block,
> To have your son come home in a box!

More than yet another antiwar song, the walking-talking blues ballad
emerged as an anthem for radicalized youth. Hippies perceived Vietnam as a contemporary heart of darkness, the source of rapidly spread-
ing nihilism. A decade later, Francis Coppola would dramatize that vision in *Apocalypse Now*, Joseph Conrad's classic novella updated for the
war in Southeast Asia. What Coppola transformed into an epic, the Fish
had earlier stated in another stanza of the "Rag":

> One, two, three,
> What are we fighting for?
> Don't ask me,
> I don't give a damn.
> Next stop is Vietnam. . . .
> Ain't no time to wonder why.
> Whoopee! We're all gonna die!

However fragile, overly idealistic, and short-lived, the Woodstock
dream offered hope—what Jean Renoir tagged a grand illusion—for
people whose old faiths in the validity of the system had been destroyed
during a turbulent decade. Understood in this context, Woodstock gave
simultaneous voice to diametrically opposed possible reactions to death.
The one articulated by Country Joe implied total acceptance, leading to
anarchic negativity. The opposite response, sentimental and narcissistic,
was conveyed by Three Dog Night:

> I just want to celebrate
> Another day of living!

Live, that is, for the moment.

Still, there existed a third possibility, midway between the extremes, and far preferable to either: accepting death *without* collapsing into a moral abyss. As Blood, Sweat, and Tears insisted, man exists as part of an ongoing cycle, driven by a firm underlying meaning that we mortals can never fully comprehend:

And when I'm dead,
And when I'm gone;
There'll be one less soul
In this world
To carry on, *carry on!*

This compromise—beneficial to the individual *and* society—implies the answers found in Zen. This helps us to grasp why that religion/philosophy became so popular in America even as the war escalated:

We should acknowledge our anxieties and contemplate death if we intend to live as enlightened and self-actualized persons. . . . We cannot be whole and mature adults unless we live with the full realization of our mortality. . . . The trick is to be aware of the fullness of life—including our mortal vulnerability—without giving way to despair.[1]

Freud sensed this at the onset of modernity: "Would it not be better to give death the place in actuality and in our thoughts which properly belongs to it?"[2]

Easier said than done! Observing changes already under way during our transformation from a nineteenth-century traditional sensibility to modernism in the twentieth, sociologist Herbert Spencer predicted that as, for better or worse, our society grew ever more sophisticated, the notion of a people living virtually at one with their dead (as Native Americans had, before the coming of the Anglo) would end.[3] "Advanced" societies purposefully create elaborate barriers of time and space between themselves and those who have passed or are passing, living and dead occupying two separate worlds on this earth. Nursing homes for the elderly came into being, while new cemeteries were located far from dwelling places.

The Woodstock Nation, reacting against what members perceived as the preceding generation's false myths, opted for earlier truths. Love beads were long gone by the early seventies, but the thinking that had accompanied such temporary symbols was transferred from an ephemeral counterculture to the center of redefined mainstream thought. As a result,

Awareness of death has increased noticeably in our society. . . . The taboo has been at least partially lifted, as witness the development of death education courses throughout the United States and more sensitive recognition of death-related problems by the media.[4]

Experts in the field of death education, which blossomed in the seventies, agree that acceptance of death as a part of life can be fully mastered by the individual only if introduced at an early age. Then, children partake in "the comfort of shared responsibility and shared mourning. It prepares them gradually and helps them view death as part of life, an experience which may help them grow and mature."[5]

In this context, it's important to recall that Disney has been criticized as the foremost Eisenhower-era sanitizer of children's entertainment. As mentioned earlier, Bruno Bettelheim, while providing a Freudian analysis of the original fairy tales in *The Uses of Enchantment*, was anything but kind to Walt. Actually, though, far from standing at the center of the mid-fifties middlebrow pack, Disney—as evidenced by the films themselves—implicitly agreed with Bettelheim's premise, that being an intense dislike for

"safe" stories [which] mention neither death nor aging, the limits to existence, nor the wish for eternal life. . . . The [true] fairy tale, by contrast, takes these existential anxieties and dilemmas very seriously and addresses itself directly to them.[6]

So too do Disney films, based on time-tested tales and a carefully selected group of contemporary stories. The noted change in our view of death, as a people—from the false enlightenment of postwar culture to the darker, more complex view of post-Woodstock America—was introduced by Disney in entertainment aimed at the very young.

THE READINESS IS ALL

THE SKELETON DANCE (1928–1929)

Death, as a moral issue and, in Shakespeare's words, a necessary end, was present in Walt's animated work from the outset. *The Skeleton Dance*, first of the *Silly Symphonies*, featured a quartet of skeletons rising from the grave and joyously cavorting in the moonlight. In an early display of deconstruction, they turn to the camera, directly confronting the audience. This horrific image upsets the child-viewer less owing to any immediate sense of suggested threat than a tacit understanding that they represent what we will all someday become. In its time, *The Skeleton Dance* served as a modern equivalent to Dance of Death paintings, elaborately displayed on rural European church walls by medieval monks.

Copyright Walt Disney Productions; courtesy Buena Vista Releasing.

THE DANCE OF DEATH. From the beginning, Disney's films confronted his audience
with stark, vivid images of death, as horrifying as those symbolic tableaus medieval monks
once painted on the walls of rural churches to terrify the populace into an awareness of
their mortality; one of the first animated shorts to synchronize visuals to a musical sound
track, *Skeleton Dance* (1928–1929) featured a portion of Edvard Grieg's *The March of the
Dwarfs*, setting the pace for *Fantasia*—with its ambitious presentation of classical music to
the popular audience—a dozen years later.

The key purpose of both visual art forms, ancient and modern, must be
considered cautionary: forcing a bland onlooker out of narcissistic leth-
argy, i.e., what in our time Ernest Becker would describe as our daily denial of death.[7]

Viewed from a contemporary viewpoint, Disney's film "brewed a
humorously macabre concoction."[8] At the time of its release, the *New
York Daily Mirror* noted this cartoon unnerved its audience by "mak[ing]
you shiver and mak[ing] you laugh."[9] The musical score by Carl Stall-
ings bears more than passing resemblance to Edvard Grieg's *March of
the Dwarfs*, likewise cryptic and comical. The bizarre use of graveyard
humor, including one skeleton detaching his leg bone and employing it
as a musical instrument, caused the *Herald Tribune* to hail Disney's
"shrewd and surprisingly Rabelaisian humor."[10]

It was not for nothing that Disney made death a central issue of his
oeuvre. Death had, for most of his life, been an ongoing obsession. Barely
an adult, the young Walt had on a lark visited a fortune-teller. Instead
of the usual mumbo jumbo, this mysterious figure peered deep into the
young man's eyes, cryptically insisting that Disney would die before

reaching his thirty-fifth birthday. Though not by nature a superstitious man, Walt found himself overwhelmed with fear as the moment drew near. One might guess that, when the decreed day came and went, he would have been relieved. That proved not to be the case.

Having survived his thirty-fifth birthday, Disney

continued to brood about [the prophecy] long after it had been proved false. The sense of mortality weighed on him, and he seemed to be in a race against time to accomplish all the work he wanted to do. "I hate to see the weekend come," he remarked, complaining of the break in his usual pace.[11]

The readiness, for Walt as for Hamlet, was all. Like the poet Andrew Marvel, Disney always heard time's winged chariot hurrying near— threatening to draw him into an emotional black hole. Unless, that is, Walt found a way to recapture his earlier, simple belief in what Shakespeare described as a

divinity that shapes our destinies,
roughhewn though it may be.

Disney's personal odyssey as a man would be propelled by that all-important search; as an auteur, drawing inspiration for his highly personal art from his own life's journey, he would regularly return to death —his most constant, pressing, and disturbing theme.

A NECESSARY END

SNOW WHITE AND THE SEVEN DWARFS (1937)
BAMBI (1942)

To achieve inner peace, for himself and his impressionable audience, Disney first had to reject the conventional wisdom of his age. At the time of his birth (1901), children were regularly exposed to death, living either in the farm-based country or crime-filled cities. During his lifetime, however, America transformed, as white-bread suburbia came into being. Believing themselves to be enlightened and progressive, those in authority hoped to create a sanitized culture for their children, parents and teachers of the 1950s

believ[ing] that only conscious reality or pleasant and wish-fulfilling images should be presented to the child—that he should be exposed only to the sunny side of things. But such one-sided fare nourishes the mind only in a one-sided way, and real life is not all sunny.[12]

However well intentioned, the 1950s approach might have proven calamitous. Such representations could have caused an entire generation to reach adulthood without any proper understanding of death as an integral part of life. As poet Rabindranath Tagore wrote (in "Fruit-Gathering"):

> Let me not pray to be sheltered from dangers
> but to be fearless in facing them.

Fortunately, Disney was present, offering heroes who serve as audience surrogates when they fearlessly face death. Disney fought against the grain by reaching back to the view of primitive peoples "not bothered by the fear of death."[13] Such thinking was developed in ever more complex form once Disney initiated his full-length animated movies.

At the end of *Snow White*, the queen-crone hurtles to a horrible death, falling from a cliff during the storm. Her demise qualifies as poetic justice, for she deserves what she gets. More impressive still—and more true to real life—the good also die, often owing to noble efforts. The huntsman who spared Snow White is imprisoned as a direct result of his decency, then tortured in the evil queen's dungeon. In the final cut, this occurs offstage, save only for a pitiful image of his skeleton, grasping for a pan of water just beyond reach. Still, we get the gist; though doing the right thing may save you spiritually, it hardly ensures survival in a cruel and unfair world. *Snow White* opens with death in the passing of the heroine's father. Over the years, this would become the most significant catalyst to set a typical Disney story in motion, as it was earlier essential to folktales and fairy stories, passed down in the oral tradition and eventually finding literary expression in the works of Perrault (1697) and the brothers Grimm (1812).[14]

Disney's most famous depiction of death is the shooting of the mother deer in *Bambi*. An element of Darwinism is present when the Great Elk of the Forest calmly informs his son: "Your mother can't be with you anymore." This is Disney's most memorable scene in which he purposefully shocks children out of their formative denials of death. Later, and as significant, there is the implied death of Bambi's father, likewise accepted in a manner that does not lead to despair. Following a forest fire, in which Bambi has proven his courage, the two male deer stand side by side atop a mountain, gazing down at nature replenished. The Great Elk quietly turns and walks away. Glancing back at him, a now mature Bambi grasps what is about to happen, without regret turning away from his father's oncoming end (implied through what, in a different context, J. P. Tellotte describes as "the phenomenon of absence")[15] to instead consider the happy scene (life) below.

As Bettelheim insists, the most worthy child-oriented stories

tell about an aging parent who decides that the time has come to let the new generation take over. But before this can happen, the successor must prove himself capable and worthy. . . . It is here that fairy tales have unequaled value, because they offer new dimensions to the child's imagination which would be impossible for him to discover as truly on his own.[16]

The inclusion of death as part of life in the natural world must be accepted by Bambi, Disney, and—ultimately and most significantly—the impressionable youth audience.

AN UNTIMELY FROST

SONG OF THE SOUTH (1946)

CINDERELLA (1950)

ALICE IN WONDERLAND (1951)

LADY AND THE TRAMP (1955)

When, at the end of *Song of the South*, a bull chases little Johnny (Bobby Driscoll) and gores him, first-time viewers believe the boy may die. This owes to Disney's refusal to guarantee a conventional happy ending. We never know for certain how any movie will conclude. Always, then, there exists an element of suspense.

With *Cinderella*, as in *Snow White*, the story begins with death in general, her father's death in particular. Later in *Cinderella*, Disney surprises his audience by allowing an animal (if a notably obnoxious one) to receive its just deserts. The well-named cat Lucifer is last seen hurtling to his death after being forced out the tower window. Death would take on cannibalistic elements with the devouring of humanized baby oysters in the "Walrus and the Carpenter" episode of *Alice in Wonderland*. Not only naughty creatures, but fatally naïve ones, can expect a horrid end in a world that, as Woody Allen once noted, resembles a giant restaurant, everyone devouring everything ad infinitum.[17] That the contemporary Disney company hasn't abandoned this concept can be seen in *The Lion King*'s grotesquely accurate food-chain song and dance sequence.

During Walt's career, *Lady and the Tramp* had initiated a different sort of film, his first lighthearted divertissement. Yet the filmmaker was not averse to dealing with death in a context that was notably removed from his traditional fairy-tale films. We sense that the rat which menaces the home must be destroyed before it bites someone. At the end, it is indeed killed, brutally but necessarily. Not only monstrous figures die, however. At one point, Lady is incarcerated in a dog pound, with less fortunate animals who, unlike her, are unlicensed. Disney makes it clear that each will, in time, be put to death. Lady (and we) actually observe one sad case. The amiable Nutsy is led along what other dogs refer to as "the long walk," an animated equivalent to "the last mile" in 1930s prison films. Though Lady's master comes for her, she leaves knowing such a fate is in store for the others. Even her beloved Tramp comes close to experiencing what Shakespeare tagged an untimely frost. When he's captured and carried off to the pound, we overhear the following:

AUNT SARAH: Destroy that animal at once!
DOGCATCHER: Don't worry, Ma'am. We've been after this one for some time. We know what to do with *him!*

The impact reaches further and deeper still. Disney's harshest critics as well as his admirers acknowledge that, Aesop-like, he employs animals as a means of commenting on the human condition. In this film's context, mutts die because they are poor; the pedigreed are not put to sleep. Likewise, in her work on conceptual approaches to the study of death, Dr. Kathy Charmaz outlined the Marxist perspective: death in terms of the social inequality that allows the poor to die at an earlier age than those with means.[18] Marxist views held by Elias Disney had been absorbed, however unconsciously, by his son. Thus, *Lady and the Tramp* offered the family audience a serious vision of the inequality of death.

BORN AGAIN

PINOCCHIO (1940)
THE ADVENTURES OF ICHABOD AND MR. TOAD (1949)
SLEEPING BEAUTY (1959)
THE THREE LIVES OF THOMASINA (1964)

Opting for another approach, *Pinocchio* features an early Disney depiction of being reborn. As Bettelheim has noted:

If there is a central theme to the wide variety of fairy tales, it is that of a rebirth to a higher plane. Children (and adults, too) must be able to believe that reaching a higher form of existence is possible if they master the developmental steps this requires.[19]

Pinocchio achieves such a transition by diving into the belly of the beast (Monstro the Whale), reemerging from that oceanic womb with his family rescued. He is the male counterpart of Grimm's Little Red Riding Hood:

The child knows intuitively that Little Red Cap's being swallowed by the wolf—much like the various deaths other fairy-tale heroes experience for a time—is by no means the end of the story, but a necessary part of it. The child also understands that Little Red Cap really "died" as the girl who permitted herself to be tempted by the wolf; and that when the story says "the little girl sprang out" of the wolf's belly, she came to life a different person.[20]

Likewise, Disney's Pinocchio. At film's end, the title character—whom we know to be drowned, having seen it happen—comes back to life in a more advanced phase. The film's fantastical vision substitutes a human being for the puppet—actually, an adolescent now, compared to the former narcissistic child. A parallel with the audience is, if on an entirely unconscious level, communicated to child viewers, who perceive themselves as being in some way incomplete, needing to prove themselves before being accepted as humans in the fullest sense.

In the compilation film *Ichabod and Mr. Toad*, both title characters undergo near-death experiences. The Headless Horseman's burning pumpkin is thrust into Crane's face; J. Thaddeus Toad apparently drowns after having fallen into a lake with ball and chain attached to his leg. Intriguingly, Disney offers no explanation as to how either survived, on any realistic level; each, we must assume, did not escape, rather died only to be reborn. The pairing of stories by Washington Irving and Kenneth Grahame strikes many observers as an odd match. Still, the tales do belong together, owing to Disney's fascination with the potential for death in life. The image of the horseman, wildly waving his rapier, and the equally dark portrait of the gallows awaiting Toad serve as parallel symbols of dread. As a result of such experience, Ichabod—learning humility—gives up his immature pursuit of the pretty but superficial Katrinka, settling for a plump wife, large family, and full table. Toad, conversely, is his foil: Too flaky to be reformed, too immersed in hubris to renounce his old ways, Thaddeus flies off on his latest obsession, the airplane. Having failed to conquer the land, he embarks on an impossible quest to master the sky.

Sleeping Beauty marked Disney's return to the traditional fairy tale. For the better part of a decade, he personally oversaw the creation of this animated film, trusting that it would be accepted as his crowning masterpiece.[21] Characteristically, Disney included the notion of being born into a second life. After slipping into an all-encompassing sleep, Princess Aurora and those in her kingdom eventually wake to begin their existence anew—to enjoy, in essence, a second chance at life, everyone's

THE CONFRONTATION WITH END GAME. Whereas most entertainments for children serve as escapist fare, allowing a youthful audience temporary respite from the dark aspects of everyday life, Disney films achieve precisely the opposite, forcing the impressionable viewer into an intense cognition of death as, in Shakespeare's words, "a necessary end"; Washington Irving's New England schoolteacher, transformed by Disney into an American Everyman, comes face-to-face with his dark destiny in *Ichabod and Mr. Toad* (1949).

unguarded dream as a child, a more secretive fantasy once we become adults.

Watching such a film does not, despite the joyous finale, offer the child viewer escapism so much as a cinematic equivalent to the therapeutic experience. Like the fairy tale,

psychoanalysis was created to enable man to accept the problematic nature of life without being defeated by it, or giving in to escapism. Freud's prescription is that only by struggling courageously against what seem like overwhelming odds can man succeed in wringing meaning out of his existence.[22]

Likewise, at the end of *Sleeping Beauty*, Walt wisely chose *not* to insist that she and her prince will live "happily ever after." Disney does not release a child from the viewing experience after depicting a fabled future in which death doesn't exist. That would prove to be only a false promise, with no bearing on the audience other than to misinform, thereby doing immeasurable harm in the long run, if making the child momentarily feel safe and secure, on the order of the mid-twentieth-century entertainment so despised by Bettelheim. Disney reveals, rather, a male-female relationship based on true equality—trusting that when "one has reached the ultimate in emotional security of existence and permanence of relation available to man," then "this alone can dissipate the fear of death," without the need for reassuring but false claims.[23]

By far, the most ambitious and unsettling such film was *The Three Lives of Thomasina*. Set in the Scottish highlands, circa 1912, the narrative begins shortly after the death of the mother to little Mary McDhui (Karen Dotrice) and wife to Andrew (Patrick McGoohan). Deeply distressed by the loss, the once sensitive, now embittered man accepts a position as veterinarian in a rural village. Rather than risk being hurt again, he develops a cool, clinical attitude toward all creatures great and small. The simple folk come to resent this modern man's scientific/logical outlook, despite his remarkable skills. In this frame of mind, they completely overlook his successful operation on a blind man's seeing-eye dog. When the title character, Mary's beloved cat, is diagnosed with tetanus, Andrew insists that Thomasina must be destroyed. As she "dies," Thomasina pays a spiritual visit to her ancestors, Bubastis and other deities of ancient Egypt. Thomasina becomes at one with them during a metaphysical flight through time and space: female and feline, woman combined with animal, another of Disney's positive variations on the Great Goddess of classical mythology. As Bubastis emits a bright light (i.e., true wisdom), Walt paves the way for the New Age thinking that would emerge from the cultural rubble created by Woodstock's dark and difficult aftermath.

We—as an audience—have been prepared for this by the opening sequence. Playful images of Thomasina are here underscored by Terry Gilkyson's theme song, which praises and accepts the cat's mythic and pagan associations:

> I don't think it's odd,
> If you are an Egyptian god.

What follows conditions an audience to reach our singing narrator's level of enlightenment. His theme song conveys, like the chorus of a Greek play, the artist's attitudes. Disney's vision includes a defense of reincarnation, a slap in the face to the Judeo-Christian theology of main-

IN PRAISE OF THE OLD GODS. Disney films consistently undermine the Judeo-Christian vision of death, ingrained into the American psyche from the Puritan era to the twentieth century; in *The Three Lives of Thomasina* (1964), Disney introduced impressionable young audiences to the pagan notion of reincarnation, as the "familiar" (in this case, the title cat) to a benign Wiccan woman dies, only to be reborn after encountering the ancient gods of Egypt, who, in Disney's vision, are as celebrated as they had been damned in Cecil B. DeMille's more conventional *The Ten Commandments* (1956).

stream America. For primitives and pagans, beliefs in reincarnation derived from a close, sympathetic observation of nature, applying lessons learned there to man's spiritual and physical existence.

Walt's earliest *Silly Symphonies* included a series of four films, each dedicated to a single season. Leonard Maltin has noted that numerous Disney films carried their animal characters, whether animated (*Bambi*) or live-action (*Perri*), through these four seasons.[24] Disney's own primitive, ritualistic celebration of nature was shared with the child audience, which ritualistically attended his films, rereleased every seven years before the advent of home video. Like Snow White, Pinocchio, and Princess Aurora in *Sleeping Beauty* before her (and, in a less fantastical vein, the upcoming Pollyanna), Thomasina dies only to rise again, via the intervention of older gods that Disney seduces his impressionable audience to, in defiance of the middlebrow culture around them, fully accept.

A DOG'S LIFE

OLD YELLER (1957)

In addition to combining elements of the historical western, the nature documentary, and *The Mickey Mouse Club* (Tommy Kirk and Kevin Corcoran were both series veterans), *Old Yeller* ultimately serves as a death-education film. Dramatically, *Old Yeller* is not in the *Lassie, Come Home* tradition, assuring children that, however difficult circumstances may be, a boy and his dog will always be reunited. Nor does it resemble Marjorie Kinan Rawlins's *The Yearling*, in which a child must accept the near-nihilistic killing of a pet deer by his father when the animal becomes a difficult pest. As with all other Disney films, the pet-oriented movies offer guarded optimism, ending with an "up-cry."[25]

Previously, Disney had created an anti-*Yearling* with *So Dear to My Heart*. The film insists that such an animal—however pesky—can, should, indeed must, be tolerated, the ultimate rewards for our humanity far outdistancing any inconveniences. *Old Yeller* extends that attitude. While his dad is away on a cattle drive, fifteen-year-old Travis Coates (Kirk) is infuriated by a stray dog that tears through their small farm, doing damage. Viewing a fence Yeller has knocked down, Travis smirks:

That old dog better not come around while I got me a gun in my hands!

This is no mean threat. Later, for the sake of his lonely little brother, Arliss, Travis allows Yeller to sleep on their porch. Before retiring for the night, Travis hangs meat precariously close to Yeller, telling the dog he'll shoot the animal if he so much as licks it. The following morning, Travis rises, grabs his rifle, and heads outside to jubilantly do just that. Travis is amazed to see Yeller has controlled himself.

There are, of course, other elements in the film besides death. Key Disney themes are present in this rethinking of Fred Gipson's novel. Such ideas are expressed in the ballad, written by Gil George and Oliver Wallace, sung over the title credits by Jerome Courtland. As Yeller chases after rabbits (which, children in the audience realized, he means to kill and eat), we are told that

> Old Yeller was a mongrel,
> Without a family tree.
> Yet he could up and do it,
> And that's how a good dog should be.

Disney's dislike of "class" through birthright is in evidence. Though he would indeed make movies about creatures with pedigrees (*Stormy, the Thoroughbred*), the true test of class is in one's actions.

Also essential is Disney's recurring concern with capitalism. The story is set immediately following the Civil War. Small-time rancher Jim Coates (Fess Parker) merges his few steers with a larger Kansas-bound herd, owing to a postwar recession. This family has love aplenty. As Jim tells his wife, Katie (Dorothy McGuire):

Cash money's all we need to get a tail-hold on the world.

In the screenplay Gipson prepared specifically for Disney, Travis and younger brother, Arliss (Kevin Corcoran), discuss this issue. As the older boy says:

If you got money, you give it to people for things. They say you can get *anything* with money.

Jim will return with enough money to maintain their little spread, as well as presents for all. Before leaving, he tells Travis:

You act a *man's* part, I'll bring you a man's horse.

The work ethic is in evidence, as well as the need for a rite of passage. Money is not—here, or in other Disney films—necessarily the root of all evil, so long as it's fully earned, then spent on a worthwhile object rather than hoarded or obsessed on for its own sake.

This is no pastoral depiction of life in the West for children, on the order of George Stevens's more "adult" *Shane* (1953). In that classic, we never once see the little boy (Brandon de Wilde) working. *Old Yeller* is another matter. No sooner has Jim left than Travis assumes his father's role. He mends fences, marks pigs, plows the cornfield, stays up all night to stand guard against raccoons that threaten to gobble up the family's crops, then goes right to work in the fields without any sleep. His mother is another of Disney's protofeminist women, sawing into logs the wood that Travis has cut down. The work ethic holds true even for Old Yeller. Travis refuses to accept the dog until he proves himself able to do chores, ranging from catching fish to chasing away raccoons.

The foil to this functional family is Bud Searcy (Jeff York), the area's good-for-nothing loafer. Bud is excluded from the cattle drive, though he promises to help local families. He instead assigns his young daughter, Lisbeth (Beverly Washburn), to do any work, Bud preferring to loaf and mooch meals. This being a Disney film, there's also a strong adolescent sexual attraction. Travis finds himself matched with Lisbeth, the two symbolized by their pets. Old Yeller has gotten her dog, Miss Priss, pregnant. Without being explicit, the film suggests the teenagers will in time wed and begin a family, thus continuing the life cycle in true Disney fashion.

Despite such attention to life and its abundant if hard-won rewards (indeed, in large part *because* of it), the threat of death is as marbled through the movie as it is in *The Seventh Seal*, produced in Sweden by Ingmar Bergman even as Disney completed *Old Yeller*. Travis heads out into the woods, hunting. He proves himself one of Walt's ecological role models by refusing to pull the trigger on a mother deer nursing her young. But when a single deer crosses his path, Travis shoots. In the following sequence, he returns with it stretched across his mule. Disney conveys to his child audience an intelligent middle ground between the extremes of total insensitivity to nature and the unrealistic sentimentality that would have had Travis returning without meat. Darwinism is accepted; some must die so that others may live. On the other hand, the continuation of any species must be consciously maintained if we are to be truly human.

Old Yeller proves himself a hero by chasing off a huge bear that menaced little Arliss, an incident that keeps the threat of death potent. When Old Yeller attacks the family's half-wild pigs in defense of Travis, who fell into their midst while marking ears, the wounded dog must be sewn up by Katie. Presaging an identical plot device in *Life Is Beautiful* (the

THE CYCLE OF LIFE. As in ancient fable, Disney films incorporate the reality of death into a concept that mythologist Joseph Campbell referred to as "sacrifice and bliss"—loss through death does not lead to pessimism but rather reaffirms that life, despite its dark edges, is ultimately a positive experience; in *Old Yeller* (1957), Travis Coates (Tommy Kirk) must shoot his beloved dog after the animal is infected with rabies; after a period of mourning, the youth finds the courage to transcend his sorrow and rebuild his life by loving Old Yeller's neglected pup.

only film about the Holocaust that could have been mounted as a Disney project), the mother in *Old Yeller* does precisely what the father opts for in Roberto Benigni's Oscar winner, creating a fantasy to shield her innocent younger son:

We're playing Old Yeller is sick, and you're going to take care of him.

Pretending he and the heavily bandaged Yeller are wounded Indians, Arliss crawls up alongside him on a travois.

The sequence is doubly remarkable considering the film's intended audience. Children in attendance were likely to be no younger than Arliss, no older than Travis. The movie speaks to both, and—inclusively —all in between. Early-teen viewers were, like Travis, forced to directly come to grips with death, as a constant potential if not always an immediate reality. Those the age of Arliss watched as caring parents (in Disney's films, the emphasis on mothers) protect them from the world's horrors for as long as possible. This creates a rite of passage for the younger viewer. By watching such parental tactics dramatized, the child is made aware of them, and—as a result of seeing the film—passes beyond that phase of life.

Not that Arliss is ever blithely unaware of death. Travis shoots the cow, having found it "staggering and slobbering" (as a wandering cowboy, played by Chuck Connors, puts it), indicating hydrophobia. Having seen this, little Arliss becomes all but obsessed with death.

ARLISS: Where will Rose go, now she's dead?
TRAVIS: Nowhere.
ARLISS: Won't she go to heaven?
TRAVIS: I don't think so.
ARLISS: Aren't there no cows in heaven for the angels to milk? And how far off is heaven? Farther than where Poppa went?

Travis, assuming the parental role, attempts to formulate an answer that will appease the child's fears without passing on unnecessarily fantastical myths.

Travis is interrupted by screams from Katie and Lisbeth, the two women menaced by that oldest of male predators, a wolf. Not that Disney reverts to any stereotypes about this animal. No normal wolf would ever attack them, we learn, only one driven mad by rabies. Yeller arrives on the scene before Travis, holding the predator at bay until Travis can get a clear shot. But Yeller has been bitten. Katie, her female wisdom intact, knows the dog must be killed. Here, Gipson alters his novel to bring the material in line with Walt's ongoing vision. In the source, Travis shoots Yeller that very night, the dog still seemingly healthy. In the Disney version, Travis locks Yeller in a pen, hoping that Yeller may yet recover, however slim the chance. Only when the dog, like Rose, begins "staggering and slobbering" (and almost bites Arliss) does Travis fire the fatal shot.

Yet the story is not over; a Disney film, like one by Capra, must always temper the darkness. Jim returns, with presents for all, including the "man's horse" that will put the official seal on Travis's coming-of-age. Arliss, who remains locked in his world of childhood fantasy, is given an Indian headdress. For Katie, there's a pretty dress and new shoes; Disney women, however feminist, maintain their femininity. And for all, the capital necessary to maintain their home, for as Jim announces while shaking a bag of coins:

Hear this, Katie? Money! *Cash* money. First we've seen since the war.

But Travis, consumed by cynicism and bitterness, threatens to surrender to an absurdist worldview. Lisbeth, his (assumed) future wife, attempts to use her female wisdom to help him. She gives Travis one of Miss Priss's pups, hoping this will reignite the life cycle, with its necessary rituals occurring once again.

> LISBETH: If you could just learn to like the pup. He's part Old Yeller.
> TRAVIS: May be part Old Yeller, but he ain't Old Yeller!

The difference between the statements contrasts a woman's instinctual wisdom with the male's limiting combination of stubbornness and sentimentality. Yet Travis will eventually accept what Lisbeth tells him, coming to terms with his female aspect, as all Disney heroes must if they are to be role models such as the quietly masculine Davy Crockett, rather than pathetic like the outrageously macho Pecos Bill.

Jim—a rugged man's man, yet influenced by his wife, even as Crockett (played by the same actor) had been—understands that the "man's horse" means nothing at this moment. Jim encourages Travis, who with Lisbeth (working as equals, a projection of their future life together) has buried Old Yeller, to move on.

> TRAVIS: How can you forget something like that?
> JIM: Isn't a thing you can forget. Maybe not a thing you *want* to forget. Life's like that sometimes. Now and then, for no good reason a man can figure out, life will haul off and knock you flat. But it's not *all* like that. There's good beside the bad. And you can't go fretting about the bad. *That* makes it *all* bad!

Here, then, Jim signifies the mature Disney—having survived his thirty-fifth birthday—speaking to the young Walt, who had just heard the fortune-teller's prophecy. Words are one thing; ultimately, we learn only by experience. Travis notices the pup stealing meat, much as Old Yeller did before being domesticated. Travis smiles through his tears. The final shots feature a montage in which Young Yeller chases rabbits across the countryside, nearly identical to the action in the opening. In this parallel, we discover a ritual end to the tale, offering the contemporary child audience a vision of life as including (but not being conquered by) death.

DEATH BE NOT PROUD

GREYFRIARS BOBBY (1961)

The inverse of *Old Yeller* (and, as such, that film's necessary complement), *Greyfriars Bobby* deals with a dog's necessary acceptance of a person's death. The story dramatizes that life does indeed go on, and that the death of a beloved can serve some positive purpose, if one only chooses to perceive it that way. Robert Westerby's screenplay follows the pattern of Eleanor Atkinson's book, itself based on the true story of an Edinburgh Skye terrier, circa 1865. Yet this is, of course, the Disney version. While mostly cleaving to the facts, Walt transformed the story into an expression of his own essentially positive yet antisentimental views.

The film opens on a rural Scottish farm, where (in the Romantic tradition) simple people work close to the earth, enjoying a positive life. The crofter (Gordon Douglas) and his wife (Rosalie Crutchley) are gentle, generous people, particularly when lovingly spending time with their daughter (Jennifer Nevinson) and the small dog they gave her. Quickly, though, we realize all is not what it seems. The farmer drives his working man, Old Jock (Alexander Mackenzie), to the city, twenty miles away. Rather than making his weekly trip with Jock to buy necessities, the crofter drops the old man off permanently. Though the crofter insists he's doing this because of financial problems, it's clearly implied that Jock is being let go owing to his years, Disney once again implying an attack against ageism within his family-film context.

The drama unfolds when the dog, Bobby, deserts the wagon to try and find Jock. In Bobby's mind, he belongs to Old Jock, though Bobby also loves the little girl. In Disney, nothing is ever made simple for the child audience, and Bobby's choice is an emotional and difficult one between two fine human beings. In Edinburgh, Bobby finally discovers Old Jock, sleeping in rags as a hard rain pours down. The sequence, as powerful as anything in Vittorio de Sica's *Umberto D* (1952), conveys Disney's concern for the homeless, perceived as in that Italian Neorealist film not as lazy and, therefore, self-doomed, but rather as cast-off members of the working class. After spending his last pennies to find shelter for Bobby and himself in a flophouse, Old Jock passes away. When, in the morning, Bobby licks his master's hand, trying to wake

Old Jock, the scene is surprisingly free of melodrama. As an attending doctor notes, Jock died of "pneumonia, and of being old, and worn out." The film conveys a sense of relief. At least he will suffer no more.

But Bobby's problems—his, to borrow from Becker, denial of Old Jock's death—have only begun. When Bobby slips into Jock's funeral procession, almost tripping several of the pallbearers, the moment is played as black comedy, introducing a child audience to gallows humor. After Jock is buried in Greyfriars, Bobby takes to sleeping on the grave. This is not, as Disney portrays it, a morbid case of necrophilia but something far more spiritual. In no way depressed by the situation, Bobby merely maintains an ongoing relationship with someone who is still very much alive to him, even if Jock has moved on to a different state of existence. Throughout the film, there will be nothing sad in their ongoing rapport. Disney presents it as a paradigm for positively dealing with the death of any loved one, if we only manage the balance that Bobby maintains.

For Bobby's devotion to Old Jock (actual name, John Gray) hardly diminishes his strong desire to go on living, and also working: Bobby voluntarily serves as the local rat catcher, thus paying his own way. Once again, Disney employs a shaggy-dog story to comment on the world of humans. "Bobby's got no respect for the law," one of the Dickensian street children observes. This, in Disney's context, is presented as positive. Children who observed the film in 1961 would become the college students who likewise expressed no respect for the law if a particular piece of legislation struck them as stupid, wrongheaded, or immoral.

That proves to be the case here. The drama centers around a court case in which the lord provost (Andrew Cruickshank) must determine Bobby's fate, after the dog is seemingly doomed by a ridiculous and worthless law. Foreshadowing the antipolice mentality of the late sixties, the nearest thing to a villain is Maclean (Duncan Macrae), a by-the-book constable who brings Bobby to court on a technicality. The dog is not licensed by any owner, which would cost seven shillings. Though everyone loves Bobby, no one actually owns him, nor will he allow anybody to tie him down, however friendly he is to all. Bobby cannot be neatly bracketed into any easy, obvious form of existence. Therefore, according to law, he ought to be taken to the pound and destroyed.

Bobby is saved by one more of Disney's Children's Crusades. Upon hearing of Bobby's fate, the kids, poor as they are, pool whatever money they can find and rush to the courtroom to pay for the license. Here again, Disney reveals his Capra-for-children populism. The pooling of resources resembles the similar action on the part of small-town residents to save George Bailey from bankruptcy in *It's a Wonderful Life*. Such selflessness (incipient if entirely unconscious socialism) so impresses the lord provost that he extends to Bobby a special honor called Freedom of the City, the dog's independence and uniqueness at last accepted and respected. Bobby's positive presence creates a true community out of what had been only a lonely crowd. As, in the final shot, Bobby nestles once again on the grave of Old Jock, the camera pans to the left as, one by one, city dwellers lean out their windows and shout "good night" to Bobby. Their voices intermingle, as they also (for the first time) react to one another. Out of Old Jock's death has come the kind of simple, pure love that seemed lost once these former farmers deserted the natural country life to try and survive in an archetype of the modern city.

A NECESSARY END

BIG RED (1962)

However much he may personally adore mongrels, Disney does not slip into any easy reverse prejudice against animals or people of class. Just so long, that is, as they prove their worth through action. For his next boy-and-his-dog story, he chose to glorify a pedigreed Irish setter. Big Red, like his forerunners—the mongrel Yeller and little Bobby—achieves great good in life by helping humans overcome their problems in dealing with death. The class system is indeed at this movie's heart, along with Disney's theme of bridging the Generation Gap. The human protagonists are Rene Dumont (Gilles Payant), a poor orphan lad who cannot come to terms with the loss of his parents, and aging aristocrat James Haggin (Walter Pidgeon), who remains in a difficult state of denial following the untimely death of his beloved son. The young man was killed during World War II, adding a patina of Disney's antiwar sensibility.

Also present is Disney's ongoing dislike of raw capitalism. Haggin's potentially tragic flaw is that he cannot love the dog (or anything else) for its own sake. All he wants are blue ribbons and cash prizes, much like Jeremiah at his moral low point in *So Dear to My Heart*. But in the Disney vision, old dogs (and people) can, like the young, learn new tricks. Initially grateful for Rene's help in training Red, Haggin banishes the boy upon realizing that the animal loves and will only respond to the lad. This leads to Red's near-death, the dog crashing through a window while trying to reach Rene. Death seems so imminent that Haggin orders his overseer, Emile (Emile Genest), to put the animal out of his misery.

Red's fate appears sealed, particularly to those who recall Old Yeller. In this case, the dog survives, thanks to Rene, who steals Red, nursing him back to health. The film includes Disney's beloved concept of life cycles as symbolic of the regeneration of all existence, life and death necessarily mixed. Red finds a mate and becomes father to a litter. But where there is life, there is also in Disney—as in the actual world that these films prepare the very young to face realistically—always the potential for death.

While attempting to save the dogs from a prowling cougar, Haggin gets his foot trapped in rocks and is almost torn to pieces himself. The boy proves himself a man through a necessary act of violence: Rene shoots the cougar, saving Haggin, Red, Red's mate, and the litter. Always, though, out of death comes some good. Thanks to Big Red acting as catalyst, Haggin and Rene find in one another the son and father that each sorely needed.

THE YOUNG SEARCHERS

SAVAGE SAM (1963)

Disney's belated sequel to *Old Yeller* stands as this filmmaker's thematic equivalent to John Ford's *The Searchers* (1956), now widely regarded as one of the great American films. While this minor and largely forgotten Disney effort cannot be compared with Ford's masterpiece on an aesthetic level, it is perhaps even more historically authentic in its depiction of the plight of Anglo children captured by Comanches and the necessity of death in retrieving them than Ford's classic.

Travis Coates (Tommy Kirk), his Uncle Beck (Brian Keith), and Bud Searcy (Jeff York) are here the counterparts of Martin Pawley (Jeffrey Hunter), Uncle Ethan (John Wayne), and Old Mose Harper (Hank Worden) in Ford's film. Lisbeth Searcy (now played by Marta Kristen) is the equivalent of Debbie Edwards (Natalie Wood). Seized with her is Arliss (Kevin Corcoran), though the film takes a surprising attitude toward the lovable little boy from the first film. He has grown up to be an insufferable spoiled brat, whose tauntings of an innocent Indian youth (Rafael Campos) are largely responsible for the plight he and Lisbeth find themselves embroiled in. In Ford, the Comanches attacked without obvious motivation, reducing them to the dangerous and evil caricatures of previous (if less inspired) traditional westerns. In Disney, they were provoked by an insensitive Anglo and therefore emerge as at least somewhat sympathetic.

The title character, Old Yeller's son, serves the function of scout. Without him, and his remarkable sense of scent, the ostensible heroes could never discover the hidden Comanche village. Like Ford, Disney accurately chronicles the racist attitudes of Texans at that time. One here refers to the Comanches as "dirty murderin' savages," a phrase that also appears in *The Searchers.* The difference is, in Ford's film the line is spoken by a member of the search party (Ward Bond) whom we are meant to admire. Indeed, most all of the Texans are glorified and sentimentalized in Ford's film. In Disney's version, the search party (peopled by such veteran western types as Slim Pickens and Royal Dano) proves so unpleasant that, in comparison, the Native American characters come off as considerably less offensive.

In achieving victory, the Anglos reveal themselves to be remarkably brutal. In one particularly gruesome sequence, young Arliss viciously smashes in the head of an Indian. He never for a moment suggests any regret about his action, as Jim Hawkins did when forced to kill in *Treasure Island.* For contrast, there is once again *The Searchers,* in which the raiding party of whites that attacks a Comanche village in the final sequence appears to kill no one, except for the one warrior done in by Hunter, the remainder of this fight played with a lighthearted comic tone. That may appease a modern audience's conscience, but has little to do with life as it was lived in the West. Clearly, it is Ford who is the sentimentalist; Disney, the realist.

A LOT OF WORK TO DO

"OPERA PATHETIQUE," *MAKE MINE MUSIC* (1946)
"JOHNNY APPLESEED," *MELODY TIME* (1948)

Rather than avoid the issue of death, Disney films face it without fear. The hero's mother dies in *Rob Roy;* a teenager learns to kill in *Johnny Tremain.* But in those movies, and the rest of the oeuvre, death is never simplified or glorified, any more than it is denied. However entertaining, these are essentially educational films that taught their young audience a truth nowhere else found in Hollywood movies tailored for children. We must accept death's inevitability without allowing ourselves to become obsessed with its more fearsome aspects. Death, in Disney, is merely another stage of life.

No film better captures and crystallizes that idea than the "Opera Pathetique" segment of *Make Mine Music.* Nelson Eddy provided all the voices for this tale of "The Whale Who Wanted to Sing at the Met," featuring Willie. He is one more of Disney's belovedly different characters who refuse to accept their obvious lots in life—daring to dream of achieving something quite out of the ordinary considering the limited expectations of their stations at birth.

Here, Disney was able to make opera accessible to the mainstream audience by containing classical music in a piece less imposing than the ambitious *Fantasia*. Also, he was able to remove all the negative stigmas from fearsome whales (ranging from Moby Dick to his own Monstro in *Pinocchio*), providing the first positive screen portrayal of that much-maligned mammal. When a human approaches Willie, singing in the ocean, the trusting whale assumes this is a producer of opera, arriving to hear Willie's audition. The human, Tetti Tatti, carrying with him the baggage of civilized prejudice, coldly harpoons and kills Willie. Animal-rights activism combines with death education, as we are informed by the narrator that "people aren't used to miracles." The filmmaker's hope, apparently, is that young people in the audience will grow up to be far more enlightened. Once more, guarded optimism prevails, since we see Willie singing in heaven and are told: "Miracles never die."

The "Johnny Appleseed" segment of *Melody Time* furthers this theme. The film was fashioned fifteen years after Walt realized that he would indeed *not* die before his thirty-fifth birthday. Yet as he hit fifty, there occurred that initial sense of the approaching end game that comes to any man who reaches the half-century mark without retreating into outright denial. This is—if far from Disney's final word on the subject—then certainly his most characteristic statement.

In detail, we see the experiences (involving a Capra-like guardian angel) that lead young John Chapman, intimidated by huskier pioneers, to accept that he, in his unique way, can play a valuable and necessary part in the taming of the frontier—planting apple trees that will feed future generations. Then, the short subject (a mere twenty-two minutes in length) leaps over most of John's life in a dissolve montage sequence, during which Johnny grows a beard that swiftly whitens. Your years, the film wordlessly informs the child viewer, will go by very fast. Almost as much time is given over to Johnny's death as allotted to his moment of inspiration. Napping beneath one of the apple trees he planted, old Johnny hears the voice of his guardian angel and leaps up to greet him. Then he notices his own body still stretched out beneath the tree. Like England's Everyman (circa 1500), he could claim: "O Death, thou comest when I had thee least in mind!"

JOHNNY: Why, what's that?
ANGEL: Hmmm? Oh, just yer husk, John. Yer mortal husk.
JOHNNY: No. Dang it, Angel, I just won't go.

Johnny steadfastly refuses to travel onward with the angel. He slips into a denial of death—not out of cowardice, but a dedication to Disney's work ethic. There are more apple trees to be planted. Realizing that's the reason for John's hesitation, the angel points upward, explaining that heaven has just about everything *except* apple trees. Intrigued, Johnny eagerly departs on this, his greatest journey. Death is for him not an end but a beginning, a happy continuation of his endless odyssey (now metaphysical), thanks to his positive attitude toward it. Those lovely pink and red colors we see at sunset, the narrator informs us, are actually celestial apple blossoms, the fruits of John's ongoing work.

For Disney, as for Dr. Johnson, "It matters not how a man dies, but how he lives."[26] Disney's films, in which characters confront death and overcome human fear of it, illustrate for children the wisdom of Donne: "Death, thou shalt die."

Copyright Walt Disney Productions; courtesy Buena Vista Releasing.

THE HILLS HAVE EYES. Bruno Bettelheim has suggested that the best fairy tales are actually horror stories, scaled down to a level children can deal with; in *Snow White and the Seven Dwarfs* (1937), Disney emphasizes that aspect, the title character's initial gestalt causing her to unfairly project dark inner fears onto the benign world of nature.

Conclusion

Popular Entertainment and Personal Art
Why Should We Take Disney Seriously?

I'VE NEVER CALLED MY WORK AN "ART." IT'S PART OF SHOW BUSINESS.
I MAKE PICTURES FOR ENTERTAINMENT, AND THEN THE PROFESSORS
TELL ME WHAT THEY MEAN.
—Walt Disney, 1952

A WARMTH WITHIN THE BREAST WOULD MELT
THE FREEZING *REASON'S* COLDEST PART,
AND LIKE A MAN IN WRATH THE HEART
STOOD UP AND ANSWER'D, "I HAVE *FELT*." (EMPHASIS MINE)
—Alfred, Lord Tennyson, 1833

However much Disney's attitudes reflect those of England's Romantic poets, the British bard whom Walt's life-journey most resembles is Alfred, Lord Tennyson (1809–1892). A post-Romantic, Tennyson admired the works of those controversial literary rebels who preceded him, emulating their style and substance in his art. Despite that, he has always been perceived as a far more conventional figure.

Like the young Disney, Tennyson was born in a rural setting, raised by a strict father who lapsed into fits of violence. As with Walt's partnership with Roy, he collaborated with his brother Charles, as well as a friend—Arthur Hallam—who was to Tennyson what Ub Iwerks would be to Disney. The harsh reviews Disney received at Bosley Crowther's hands had their counterparts in those visited upon Tennyson by John Wilson Crocker. Despite such relentless attacks, though, Tennyson's poems—like Disney's films—swiftly won him public acclaim. As Disney early on moved to Los Angeles, so did Tennyson relocate to London. Like Disney, Tennyson remained an earthy realist in everyday life, while expressing in his work a mysticism that embraced "the Reality of the Unseen." Accused of sentimentality for his unabashed adoration of nature, Tennyson's "most passionate desire" was to "have a clearer and fuller vision of God"; nonetheless, he expressed only cynicism toward organized religion. Despite the fact that his name became a household word in his own lifetime, Tennyson often found himself deep in debt; Disney would know just such a paradoxical fate.

In Memoriam (1833–1850) stands today as Tennyson's major attempt to reconcile nature with science, which (like Shelley and other Romantics and in our time Disney) he adored equally. After the publication of Tennyson's much-loved epic *Idylls of the King* (1859), in which the author combined fervent patriotism with liberal attitudes, he lived the final third of his life as "a national or international institution,"[1] a phrase that describes no other Hollywood filmmaker so well as Disney, until the advent of his most notable successor, Steven Spielberg.

Tennyson resembled Disney in one other respect. Few things offend academics so much as commercial success, which explains the gradual sagging of Tennyson's reputation. Elitist critics perceived in the public's great love for him (adoration might be a more accurate term) a hint of something shallow. After all, if the groundlings enjoyed *The Princess* (1847) and *Maud* (1855), didn't that suggest the poet had pandered to a lowest common denominator? Of course, Shakespeare earlier suffered just such treatment at the hands of the intellectual elite, who pronounced him inferior to Christopher Marlowe, Ben Jonson, and Thomas Kyd. Likewise, Spielberg would have to wait for an inordinately long time before being taken seriously with *Schindler's List* (1993).

Disney qualifies as another such figure. Following the commercial and critical failure of the ambitious *Fantasia*, his seemingly less ambitious work was dismissed as popular entertainment, rather than the output of a serious artist, a situation that had less to do with any failings in the work than the public adoration it engendered. Yet no less a literary star than T. S. Eliot, generally considered one of the greatest of all modern poets, insisted that one could be considered a true artist rather than a mere artisan if one's oeuvre displayed all three of what Eliot considered the key criteria for such status: An *abundance* of work, a *variety* of genres within that canon, and a complete *competence* at one's craft.[2] In combination, these must also convey a consistent worldview, at once expressive of the individual creator, yet broad enough to move the public of his or her own time—then, ideally, future generations for all time.

Judged by these standards, Disney rates as a serious artist who—like Shakespeare, Tennyson, and Spielberg—presented personal statements in the guise of popular entertainment. This final portion of the book will scrutinize four oft-forgotten movies, as well as two commercial blockbusters that have always been critically drubbed, to reveal a consciousness at once unique to Disney yet universal in its appeal. Just as significant, Disney's vision finds perfect expression in a distinct aesthetic approach that is organically related to his ideas. When form and content so perfectly fuse, the result extends beyond technical craftsmanship, becoming authentic (as opposed to "corrupt") popular art.

DISNEY'S HEART OF DARKNESS

SO DEAR TO MY HEART (1948)

The film's title has as much to do with Walt's own feeling for the time and place (small-town America, circa 1906) as a little boy's love for his pet lamb. As Disney openly admitted, "*So Dear* was especially close to me. Why, that's the life my brother and I grew up with as kids out in Missouri."[3] Many plot elements are not found in Sterling North's pleasant if minor book *Midnight and Jeremiah* and were added by screenwriter John Tucker Battle at Disney's suggestion. The legendary racehorse Dan Patch did indeed stop over in Marceline, where Walt, like the film's Jerry (Bobby Driscoll), petted him and fed him an apple.[4] North's story served merely as a source, leading not to the mythic "Disneyfication" (i.e., sentimentalization) of the material, but, in fact, its opposite.

Most notably: In North's book, Jerry's lamb wins the grand prize at the county fair, an unlikely and ultimately faux happy ending. In Disney, Danny loses to a more conventionally bred lamb, receiving instead a special ribbon (though no *cash* prize) from the common-man judge (Harry Carey). Disney's ending is not only tougher, but transformed in other key ways to express his views. The judge, rustic symbol of true American values, acknowledges that Danny is truly "in a class by himself," expressing Disney's abiding love and respect for individuality—the greatness of unique personages (here symbolized by an animal), even if they do not fit into society's usual mold for "winners."

Likewise, Disney's obsession with death, at most a minor element in the brief novel, is essential here. The opening sequence, a marvelous animated montage by Ub Iwerks, focuses on a scrapbook chronicling the changing of the seasons. In particular, Walt focuses on autumn, specifically a leaf contained in the child's collection of stored-away memories. For a moment, the leaf is vibrant with red and orange hues. Then, it swiftly dies before our eyes, all the colors gone. No matter how desperately we may want to preserve the past, there are limits to what anyone can achieve in this ambition. Suddenly, the dead of winter dominates. Disney then does something rare in his films, focusing on a specific religious artifact, a manger scene. Yet the light shining from Joseph, Mary, and the Christ child seems, in context, less an instance of devout Christian imagery than a broad symbol of hope. However cold the winter (death), a ray of light (hope, life) remains.

Disney constantly employs the scrapbook (and voice-over narration spoken by John Beal, combining fragments from North's book with Walt's own personal recollections) to deconstruct the viewing experience. This reminds us that an entire way of life, depicted in the film, is itself dead and gone. Jerry lives on the farm with his grandmother (Beulah Bondi), though no explanation is given (or needed) as to what happened to his parents. Clearly, they have passed, the film (and its audience) taking this for granted. Death is a part of life, needing no great debate. Then come the birth of baby lambs on the Kincaid farm and the admission that, if Jezebel won't allow her black lamb to suckle, "he'll surely die."

Grandmother quietly insists:

The ways of nature seem cruel sometimes, and hard. But there's a plan behind it all. "He knoweth every sparrow that falleth."

Her words express Walt's belief that science (survival of the fittest) and religious faith are not at odds; God is inherent in nature, even its darker side. Yet, Disney insists, man must not simply accept this, employing it as an excuse for Social Darwinism. The child being father to the man, Jeremiah convinces Grandmother to keep Danny alive.

Not that the lamb is easy to have around. There are times when it appears Granny has reached the end of her tether with Danny's mischievousness. As Uncle Hiram (Burl Ives) sings, only half kiddingly, and with dark humor:

> If you git outta that pen,
> You ornery critter,
> You'll end up a fried lamb fritter.
> If you don't learn to settle down,
> You'll be roasted a golden brown!

Danny, given time, proves his worth. Disney taught his young audience a precept that would prove essential to 1960s thinking: Love is meaningless unless it is entirely unconditional.

In true Disney form, the issue of death here merges with two other concerns, capitalism and spirituality. Hoping to go to the county fair and enter Danny in competition, Jeremiah is informed by Granny that they don't have enough money.

> JERRY: We can pray for it.
> GRANNY: In this house, we don't pray for cash money. Only things of the spirit.

To earn the necessary funds, Jerry and his companion Tildy (Luana Patten) search for a wild honey tree, the contents of which could bring in a small fortune. This compares nicely with Ross Lockridge's fabled literary county and its "raintree," the source of all ancient wisdom that can unlock the mysteries of the universe for jaded moderns. Disney's children do indeed find one, but not before entering the dark bog that exists alongside bright country scenery, precisely as in the Lockridge novel.

As they drift farther into the primordial nightmare-by-daylight, Jerry and Tildy pass a cow's skeleton.

> TILDY: What killed it?
> JERRY: Nothin'. It just died.

Within moments, Tildy is nearly sucked into a bog hole. This is Conrad's heart of darkness, Disney-style; wild dogs, howling beyond the trees, threaten to tear the children apart. Though Walt never filmed *Hansel and Gretel*, this suffices. In the sequence, everything that Bettelheim ever wrote about the horrific aspect of fairy tales is vividly realized.

Like Perseus and Mirope of Greek myth, Disney's diminutive heroes must pass through the land of the dead to reach the light.

However innocent to a Romantic imagination, rural folk are not in Disney portrayed as simple swains, pure and incorruptible. During the course of his coming-of-age, Jerry nearly loses track of all that's important. He comes to care less about Danny's being acknowledged as a true winner than about the money involved. When Danny escapes his pen and is lost in the storm, little Jerry goes out searching, almost dying after a brutal battering by wind and rain. When Granny drags the boy back to the farm, cradling him in a coverlet, she attempts to explain that Danny may not survive the night, phrasing this in a spiritual—if not narrowly religious—fashion.

GRANNY: The Lord giveth, and the Lord taketh away.
JERRY: He can't have him! He can't have Danny.
GRANNY: You're not tellin' the Lord what he can do, and can't do. *He'll* do the tellin'.

When Danny continues to object, she reveals the true reason for her anger. Jerry's attempt to save Danny cannot be considered truly heroic, owing to Jerry's now-corrupted motivation. Granny here expresses perfectly the Disney code:

You've turned your heart away from the things I taught you since you were a baby. Started out loving the lamb. *True* love ain't a harmful thing. It's a good thing, good for the *spirit*. But you don't love that lamb anymore. All you're thinking about is *cash awards*. . . . You aren't thinkin' about the lamb. You're just thinkin' about *yourself*.

Jerry turns away and weeps, because he knows in his heart that she's absolutely right. In Disney, nothing is more reprehensible than self-interest, particularly raw capitalism. Even the finest among us, here Jerry, are tempted by living within the American system. Yet Walt will not—like his socialist father—simplistically condemn that system. Instead, Walt Disney insists on the need to redeem the corrupted American dream through an individual's difficult relearning of how to act in an honorable way.

This is, finally, a redemption saga, as much so as any ever conceived by a Catholic artist. Danny doesn't die, so when Jerry finds him, he brings Tildy to tears by insisting they aren't going to the fair after all. When questioned about this by Granny, Jeremiah reveals he has, in essence, been born again:

JERRY: I made a promise to the Lord. If I found Danny, we wouldn't take him to the fair.

GRANNY: Well, I made a promise to the Lord, too. I promised if we found him, we *would* go to the fair. And since I knowed Him longer than you, I think it'll be all right if I keep my promise.

This is pure situation ethics. As Granny notes, once the happy boy is gone:

Forgive me, Lord.

In the strictest sense, her lie might be considered a sin. She, Disney, and we all know better.

AMERICANIZING NEOREALISM

THE LITTLEST OUTLAW (1955)

In Mexico City, a ten-year-old orphan, Pablito (Andres Velasquez), assists his cruel stepfather, Chato (Rodolfo Acosta), as horse trainer to General Torres (Pedro Armendariz). When the general's daughter, Celita (Laila Maley), attempts to ride spirited Conquistador over a high wall, she is thrown and left paralyzed. Outraged, the general orders the animal shot. Unable to stand by and let this happen, little Pablito steals the horse, embarking on an odyssey in which he traverses Mexico's diverse countryside. His own uncle pursues on the general's orders. Adventures experienced by boy and horse range from the dramatic to the comic; always, the sense of a dark destiny hovers about them.

Outlaw was conceived by studio veteran Larry Lansburgh, who had been allowed to work independently in Mexico after receiving Walt's blessing to move ahead with the project. Rather than contradict a notion of Disney as guiding consciousness, the film attests to how completely he controlled even modest programmers. Lansburgh would not have received his go-ahead if Disney hadn't sensed, from the blueprint, that *Outlaw* would fit in with a then-expanding notion of what constituted Disney entertainment. Likewise, Lansburgh would never have brought the idea to his boss if he hadn't been certain it would receive the stamp of approval.

Technically, *Outlaw* represented something new for the studio, as the first feature shot in a style called Neorealism. This approach had been developed in postwar Italy by screenwriter Cesare Zavattini, in collaboration with such directors as Roberto Rossellini and Vittorio de Sica.

Their movies—most memorable among them *The Bicycle Thief* (1949)—relied on ordinary people rather than professional actors, to increase the sense of realism, and were shot on location for the same purpose. Always, they emphasized social themes, forsaking any simplistic notion of heroes and villains. All people, according to this view, are victims of the abiding power structure. In Italian Neorealism, as in Disney, death is a constant possibility, hanging over awkward attempts of common people to survive. Rather than create a sense of nihilism, such a threat allows us to live our lives with meaning. What we do, while struggling in an often incomprehensible world, allows each humble individual the potential for a new and modern brand of heroism.

Lansburgh had, for Disney, already created several Neorealist featurettes—e.g., *Stormy, the Thoroughbred* (1954)—combining a documentary sense of realism with a carefully scripted drama. Though several lesser-known professionals are included, in *Outlaw* Disney developed the docudrama, Americanizing (and Disneyizing, the terms all but synonymous) *Bicycle Thief*, as well as its leftist theme. No one is ever born a thief, outlaw, or criminal; fundamentally decent people are reduced to such by those controlling an insensitive system that, ironically, we call by the lofty title "civilization."

Within this altered stylistic context, Lansburgh was able to include several key Disney themes. There is an ambiguous attitude toward the military; General Torres, though fundamentally a decent person, has become a martinet owing to his position of power. He makes the mistake of ordering his daughter about; though only ten, Celita soon proves herself to be one of Disney's feminist heroines in embryo. At one point, she makes her father face his previously unconscious sexism:

If I were a *son*, you'd let me ride Conquistador!

Torres has no answer, because she is right. *Outlaw* also includes a criticism of animal abuse. Conquistador is afraid of leaping walls because Chato, while training him, used sharp spikes to frighten the horse into jumping higher. When Conquistador becomes hysterical, Chato tries beating the animal into submission. This situation would be brutal for an "adult" feature; in a family film, it proves so intense that many observers might wonder if Disney had lost his sense of his captive audience. In fact, he knew *precisely* who they were. Disney's definition of a family film is not merely a divertissement to provide temporary escape from the horrors in the world. He instead oversaw the creation of diverse works—animated, live-action, and various combinations thereof

MORAL BUT NOT MORALISTIC. Disney films consistently convey the traditional notion that moral behavior is imperative, while simultaneously undermining all conventional concepts of simplistic morality; as the title of *The Littlest Outlaw* (1955) indicates, the young rebel-hero (Andres Velasquez) is absolutely right in stealing a beloved horse from those who would harm it, while a priest lies—and feels justified in doing so—to aid the child and the animal in their attempt to escape from corrupt adults.

—that demonstrate a sense of thematic continuity and a consistency of artistic ambition characterized by a willingness to force the entire family to deal with—and, Disney hopes, change—horrific situations that are all too real in the world around us.

The anticapitalist theme is as present here as in any Italian Neorealist film. Chato's motivation for his abusive behavior is a series of bets, for he greedily hopes to amass a small fortune for himself, at any cost to the animal. The class system, and the lack of interest on the part of enlightened young people in this by-product of adult greed, appears in the attitude of Celita toward Pablito. They are best friends, the girl's eyes always suggesting that she may be considering some possible future romance. The Generation Gap is in evidence, as innocent Pablito rightly rebels against his corrupt foster father.

Shortly, he is a young runaway, a term that would describe a considerable portion of America's youth only a decade later. Disney makes us aware that, when such a situation occurs, it is not the runaway's fault, rather the result of an adult system that failed to hear his cry for help. And there is a suggestion of Disney's metaphysical theme. Immediately after fleeing, Pablito prays. But as one would expect from Disney, he does not do this in a church, but pantheistically—standing before an immense cross placed in a beautiful natural location. He can pray with a clear conscience because his theft of the horse was not a self-serving act, which Disney could never condone, but the moral breaking of a law. This would likewise prove a key issue for 1960s rebels, as they burned draft cards and destroyed military machinery.

Ultimately, Pablito must trust a priest in the small village of San Miguel de Allende. Luckily for the boy, the padre (Joseph Calliea) is a radical and, as such, a predecessor to the Berrigan brothers. He hides boy and horse in the church, misinforming Chato as to their whereabouts. Then, the priest immediately kneels to confer with God:

Did I do wrong? I don't think so. Yes, I lied just then. Am I not protecting the soldier's horse? Yes, but the boy says they will kill it. I don't *feel* as though I've done wrong!

The padre rises and is clearly content. The controversial concept of situation ethics, which would make morality in America more complex during the 1960s and exists in sharp contrast to stiff traditional views, remains omnipresent in Disney films. His good characters lie, cheat, and steal. Moreover, their doing this is presented as proper behavior, so long as it is performed for a just cause.

There is an enlightened capitalist on view here. Don Pepe (Pepe Ortiz), a vaquero, allows his doctor (Carlos Ortigoza) to care for the wounded horse. Money, as always in Disney, is neither good nor evil in and of itself. And, lastly, there is a sequence involving the bullring, when Conquistador will be ridden by a picador. Disney had previously let his negative attitudes about this sport be known in the animated *Ferdinand the Bull*; here, he shows an actual bullfight in more brutal fashion than had ever been the case in adult Hollywood movies like *Blood and Sand* (1941) and *The Bullfighter and the Lady* (1951). In them and other such cinematic depictions, the matadors were inevitably glorified. Not, of course, in Disney. When one matador is knocked down and gored, child audiences attending Saturday matinee screenings across the country spontaneously cheered and applauded. A growing radicalization against animal abuse among the next generation of Americans began at that moment. At the end, the general has—impacted by his "princess" daughter and the pauper boy—come to see his mistakes. Having grown as a result of their gentle teaching through example, he relents on his previous order of death for the animal.

There is, fortunately, no sentimental ending. We never learn whether Celita will ever walk again. Even if she cannot, she can still ride. In the final shot, she and Pablito sit atop Conquistador, together. The horse is cured, owing to loving treatment. The looks that pass between boy and girl suggest they may yet become a romantic couple. Disney, as always, presents mixed marriages across class and/or race (she pureblood Spanish, he mestizo, they a human Lady and the Tramp) as highly desirable. The young people, and their horse, have denied death—not by refusing to look it in the face, but by choosing to live meaningful lives.

THE READINESS IS ALL

DARBY O'GILL AND THE LITTLE PEOPLE (1959)

As Shakespeare said, through the person of Hamlet: "If it be not now, it will yet be to come: The readiness is all." All Disney films are, on some level, about living one's life in such a way. When death does come, as it inevitably must, the central character is ready. None of the films, though, is so all-consumed with death's ever-present shadow as *Darby O'Gill*. In the opening sequence, Sheelah Sugrue (Estelle Winwood), a village crone (it is strongly hinted that she may be a witch) in rural Ireland, visits the simple cottage inhabited by the governor's gamekeeper, Darby (Albert Sharpe), and his lovely daughter Katie (Janet Munro). Learning that Darby is off at the pub, Sheelah attempts to win over independent-minded Katie for her own bullyboy son, Pony (Kieron Moore). One more of Disney's protofeminist role models, Katie has no interest in marrying Pony or anyone else; she'll marry only if and when she finds a man whom she considers worthy of herself. In response, Sheelah tries to frighten Katie:

SHEELAH: Your father is getting no younger, and when the time comes, we must all "step down."
KATIE: Don't put me father in the grave just yet.

Like Prospero, Darby is something of a magician, certain he can conjure up the King of the Leprechauns, Brian (Jimmy O'Dea). Like Disney, Darby is an inveterate storyteller. Intriguingly, his small, loyal audience is composed entirely of locals who frequent the village pub; there are virtually no children in the village or surrounding countryside. *Darby* is the first film ever made for young people that features no counterparts for them onscreen. Perhaps this was Walt's way of implying that the perception of him as an entertainer of children was a media-created myth. When Darby tells what might seem to be children's stories (about the wee people) to grown-ups, he can be taken as an autobiographical figure —that is, Disney's means of informing us his films had been intended for, as the filmmaker himself put it on numerous occasions, "children of all ages."

Initially, Darby hopes to capture King Brian and procure three wishes. The first is a big pot of gold. Though this might initially seem to contradict Disney's ongoing criticism of raw capitalism, that proves not to be the case. The gold will provide a dowry for his still-unmarried daughter, allowing Katie to live independently for as long as she chooses. Conversely, the villains are motivated by self-interest. Pony wants to marry Katie not because she's charming and beautiful, but to put himself in line for a position as replacement gamekeeper. Michael (Sean Connery), who wins that job, loves Katie for herself. He proves too shy to kiss her. As always, it is the woman who must take control of the situation and apply the first kiss.

Pony refuses to do a favor for the lovable local priest, Father Murphy (Denis O'Dea)—retrieving the poor parish's bell from a nearby town without being paid for the trip. Darby, Disney's hero, makes that trek without asking for or accepting recompense. Darby, when working in the fields, carries either a hammer or a sickle and, on some occasions, both—a semiotic reminder that Walt's considerable qualms about capitalism originated with his father's firm socialist beliefs. Even the initial plot mechanism, in which Lord Fitzpatrick (Walter Fitzgerald) retires Darby (with a decent, even generous, pension), connects to Disney's social thrust. *Darby* was one of Hollywood's first attacks on ageism, since Darby still can clearly do his work.

Toward the end of the first act, Darby essentially "dies." After chasing his old horse Cleopatra up a hill toward the remains of an ancient Celtic holy ground, Darby is surprised when the animal suddenly turns white—i.e., becomes the pale horse of death. As the animal rears on her hind legs, Darby falls backward, down a deep, dry well, landing hard. When he opens his eyes, he's in the Great Hall of Knocknasheega, singing and dancing with the little people. When Darby speaks of returning to Katie, King Brian insists: "Once you're here, there's no going back!" As to Darby's daughter, Brian adds: "Don't worry about Katie. She'll throw you a good wake, then forget all about you."

Darby is, for all intents and purposes, dead. Darby's reasoning, in seeking to earn his escape, is not unlike that of Johnny Appleseed, who didn't want to expire only because there were more trees to plant. Darby insists that, since he's the village storyteller, the locals would cease to believe (however tenuously) in leprechauns once he stopped relating the tales. Possibly, this novel approach reflects Disney's own denial of death. Who would modernize those wondrous old fairy tales if he were gone? The answer, of course, is Steven Spielberg, in films like *E.T.* (1982) and *Hook* (1991). Darby does manage to return to the real world. In this, he clearly precedes Thomasina, the cat who will also lead three lives. In Darby's second existence, he gives up all interest in riches: "I'll not wish for the gold; nine times out of ten, it leads to unhappiness." His character arcs, proving that an old dog *can* be taught new tricks. Now, Darby hopes to trick his longtime adversary Brian into bringing Katie and Michael together as a couple.

The final act opens when Katie—like the heroines of *The Littlest Outlaw*, *Pollyanna*, and *Thomasina*—is seriously injured in a fall. First, Disney establishes the limits of conventional religion. However well intentioned, Father Murphy can offer nothing but dim prayers. The dread Costa Bower, the death coach, comes for Katie; Darby calls up Brian to grant the old man an entirely selfless wish, changing places in the coach with his daughter. As the coach ascends, we see what Darby sees, joining him (through marvelous special effects, state-of-the-art in their time) in a near-death experience—the world fading away as it would for a dying man. But King Brian appears and tricks Darby into making a fourth wish (that he could see Katie and Michael married). According to legend, the request for a fourth wish cancels out the earlier ones. So Darby is returned to earth to live, like Thomasina, a third life. Considering his advanced age, this will clearly be brief, as the bittersweet finale suggests. No matter. For he, like Hamlet, knows that the readiness is all, and in the preceding dramatic comedy, he has fully prepared himself. For Disney's old hero, like the Bard's young prince, the rest will be happily silent.

TIGER, TIGER, BURNING BRIGHT

SWISS FAMILY ROBINSON (1960)

In 1960, at the height of his interest in creating live-action features, Disney mounted (in his own words) "a wonderful show."[5] Yet beneath its surface of highly entertaining romance, comedy, and action, *Swiss Family Robinson* served as an apotheosis for Disney's Romantic ideas, all suggested and then developed in earlier projects, on reclaiming humankind's gloriously primitive connection to the natural world. The film serves as a Romantic's paean to our discovering, if only by accident, the lost Eden, and—after gradually finding the way out of civilization's shackles—learning to understand that the difference between a garden and a jungle exists not in the landscape but in one's point of view.

Swiss Family Robinson, as a film, has little to do with the themes or narrative of Johann Wyss's 1812–1813 novel. Disney retained only the characters' names and the central concept of a European family attempting to emigrate to the New World, cast away on an isolated island; Tobago, near British Guiana, provided the perfect shooting site. Essentially, Disney reversed the attitudes of Wyss, which from our perspective can only be considered Classicist, conservative, and ultimately imperialistic. Wyss's family, originally distraught at their predicament, realize in time that they can survive if, as Anglos facing the primitive heart of darkness, they impose old religious values and recent scientific knowledge upon nature. In the film, the opposite proves true. Though for Walt, as they were for Wyss, religion and science will prove significant in the family's survival, both are in the film drawn *from* the natural world rather than imposed *upon* it.

What we witness onscreen is Disney's creation of an archetype for what, in the sixties, would become the enlightened modern family, adjusting to and then living in harmony with nature, rather than attempting to subdue the primordial world. In this context, Disney's essentially Romantic leanings are obvious from the opening sequence. While making their way in makeshift boats from the wrecked ship, stuck on rocks, to the island's shore, the youngest child, Francis (Kevin Corcoran), worries about the animals. Youth's positive connection to the natural world far exceeds that of the adults, however positive they may be. The father (John Mills) is initially unconcerned. He will arc during the course of the story, becoming a better—and more natural—man in the process. The mother (Dorothy McGuire), a true Disney woman, shows considerably more sensitivity than her male counterpart from the very beginning.

The notion of the child as Wordsworthian swain continues as the narrative progresses. Francis has no sooner arrived than he's riding on a tortoise's back, later doing the same with a baby elephant. The middle son, Ernst (Tommy Kirk), has an easier time adjusting to nature than the oldest, Fritz (James MacArthur); with age has come the baggage of civilization. He must unlearn the imitation of civilized adults before he can achieve transcendence with the natural world and, with it, achieve the spiritual rebirth that comes easier to the very young.

"A HOUSE SHOULD NOT BE *ON* A HILL, BUT *OF* A HILL." The architectural ideas of Frank Lloyd Wright were adapted to the cinema by Disney; as the title characters in *The Swiss Family Robinson* (1960) grow ever more natural (i.e., "good"), their moral regeneration is reflected by the tree house, like them inseparable from the natural world with which they are now at one.

Mother and father are those rare modern adults who are still in touch with their primal sympathy. After all, Father chose to leave Switzerland for the New World, despite the fact that "other men in offices stay there." He couldn't; like such diverse Disney heroes as Davy Crockett and *The Happiest Millionaire*'s Angie Duke, Father Robinson set out with hopes of finding something new and better. The mother understands her husband's leanings, drawing her personal philosophy (consciously or not) from Rousseau: "You wanted to give our sons a chance to be free!" These were middle-class people, not indentured servants, in Switzerland. By "free," she does not mean an escape from literal enslavement—rather from the symbolic enslavement of a conformist lifestyle, the nineteenth-century equivalent of postwar America's suburban culture. Also, Disney's incipient pacifism is implied. Another reason for leaving was Napoleon's imperialist attempts to conquer Europe, which disgusted the family. Like so many newly enlightened people of the sixties, they oppose all wars fought for imperialist purposes, supporting only those that are revolutionary.

The film opens the way for the back-to-nature movement, which would flourish during the following decade. Not surprisingly, then, the mother transforms their traditional Christian faith, while living in nature, into a more pantheistic religion. After their deliverance from the wreck, she insists everyone kneel and pray. Instead of scripture, however, they silently pray (without ever referring to the Christian notion of God as the Father) to the natural world around them, as embodied by the Great Goddess (i.e., Mother Nature).

Owing to the civilized baggage they carry, the island originally appears to the adult couple as a jungle. In time, they come to perceive it, like their children, as a garden. A garden that must, however, be cultivated; Disney, like Shakespeare, expresses great reverence for the good gardener. Ernst implicitly understands science, always a positive/progressive force in the Disney worldview. As they create their new home, it is he who comes up with varied inventions to heat and light their rooms, as well as provide fresh running water. There's even an elevator.

Importantly, though, Ernst fashions all such innovations from the natural materials at hand. He is a consummate Disney hero, traditional in his gradual growth of ability to accept the beauty and spirituality of nature; liberal in that he believes man, at his best, is a part of that nature, possessing like all other animals a right to adapt himself into that environment. It makes perfect sense, then, that their home is a tree house. For the tree is as much Disney's key symbol of nature at its purest as it was for practitioners of early pagan religions. Completed, their home offers a balance Shelley would have admired: nature and science, harmonized rather than at odds. Moreover, our view of it recalls the architectural ideas of Frank Lloyd Wright: the tree on a hill, and the house in a tree, totally integrated into the environment. Science and nature are completely compatible; man and nature are at one.

The father fully realizes that, in their own conformist times, this makes them unique, even eccentric:

The world is full of nice, ordinary people who have nice, ordinary homes.

At that moment, he is less the hero of a period-piece film than a contemporary critic of suburbia, with its little houses made of ticky-tacky, and they all look just the same, as do the people living in them.

At one point, Ernst's scientific mind grasps that once, there must have been a land bridge connecting their island to Asia. How else explain the diversity of animals never found to coexist in any known country? Though the film is shot on location, what we see is clearly an island of the mind, a creative geography, less a spot on the map than Disney's apotheosis of nature itself.

Along with the flamingos, monkeys, and other adorable creatures roams a potential figure of menace: a wild cat that, prowling in darkness, embodies Blake's vision of a

Tiger, tiger, burning bright.
In the forests of the night.

He is a menace, however, only so long as perceived (by the still-civilized —thus unenlightened, from a Romantic viewpoint—people) as such. Once they too have become natural, even the tiger is seen as an ally, employed to help them fight the pirates (society at its worst) who menace the island.

By movie's end, the father has regained a sense of childhood playfulness, any residing stuffiness (a holdover from the civilization he consciously wanted to leave behind) set aside as he joins in animal-riding races with the boys. Both adults literally appear to become younger; the Fountain of Youth, in Disney, is not some specific spot found hidden away in nature. It is inherent in nature itself and a full, open appreciation of the natural world.

As the father says to his wife:

Don't you sometimes feel that this is the kind of life we were *meant* to live on this earth?

By "we," he means more than the two of them as a couple, or even the family. He refers, as Disney's spokesman, to the race of man. And, more specifically, to the American people of 1960, grown conformist and self-satisfied. Yet in the sixties, an audience weaned on this and earlier Disney films would answer the father's question with a wholehearted "yes," as the back-to-nature movement emerged. As, at the end, his wife says, in full agreement:

Funny, how you can change your mind about what you *really* want. What's actually *important!*

The American people would change their mind, too, as do these supposedly nineteenth-century Swiss. Upon rescue, mother and father grasp how fully they have arced when they choose to stay on the island. So do Fritz and Roberta, he having given up his dream of taming some new, other frontier, she forsaking the London civilization to which she earlier hungered to return. Little Francis is allowed to stay as well, with the clear implication that in time, he will return to society for an education, so he can then make an informed choice as to where he will live his life. In this he mirrors Disney's own daughter, encouraged to attend Protestant and Catholic churches and then make up her own mind as to which —if any—organized religion was right for her. Of course, we can't help but believe Disney secretly hoped she would, like him, reject all communal religious systems in order to develop her own highly individualized form of spirituality.

Ernst does sail for Europe—not to join the conformist crowd there but to get a university education, something Disney always favors. Ernst will hone his already sharp mental skills and find a woman of his own. Then, very possibly, he will return to the island, which we are told will develop into a new colony, the father serving as its governor. He rather likes this idea, representing as he does one of Disney's common-man heroes who, by proving himself in the real world, transforms into one of the new aristocrats—not owing to birth, but achievement.

The film's final words, though, go to the young, as Roberta and Fritz embrace in their garden.

> ROBERTA: Two people! If they love each other, what more can they want?
> FRITZ: To be *alone!*

A DIFFERENT DRUM

THOSE CALLOWAYS (1965)

When Christmas is celebrated by the film's title clan, the ceremony takes place in their simple cabin, deep in the woods, not in the town-based church where neighbors meet for services. For Disney, spirituality, like charity, begins at home—particularly a home located close to nature. The film concerns an attempt by this early-twentieth-century family to create a bird sanctuary near the small Vermont town of Swiftwater. Their opponents range from local rednecks, less intent on hunting the wild geese for food (which Disney would never argue with) than shooting migrating fowl for the fun of it (something he despises), to big-city types, wicked raw capitalists who scheme to turn Swiftwater into a resort area by creating a hunter's paradise.

As one, observing migrating geese, marvels:

There's a flying fortune up there, if someone could just find a way to use it!

BACK TO NATURE. Disney films preceded—and, if one accepts that movies can impact and alter the public consciousness—helped create a heightened interest in ecology during the late sixties and early seventies; *Those Calloways* (1965) concerned a father (Brian Keith) and son (Brandon de Wilde) who construct a bird sanctuary, despite interference by raw capitalists eager to employ the land for commercial purposes. Himself an enlightened capitalist, Disney delicately balanced the commercial theme parks with plentiful nature reserves in the concept for Walt Disney World, Florida.

The "use" they devise entails commercialization of a quiet village, replacing the general store with a hot dog and souvenir stand. Though the residents have always adored their easygoing lifestyle, they are sorely tested by their own greed, yearning for the money that would come with a corporate takeover.

In *Calloways*, Disney presents his most complex portrait of small-town America. The people are fine and decent enough to help the Calloways, who have lost their old home to a shallow banker, build a new one. Like Capra and Ford, Disney understands that America's greatness resides in its delicate balance of opposite extremes. Even the most rugged of rugged individualists occasionally need the support of a positive community. However good, though, they are tempted by the possibilities of big profits.

Some might raise the issue of central Florida's selection for Disney's immensely ambitious theme-park project during the 1960s. Aren't his actions, as incarnated by the vast invasion, in direct contrast with what he has to say in this film? Not if one studies the research preceding the selection of Orlando. Always, the idea was to locate a large stretch that had proven unusable for commercial growth or any natural purpose as a reserve. Only when such a fallow area was discovered did the Disney Corporation decide to develop it. Small towns like nearby Kissimmee were cautiously avoided, so that their long-standing lifestyle would remain untouched. In addition to state-of-the-art theme parks, emphasis would be placed on creating new wildlife sanctuaries—Discovery Island for tourists, others that would remain off-limits to people other than professionals dedicated to the conservation of nature.

The eventual creation of Disney's Animal Kingdom in the late nineties proved that the commercial theme park and serious-minded wildlife sanctuary could coexist. Diversions would bring in large numbers of people eager to enjoy thrill rides with the knowledge that, while on-property, they could also be educated as to ecology. The Disney Corporation (operating as Walt's vision of an extended and enlightened institution that would outlive him as a person while continuing his values) followed through on Disney's long-standing desire to break down the barriers between entertainment and education.

What Disney criticizes in *Those Calloways* is not corporate commercialism. His father's extreme form of socialism was considered by Walt, then rejected in favor of the enlightened capitalism espoused by both Roosevelt presidencies. Such institutions—Theodore (the last great liberal Republican), FDR (the first great liberal Democrat), and Walt (who combined the best qualities of both) all believed—become villainous only when, as in this particular movie, they display no respect for the natural world. In this context, Swiftwater emerges as Disney's ultimate symbol of the American community. No sooner do a fast-talking, suited salesman (Philip Abbott) and his elegantly attired big-city boss (Roy Roberts) offer to make each local a stockholder in their venture than most everyone is cowed into submission. They change their minds only when Cam Calloway (Brian Keith) takes ever more violent umbrage at arriving hunters. In time, Cam is shot (if accidentally) by one. In a tradition launched by *Bambi*, *Those Calloways* is a rare commercial movie that goes firmly on record as antigun.

Upon realizing that Cam lies near death in his cabin, attended only by his loyal wife, Liddy (Vera Miles), and teenage son, Bucky (Brandon de Wilde), the townsfolk—again, like those in a Capra or Ford film—finally transform from self-interested rugged individualists into a true community. Earlier, many went so far as to call him "Crazy Cam," much as *The Absent Minded Professor*'s Brainard (Fred MacMurray) became known within his own community as "Ned the Nut." It is the eccentrics, the outcasts, those rebels who march to the beat of a different drum yet continue to work within the system to clean it up, whom Disney lionizes.

One difference between Disney and Capra, however, is that Disney offers far less sentimental heroes than those played by James Stewart and Gary Cooper. Cam is first seen returning to his family after being absent for an extended time, owing to chronic alcohol addiction. That problem will recur throughout the film, as the seemingly strong Cam reaches for a bottle every time trouble appears—saved time and again by his loyal and far stronger wife. In addition to his complex personality, Cam's morality is at best dubious. He is dedicated, almost to the point of obsession, with preserving the wild geese as a species; Cam was raised by the Nick-Nacks, a local Indian tribe, who worship the geese. Cam has passed this obsession on to his son. In the opening sequence, Bucky becomes embroiled in a fistfight while trying to stop Whit Turner (Tom Skerritt), worst of the local rednecks, from shooting birds for sport. In true Disney form, a young woman, Bridie (Linda Evans), stops the fight, enacting a deeply felt and protofeminist pacifism that men—even the best of men—can't comprehend.

Shortly, though, the morality of the Calloways grows murky. Cam and Bucky plan to finance their wild bird reserve by trapping fur-bearing animals and selling their skins. They hope to underwrite a moral mission by amoral means. At this point, the Calloways cannot be considered true naturalists, merely obsessive eccentrics. Only when they arc enough to reject the fur trade do they, in the film's second half, rise to truly heroic proportions. For then they care for *all* of nature in a magnanimous sense, not just some single part of it owing to an old obsession. This is what we expect from one of Disney's multicultural heroes. Cam, at one point, is referred to by his Native American blood brother, Nigosh (Frank de Kova), as "the only Irish Nick-Nack."

Not only the rugged individualists pass the test, however. So too does the community at large. Even the banker, Doane Shattuck (Parley Baer), finally comes around. Cam had cursed this man when Doane foreclosed on his mortgage:

CAM: You've got the might of the almighty dollar. That's *your* tablet and commandments.

DOANE: Cam, we've been friends for years.

CAM: You don't have any friends. All you've got is those coins you love to jingle in your pockets.

Though he wears a suit, Doane is not one of the big-money boys from Burlington, even if he has become involved (temporarily) with their scheme. When push comes to shove, Doane proves himself a small-town boy at heart. There was still a touch of primal sympathy even in him, however remote, waiting to be tapped. So Doane votes with the others to keep the town pure, in a way that no character of Capra (forgiving to most everyone in his movies *except* bankers) would ever do. As with Capra, so with Ford, whose banker in *Stagecoach* (1939) never reunites with the others. This distinguishes Disney from those "adult" artists: Capra may have retaught a jaded American audience how to love; Disney taught us how to love *unconditionally*.

THE BEAR NECESSITIES

THE JUNGLE BOOK (1967)

Unconditional love is at the heart of this, the last animated feature overseen by Disney before his death. The opening sequence reveals his precarious balance between fidelity to the source (in this case, Rudyard Kipling's 1894 volumes of stories for children) and a willingness to divert from it to achieve personal expression. Whenever Kipling and Disney are on the same wavelength, nothing is changed. The idea of an Indian boy raised by wolves, growing up in nature and thus superior to those maturing in civilization, could hardly help but appeal to the filmmaker who had already told the story of Pecos Bill, an American child nurtured by coyotes. But in Kipling, the child Mowgli wanders away from his rural village; in the Disney version, he is found by Bagheera the Panther in an abandoned boat, lost in the bulrushes. A reference to Moses, this hints at a spiritual element to the Disney version that is not present in Kipling.

Always refusing to simplify any species, Disney appreciated Kipling's decision to achieve a moral balance by casting both Mowgli's mentor and his worst enemy as giant cats, the latter Shere Khan the Tiger. Disney's adoration of mothers was present in Kipling's having the mother wolf accept this foundling before any of the males do; his desire to redeem animals previously caricatured as evil was likewise found in Kip-

SHAPING A GENERATION'S GESTALT. Even in seemingly escapist fare, such as his genial 1967 musicalization of Kipling's *The Jungle Book*, Disney conveyed a worldview that remained entirely consistent with the vision offered in his earlier films; Mowgli, like America's Pecos Bill—superior to other men because he has been raised in nature and thus remains unspoiled by civilization's hypocrisies—enjoys a pastoral interlude with best pal Baloo the Bear.

ling, the wolf as positively presented here as it always had been in Disney's nature films. And Disney's appreciation of community endeavor is highlighted in the depiction of the functional democratic "pack."

The most memorable of Kipling's stories traced Mowgli's early adventures with his "brothers," and this was the essence of Zolton Korda's memorable 1942 live-action feature starring Sabu. Surprisingly, then, Disney's version scraps all those tales. The narrative quickly skips to Mowgli at age ten, that moment when his mentors realize the boy must return to civilization. This allowed for the exploration of several recurring Disney themes, including the coming to grips with one's own racial identity (*The Ugly Duckling*, *The Light in the Forest*) and the bittersweet parting of the ways with friends found in nature to accept one's role in society (*Snow White*, *The Fox and the Hound*).

This transitional journey always involves death, if not its actuality then at least a cognition of its presence. Disney employed Kaa, Kipling's mesmerizing snake, for this symbolic purpose in his radically altered context. Disney also includes his ongoing satire, some of it savage, on the military by reimagining Kipling's elephants as a platoon led by well-meaning, incompetent Colonel Hathi. For feminism, there is the colonel's wife, who grows annoyed with his self-importance and takes over the command herself, to the betterment of all. The Generation Gap is also present, as Hathi's child likewise rebels against his father's bigoted attitudes. Baloo the Bear is, in the Disney version, as complex a character as Shakespeare's Falstaff. Mowgli comes to admire Baloo's unpretentious rejection of those details in life that can constrict individual enjoyment, opting instead for the "bear necessities." Still, Mowgli (and we) are asked to eventually reject, like Prince Hal transforming into Henry V, the plump character's avoidance of the work ethic.

King Louis of the monkeys is employed as a foil to Mowgli. What makes him dangerous in Disney is not (as in Kipling) spasmodic and wild behavior, but his aspiration to become human, literally "aping" Mowgli. This sequence helps to teach the boy that his own opposite desire—to become a bear—is also a denial of his true self. As lost as Dumbo, the child finds sincere friendship with a group of outsider birds who prove themselves as decent as the earlier film's black crows: Four vultures, modeled on the Beatles, one in particular a dead ringer for Ringo.

Ultimately, though, the film is about our need to grasp the unconditional nature of love at its truest, as Mowgli's mentors debate whether he ought to be returned to humankind:

> BALOO: I love that kid, as if he were my own cub.
> BAGHEERA: Then think what's best for *him*, and not *yourself!*

Baloo realizes that self-interest has nothing to do with true love. Mowgli—like Bambi and so many other Disney heroes before him—likewise realizes that romantic love is the ultimate life force. Having clung to his childhood—and male bonding—for as long as possible, Mowgli finds himself "twitterpated" by a comely village girl. Irresistibly drawn to her —and toward maturity and responsibility—he casts a final glance back at his two friends. The voice-over narration offers no final statement, leaving the movie's message implicit in the imagery and fully consistent with an oft-recurring Disney idea: the total tolerance of one race by another, perhaps the most significant concept to be advanced by the post-Woodstock generation. This would be most perfectly articulated at the end of *A Tale of Two Critters:*

Though they could never again be friends, at least they would never afterwards be enemies.

That tolerance was not won without a stiff price. The death of three civil rights workers in Mississippi during the summer of 1964 remains the single incident that symbolically marks a changeover from the long preexisting America to one that, toward the beginning of a new millennium, is still evolving. As student radical Mark Rudd said of such dark days:

It was . . . the time that we were resolved to fight—to disregard all the liberal[s] warning us of the horror of the police bust *and* the right-wing reaction. In a sense it was a time when we overcame our own middle-class timidity and fear of violence.[6]

A time when old politics, right or left, became all but irrelevant. The New Politics—like Disney's own values—transcended such concepts as liberal and conservative. How else explain the fact so many counterculture heroes of the late sixties—Bob Dylan, Jerry Rubin, Eugene McCarthy, Eldridge Cleaver, Dennis Hopper, Mort Sahl, all then perceived as leftish—had, little more than a decade later, taken a right turn, becoming fervent supporters of Ronald Reagan's campaign for the presidency?

Conversely, Disney—a Republican throughout the 1960s, then perceived as the ultimate bastion of traditional values—may now be reconsidered and viewed as something of a radical. As to the charges that Disney is too commercial, recall a statement by countercultural hero John Lennon concerning the Beatles: "We'd rather be rich than be famous."[7]

As to the charges that Disney is too vulgar, embracing the ordinary, another Walt—Whitman—might have been speaking for Disney when, in *Leaves of Grass* (1855), he expressed his love for "what is commonest, cheapest, nearest, easiest." That is, everything about the crude American democratic lifestyle, as well as the poet himself, "is *me*."[8] Or, as one social/cultural observer put it:

For Whitman, the political form of the commonwealth of Happiness is democracy and its boundaries are the universe. Work and sex are the healthy diet of this democratic universe.[9]

This is as true of the vision gleaned from Disney as from Whitman. Walt's own epithet for Disneyland, "the happiest place on earth," offers a notion more profound in its implications than the bit of commercial jingoism it has been widely considered to represent.

According to Bettelheim,

for a story truly to hold the child's attention, it must entertain him and arouse his curiosity. But to enrich his life, it must stimulate his imagination, help him to develop his intellect and to clarify his emotions; be attuned to his anxieties and aspirations; give full recognition to his difficulties, while at the same time suggesting solutions to the problems which perturb him . . . simultaneously promoting confidence in himself and his future.[10]

Only such stories will "prove successful at enriching the inner life of the child."[11]

All of which serves as perfect description of Disney entertainment. This provides a richer understanding of the real reason his stories have survived, and will continue to do so, despite long-standing intellectual and academic condemnation. In such quarters, Disney continues to be written off as a cinematic equivalent of Longfellow, whose poetry— once considered the building block of a solid American education—is now all but forgotten, relegated to what Woody Allen, in *Manhattan* (1979), referred to as the Academy of the Overrated. As Baudelaire insisted, "The charges leveled by bad critics against good poets are the same in all countries."

However true the charge may be of Longfellow, largely banished now from public school curriculums and literature classes at universities, it hardly describes Disney. His films have survived the social shakeout of the post-Woodstock era, during which most of American culture— low, middlebrow, and high—was scuttled. If anything, Disney films— endlessly experienced on videocassette, DVD, and cable TV's Disney Channel—grow ever more essential with each passing year.

The reason for this is perhaps best expressed by a revered Harvard professor of a half century ago summing up why the work of Alfred, Lord Tennyson would not be cast away as mere annoying cultural baggage:

Tennyson's central affirmation, which worked its way out of despair, was subjective, intuitive faith in love as the supreme experience and reality of life, a reality that implied a God of love and individual immortality.[12]

The desire of all moderns is to recover some source of faith by a "search for wholeness"[13] in a confusing, complex world, once we have all, like Forster's Mrs. Moore, stared into our own Marabar Cave and come away fearing that "everything exists, and all is nothing."[14]

Tennyson inherited such a guardedly optimistic vision from the Romantics who preceded him. It remains the pervading vision of people who somehow cling to a positive outlook in the present, embraced by people who peer into the black abyss, understand the dark implications of what is perceived there, yet somehow find the courage to proceed with their lives in a non-nihilistic manner. It provides tools for living that have become the themes of the world's best-loved philosophy and poetry, from Plato to Tennyson, Wordsworth to Whitman.

And, in our time, America's best-loved popular culture: our longest-lasting motion picture and musical favorites, from Walt to Woodstock.

Notes

INTRODUCTION. DISNEY'S VERSION/DISNEY'S VISION:
The World According to Walt

1. Bob Thomas, *Walt Disney: An American Original* (New York: Hyperion, 1976), p. 354.
2. Bosley Crowther, "Review," *New York Times*, April 6, 1962.
3. "Review," *Time*, April 20, 1962, p. 79.
4. Dave Smith, *Disney A to Z: The Updated Official Encyclopedia* (New York: Hyperion, 1998), p. 551.
5. Robin Wood, *Hitchcock's Films* (New York: A. S. Barnes, 1965); p. 18.
6. Ibid., pp. 18–19.
7. Letters to the Editor, *Syracuse Herald-Journal*, October 6, 2000.
8. H. J. C. Grierson, "The Leslie Stephen Lecture, 1923," reprinted in *Classical and Romantic* (Cambridge University Press); also reprinted in *Romanticism: Points of View*, ed. Robert F. Gleckner and Gerald E. Enscoe (Englewood Cliffs, N.J.: Prentice-Hall, 1962), pp. 20–33.
9. W. K. Wimsatt, Jr., and Monroe C. Beardsley, cited by Walter Sutton and Richard Foster, eds., *Modern Criticism: Theory and Practice* (New York: Odyssey, 1963), p. 250.
10. I. A. Richards, cited by Sutton and Foster, *Modern Criticism*, p. 167.
11. Richard Schickel, introduction to *The Hollywood Hallucination* (New York: Simon and Schuster, 1970), p. viii.
12. Dr. Lester D. Friedman in *Planks of Reason*, ed. Barry Keith Grant (Metuchen, N.J.: Scarecrow Press), p. 140.
13. Richard Schickel, *The Disney Version* (New York: Simon and Schuster, 1968), p. 23.
14. Ibid.
15. David Low, "Leonardo da Disney," *New Republic*, January 5, 1942, p. 18.
16. Mark Van Doren, "Fairy Tale," *Nation*, January 22, 1938, pp. 108–109.
17. Steven Watts, *The Magic Kingdom: Walt Disney and the American Way of Life* (Boston: Houghton Mifflin, 1997), p. 121.
18. François Truffaut, "Politique des auteurs," *Cahiers du Cinema*, no. 31, January 1954.
19. Andrew Sarris, *The American Cinema: Directors and Directions* (New York: Dutton Paperbacks, 1969), p. 37.
20. Robert Warshow, "Preface to *The Immediate Experience*," as originally submitted as the proposal for a Guggenheim Fellowship, October 1954.
21. Ibid.
22. Ibid.
23. Hans Richter, "Film as an Original Art Form," originally in *College Art Journal*, College Art Association of America, Winter 1950–1951, pp. 49–50.
24. Robert D. Feild, *The Art of Walt Disney* (New York: Macmillan, 1942), p. 53.
25. Ibid., p. 56.
26. Wood, *Hitchcock's Films*.
27. Matthew Arnold, cited by Sutton and Foster, *Modern Criticism*, p. 102.

28. Sutton and Foster, *Modern Criticism*, p. 102.

29. Bruno Bettelheim, *The Uses of Enchantment: The Meaning and Importance of Fairy Tales* (New York: Random House, 1977), p. 5.

30. Gilbert Seldes, "The Lovely Art: Magic," from *The Public Arts* (New York: Simon and Schuster, 1956), cited by Gerald Mast and Marshall Cohen, eds., *Film Theory and Criticism* (New York; Oxford University Press, 1974), p. 382.

31. Ibid., p. 383.

32. "Taking on Disney: Southern Baptist Convention and Other Organizations Boycott Disney," *60 Minutes* (Anchor, Lesley Stahl), Sunday, November 23, 1997.

33. Ibid.

34. Ibid.

35. Schickel, *Disney Version*, p. 10.

36. Michael Eisler, interviewed on *60 Minutes*, CBS Television, November 23, 1997.

37. T. S. Eliot, cited by Sutton and Foster, *Modern Criticism*, p. 150.

38. Ibid., p. 152.

39. Albert Gerard, "On the Logic of Romanticism," *Essays in Criticism* 7 (1957): 262; translated by George Watson from an article in *L'Athenie* 45 (1956).

40. Schickel, *Disney Version*, p. 10.

41. Anthony Storr and Anthony Stevens, *Freud and Jung: A Dual Introduction* (New York: Barnes and Noble Books, 1998), pp. 33–43.

42. Kenneth Burke, cited by Sutton and Foster, *Modern Criticism*, pp. 242–246.

43. Joseph Campbell, *Historical Atlas of World Mythology* (London: Summerfield, 1983).

44. Joseph Campbell, *The Power of Myth* (videotape) (New York: Mystic Fire Video, 1988).

45. Storr and Stevens, *Freud and Jung*, p. 57.

46. Ibid.

47. Ibid.

48. Pauline Kael, as cited on cover of paperback release of Schickel, *The Disney Version*, Avon Books.

49. Gerard, "Logic of Romanticism," pp. 262–263.

50. Ibid., p. 262.

51. Watts, *The Magic Kingdom*, p. vii.

52. Peter Noble, *The Negro in Films* (New York: Arno Press and New York Times, 1970), p. 8.

53. Eisler, *Private Lives*, pp. 54–55.

54. Erika Doss, *Elvis Culture* (Lawrence: University of Kansas Press, 1999), p. 27.

55. Jean-Luc Godard, as quoted by Annette Michelson in "Film and the Radical Aspiration" (talk delivered at New York Film Festival in 1966), contained in Mast and Cohen, *Film Theory and Criticism*, p. 289.

56. Judith Crist, *New York World Journal Tribune*, November 1966.

57. Leonard Maltin, *The Disney Films* (New York: Crown, 1973), p. 143.

58. Bosley Crowther, "Living Desert Review," *New York Times*, November 10, 1953, as well as other articles in the same paper.

59. Eliot, cited in Sutton and Foster, *Modern Criticism*, p. 148.

60. Wendy Steiner, *The Scandal of Pleasure: Art in an Age of Fundamentalism* (Chicago: University of Chicago Press, 1995), p. 156.

61. Plato, *Collected Dialogues*, ed. Edith Hamilton (New York: Pantheon).

62. *New York Times*, August 1984, cited in *The 60s Reader*, ed. James Haskins and Kathleen Benson (New York: Viking Kestrel [Penguin], 1988), p. 103.

63. Alexis De Tocqueville, *Democracy in America*, ed. J. P. Mayer (New York: Doubleday, 1969), p. 487.

64. Robert Pattison, *The Triumph of Vulgarity* (New York: Oxford University Press, 1987), p. 81.

65. Harold Bloom, *Shakespeare and the Invention of the Human* (New York: Riverhead Books, 1998).

66. Mick Jagger, televised interview the following day on various stations and networks.

67. James Haskins and Kathleen Benson, eds., *The 60s Reader* (New York: Viking Kestrel [Penguin], 1988), p. 104.

1. SEX, DRUGS, AND ROCK 'N' ROLL: Disney and the Youth Culture

1. J. Ronald Oakley, *God's Country: America in the 1950s* (New York: W. W. Norton, 1986), p. 1.

2. Doss, *Elvis Culture*, p. 131.

3. Walt Disney, "Studio Memo to Don Graham," December 23, 1935, Disney Archives, Burbank, California.

4. Gilbert Seldes, "Motion Pictures," *Scribner's*, May 1, 1938, p. 66.

5. Anonymous Angry Reader, Letters to the Editor, *Atlantic City (N.J.) Press*, January 21, 1931.

6. Pattison, *Triumph of Vulgarity*, pp. 184–185.

7. Disney, "Studio Memo to Graham."

8. F. Nietzsche, *Twilight of the Idols 10* (New York: Penguin, 1968), p. 73.

9. Watts, *Magic Kingdom*, 12.

10. Ibid., 13.

11. Roy Disney, interview with Richard Hubler, November 17, 1967, p. 2, Disney Archives, Burbank, California.

12. Pattison, *Triumph of Vulgarity*, pp. 184–185.

13. Walt Disney, quoted by Harry Carr, "The Only Unpaid Movie Star," *American Magazine* (1931), p. 56.

14. Roy Disney, Hubler interview, p. 2.

15. Haskins and Benson, *60s Reader*, p. 82.

16. Oakley, *God's Country*, p. 280.

17. Ibid., p. 274.

18. Arnold Shaw, *Rockin' '50s* (New York: Hawthorne Books, 1974), p. 154.

19. Trent Hill, "The Enemy Within: Censorship in Rock Music in the 1950s," *South Atlantic Quarterly* 90 (1991): 686.

20. *Newsweek*, April 23, 1956, p. 32.

21. Originally published in *Music Journal*, since cited in such studies of the early years of rock 'n' roll as Ian Whitcomb, *After the Ball: Pop Music from Rag to Rock* (New York: Simon and Schuster, 1972); *The Rolling Stone History of Rock 'n' Roll* (New York: Rolling Stone, 1976); Nik Cohn, *Rock: From the Beginning* (New York: Stein and Day, 1969); and Arnold Shaw, *The Rock Revolution* (London: Crowell-Collier, 1969). Quotation from Jonathan Kamin, "The Social Reaction to Jazz and Rock," *Journal of Jazz Studies* 2 (1974): 99.

22. Oakley, *God's Country*, p. 283.

23. Dave Smith, ed., *Walt Disney: Famous Quotes* (Lake Buena Vista, Calif.: Kingdom Editions, 1994), p. 18.

24. Dave McAleer, *The All Music Book of Hit Singles* (San Francisco: Miller Freeman Books, 1994), p. 31.

25. Pattison, *Triumph of Vulgarity*, p. 97.

26. Oakley, *God's Country*, pp. 280–282.

27. Haskins and Benson, *60s Reader*, pp. 202–204.

28. Oakley, *God's Country*, p. 403.

29. Maltin, *Disney Films*, p. 45.

30. Watts, *Magic Kingdom*, p. 113.

31. Theater program for *Fantasia*, 1940, Disney Archives, Burbank, California.

32. Walt Disney, quoted in "Films on Ideals of Youth Proposed," *New York Times*, November 17, 1940.

33. Emily Genauer, "Walt Disney's Music Pictures Range from Beautiful to Banal," *New York World-Telegram*, November 16, 1940.

34. Dorothy Thompson, "Minority Report," *New York Herald-Tribune*, November 25, 1940.

35. Pattison, *Triumph of Vulgarity*, p. vi.

36. Pare Lorenz, *Lorenz on Film: Movies 1927 to 1940* (New York: Hopkinson and Blake, 1970), pp. 207–208.

37. Walt Disney, quoted in Maltin, *Disney Films*, p. 45.

38. Maltin, *Disney Films*, p. 52.

39. Timothy Leary, "You Are a God, Act Like One," *East Village Other*, 1966, quoted in Haskins and Benson, *60s Reader*, p. 205.

40. William Burroughs, "Academy 23: A Deconditioning," *Village Voice*, 1967, quoted in Haskins and Benson, *60s Reader*, p. 87.

41. Haskins and Benson, *60s Reader*, p. 206.

42. Ibid., p. 207.

43. Ibid.

44. Jerry Rubin, open statement to the press, reprinted and reconsidered at length in Jerry Rubin, *We Are Everywhere* (New York: Harper and Row, 1971).

45. Ollie Johnston, quoted by Bob Thomas in *Disney's Art of Animation: From Mickey Mouse to Hercules* (New York: Hyperion, 1977), p. 102.

46. Burroughs, "Academy 23."

2. LITTLE BOXES MADE OF TICKY-TACKY:
Disney and the Culture of Conformity

1. Roy Disney, Hubler interview, p. 4.

2. Ben Sharpstein, quoted in Richard Hubler interview, October 29, 1968, Disney Archives, Burbank, California.

3. Walt Disney, in a letter to wife, Lillian, dated October 29, 1928.

4. Schickel, *Disney Version*, pp. 31–33, 41–50.

5. Peter Martin/Diane Disney Miller interview, Audio Reel 11, transcription pp. 9–10, Disney Archives, Burbank, California.

6. Jay Leyda, ed., *Eisenstein on Disney* (Calcutta: Seagull Books, 1986), p. 42.

7. Ibid.

8. Frank Thomas and Ollie Johnston, *Disney Animation: The Illusion of Life* (New York: Abbeville Press, 1981), p. 188.

9. Watts, *Magic Kingdom*, 184.

10. "Disney Again Tries Trailblazing," *New York Times Magazine*, November 3, 1940.

11. Mark W. Schwab, "The Communalistic Art of Walt Disney," *Cinema Quarterly* (Spring 1934): 150–153.

12. Barnet G. Braver-Mann, "Mickey and His Playmates," *Theatre Guild Magazine*, March 1931, p. 14.
13. Gilbert Seldes, "Motion Pictures," *Scribner's*, March 1, 1938, p. 65.
14. Ibid.
15. Transcript of the *Snow White* story conference, October 2, 1936, Disney Archives, Burbank, California.
16. Quoted in Watts, *Magic Kingdom*.
17. "People's World," *Daily Worker*, January 15, 1938.
18. *March of Time*, filmed series, Henry Luce media, 1943.
19. Ward Kimball interview with Klaus Stryz, *Comics Journal*, March 1988, p. 96.
20. Walt Disney, quoted by Diane Disney Miller in *The Story of Walt Disney* (New York: Holt, 1956), p. 173.
21. Ward Kimball, quoted in John Canemaker, *Walt Disney's Nine Old Men and the Art of Animation* (New York: Disney Press, 2001), p. 28.
22. David R. Smith, quoted in ibid., p. 3.
23. Pattison, *Triumph of Vulgarity*, p. 173.
24. Phineus J. Biron, "Strictly Confidential," *Los Angeles B'nai Brith Messenger*, January 3, 1947.
25. Pattison, *Triumph of Vulgarity*, p. 154.
26. Schickel, *The Disney Version*, pp. 219–220.
27. Walt Disney, "To My Employees on Strike," July 2, 1941, located in the Disney Strike Portfolio, Disney Archives, Burbank, California.
28. "Walt Disney's Speech to His Staff," transcript, February 10, 1941, pp. 18–19, Disney Archives, Burbank, California.
29. Walt Disney, Personal Memo to Westbrook Pegler, August 11, 1941, pp. 1–3, Disney Archives, Burbank, California.
30. U.S. House of Representatives, Committee on Un-American Activities, *Hearings Regarding the Communist Infiltration of the Motion Picture Industry*, 80th Congress, 1st session, October 24, 1947, pp. 280–286.
31. MPA's "Statement of Principles," currently contained in the Motion Picture Alliance file at the Margaret Herrick Library, Motion Picture Academy of Arts and Sciences, Beverly Hills, California.
32. Pattison, *Triumph of Vulgarity*, p. 158.
33. Dan Ford, *Pappy: The Life and Times of John Ford* (Englewood Cliffs, N.J.: Prentice-Hall, 1979).
34. Walt Disney, "Television Meeting," held on May 14, 1954, to discuss upcoming ABC project; currently contained in the "Man in Space/Moon Picture" portfolio in the Disney Archives, Burbank, California.
35. Walt Disney, quoted by Jane Werner Watson in *Walt Disney's People and Places* (New York, 1959), p. 3.
36. Louis Giannetti, *Understanding Movies*, 8th ed. (Upper Saddle River, N.J.: Prentice-Hall, 1999), p. 406.
37. Ibid., p. 402.
38. Ibid.
39. Michael Lofaro, *Davy Crockett: The Man, the Legend, the Legacy* (Knoxville: University of Tennessee Press, 1985).
40. Watts, *The Magic Kingdom*, p. 274.
41. *Time*, May 30, 1955, pp. 9–10.
42. Smith, *Famous Quotes*, p. 70.

43. Giannetti, *Understanding Movies*, p. 406.

44. Ibid., pp. 402–403.

45. Ibid., p. 407.

46. Ibid., p. 408.

47. William K. Everson, *A Pictorial History of the Western Film* (New York: Citadel Press, 1969), pp. 5–13.

48. Maltin, *The Disney Films*, p. 172.

49. Giannetti, *Understanding Movies*, pp. 115–120.

50. Martin Luther King, "Open Letter from a Birmingham Jail," composed April 16, 1963, quoted in Haskins and Benson, *60s Reader*, p. 25.

51. Stokeley Carmichael, quoted in *New York Review of Books*, September 1966.

52. Thomas, *Walt Disney*, p. 339.

53. Pattison, *Triumph of Vulgarity*, p. 159.

54. Irving Babbitt, *Rousseau and Romanticism* (Boston: Houghton Mifflin, 1919), pp. 390–393.

55. Pattison, *Triumph of Vulgarity*, p. 163.

3. THE MAN WHO SAYS "NO": Disney and the Rebel Hero

1. Henry Steele Commager, "The Literature of Revolt," in *The American Mind* (New Haven, Conn.: Yale University Press, 1950), p. 247.

2. Ibid.

3. Robert H. Woodward and James J. Clark, eds., *The Social Rebel in American Literature* (New York: Odyssey Press, 1968), p. vii.

4. Maltin, *Disney Films*, p. 97.

5. Haskins and Benson, *60s Reader*, p. 130.

6. King, "Letter from a Birmingham Jail."

7. Mario Savio, speaking to *Life* magazine, interview edited by J. Fincher, February 26, 1965, pp. 100–101.

8. Eldridge Cleaver, quoted on the *Night Calls* radio program in California, host, Dell Shields, July 3, 1968.

9. James Farmer, "New Jacobins and Full Emancipation," Kenyon College Public Affairs Conference Center, 1964.

10. Haskins and Benson, *60s Reader*, p. 43.

11. James Forman, *The Making of Black Revolutionaries* (Washington, D.C.: Open Hand Publishing, 1972), p. 39.

12. Ibid., pp. 40–41.

13. Davy Crockett (with James Atkins Shackford), *A Narrative of the Life of David Crockett of the State of Tennessee* (1834; Knoxville: University of Tennessee Press, 1973).

14. Haskins and Benson, *60s Reader*, p. 49.

15. Farmer, "New Jacobins."

16. Whibley, quoted by Ernest Bernbaum in "The Romantic Movement," in *Guide through the Romantic Movement*, 2d ed. (New York: Ronald Press Company, 1930), p. 52.

17. Dr. King, "Letter from a Birmingham Jail."

4. TOWARD A NEW POLITICS: Disney and the Sixties Sensibility

1. Haskins and Benson, *60s Reader*, p. 51.

2. Ibid., p. 50.

3. Ibid.

4. SDS Statement, 1962, Port Huron, Michigan, released by student group at the Uni-

versity of Michigan; reprinted in James Miller, *Democracy Is in the Street: From Port Huron to the Siege of Chicago* (New York: Simon and Schuster, 1987), p. 333.

5. Mario Savio interview, *Life*, February 26, 1965, pp. 100–101.

6. Haskins and Benson, *60s Reader*, p. 49.

7. Irving Babbitt, quoted by Ernest Bernbaum in *Guide through the Romantic Movement*, p. 151.

8. Watts, *Magic Kingdom*, p. 187.

9. Maltin, *Disney Films*, p. 187.

10. Smith, *Famous Quotes*, p. 70.

11. *Variety*, quoted by Maltin, *Disney Films*, p. 187.

12. Watts, *Magic Kingdom*, pp. 228–230.

13. Maltin, *Disney Films*, p. 220.

14. Canemaker, in *Walt Disney's Nine Old Men*, "Kimball," p. 8.

15. Maltin, *Disney Films*, p. 220.

16. Giannetti, *Understanding Movies*, p. 402.

17. Thomas, *Walt Disney*, p. 195.

5. MY SWEET LORD: Romanticism and Religion in Disney

1. John Lennon, quoted in "The Jesus Revolution," *Time*, June 21, 1971, p. 56.

2. Ibid.

3. Mark Rudd, "Columbia Notes on the Spring Rebellion," Summer 1968, reprinted in Haskins and Benson, *60s Reader*, p. 68.

4. Ibid., p. 70.

5. Rene Wellek, "The Concept of 'Romanticism,'" *Comparative Literature* 1 (1949): 147–148.

6. Thomas, *Walt Disney*, pp. 194–195.

7. Frank Lloyd Wright, *An Autobiography* (New York: Horizon Press, 1977 reprint), p. 26.

8. Earnest, quoted by Bernbaum, *Guide through the Romantic Movement*, p. 111.

9. Adrian Bailey, *Walt Disney's World of Fantasy* (New York: Gallery Books, 1987), pp. 152–160.

10. *Bambi* review, *New York Times*, August 14, 1942.

11. Ibid.

12. Leonard Maltin, *Of Mice and Magic: A History of American Animated Cartoons*, rev. ed. (New York: New American Library/Plume Books, 1987), pp. vi–ix.

13. Andre Bazin, *What Is Cinema?* Vol. 1, translated by Hugh Gray (orig. Berkeley and Los Angeles: University of California Press; reprinted New York: Grove Press, 1967).

14. *Bambi* review, *New York Times*, August 14, 1942.

15. Wellek, "Concept of 'Romanticism,'" p. 147.

16. Robert E. Gleckner and Gerald E. Enscoe, eds., *Romanticism: Points of View* (Englewood Cliffs, N.J.: Prentice-Hall, 1962), pp. viii–xii.

17. Walt Disney speaking before the U.S. House of Representatives, 1st session, October 25.

18. Wellek, "Concept of 'Romanticism,'" p. 152.

19. Bernbaum, *Guide through the Romantic Movement*, p. 35.

6. GOTTA GET BACK TO THE GARDEN:
Disney and the Environmental Movement

1. Paul Brooks, Foreword to the 1987 edition of Rachel Carson, *Silent Spring* (Boston: Houghton Mifflin, 1987), p. xii.

2. Carson, *Silent Spring*, p. 5.

3. Watts, *Magic Kingdom*, p. 305.

4. Smith, *Famous Quotes*, p. 4.

5. Gerald Mast, *A Short History of the Movies*, 3d ed. (Indianapolis: Bobbs-Merrill Educational Publishing, 1981), p. 150.

6. Dave Smith, *Disney A to Z: The Updated Official Encyclopedia* (New York: Hyperion, 1998), pp. 489–490.

7. Ibid.

8. Bernbaum, *Guide through the Romantic Movement*, 93.

9. Smith, *Disney A to Z*, p. 53.

10. Wellek, "Concept of 'Romanticism,'" pp. 165–166.

11. Watts, *Magic Kingdom*, p. 305.

12. Wellek, "Concept of 'Romanticism,'" pp. 150–151.

13. Justin Gilbert, "Disney's 'The African Lion' Teaches, Thrills, Fascinates," *New York Daily Mirror*, September 15, 1955.

14. Bill Diehl, "Walt Disney Series Unmasks Nature," *St. Paul Sunday Pioneer Press*, August 10, 1952.

15. 1954 Picture of the Year award article, *Christian Herald*, March 1955.

16. I. A. Richards, *Coleridge on Imagination* (London: K. Paul Trench, Trubner, and Company, 1934), p. 145.

17. Schickel, *Disney Version*, p. 246.

18. Watts, *Magic Kingdom*, p. 306.

19. Clarence D. Thorpe, *The Mind of John Keats* (New York: Oxford, 1926), p. 126.

20. *Living Desert* review in *Time*, November 16, 1953, p. 106.

21. Bosley Crowther, *Living Desert* review in *New York Times*, November 10, 1953.

22. Giannetti, *Understanding Movies*, p. 310.

23. Ibid., p. 314.

24. Richter, "Film as an Original Art Form."

25. Percy B. Shelley, *A Defence of Poetry* (originally published, 1821).

26. Wellek, "Concept of 'Romanticism,'" p. 149.

27. Ibid., p. 150.

28. Schickel, *Disney Version*, p. 247.

29. Shelley, *Defence of Poetry*.

30. Robert Gottlieb, *Forcing the Spring* (Washington, D.C.: Island Press, 1993), p. 148.

31. Christopher Manes, *Green Rage* (Boston: Little, Brown, 1990), p. xi.

32. Ibid., p. 28.

33. Gottlieb, *Forcing the Spring*, p. 121.

34. Ibid., p. 89.

35. Manes, *Green Rage*, p. 78.

7. "HELL, NO! WE WON'T GO!": Disney and the Radicalization of Youth

1. Haskins and Benson, *60s Reader*, p. 52.

2. Ibid., p. 50.

3. Savio, *Life*, pp. 100–101.

4. Woodward and Clark, *The Social Rebel in American Literature*, p. 2.

5. Kenneth Rexroth, "The Students Take Over," *Nation* 100 (July 2, 1960): 7.

6. Randolph S. Bourne, "For Radicals," in *Youth and Life* (Boston and New York: Houghton Mifflin, 1913), pp. 291–292.

7. Rexroth, "The Students Take Over," p. 9.

8. Major General Smedley Butler, USMC, speech delivered in 1933, as quoted in *International Spectator* 22 (3): 8.

9. Doug Casey, "Editorial," *International Spectator* 22 (3): 8.

10. Butler speech, p. 8.

11. Maltin, *Disney Films*, p. 97.

12. Ibid., p. 99.

13. William Empson, "Ignorance of Death," in *Collected Poems of William Empson* (New York: Harcourt Brace Jovanovich, 1949), p. 121.

14. Jack Kerouac, *On the Road* (New York: Viking, 1957), pp. 10–11.

15. Giannetti, *Understanding Movies*, p. 349.

16. William Pittinger, *The Great Locomotive Chase* (Washington, D.C.: Library of Congress, 1866).

17. Woodward and Clark, *The Social Rebel in American Literature*, pp. 1–2.

18. A horse named Comanche was indeed the mount of Major Myles Keogh, killed in action at the Little Big Horn on Sunday, June 25, 1876; his remains were sent to Auburn, New York, to be buried in the town where he had enjoyed his vacations in the East. Though there were several Sioux and Cheyenne warriors named White Bull, one of whom has claimed to have killed Custer, none of them ever owned Keogh's horse at any time, the mount being procured from an army stable.

19. Rexroth, "The Students Take Over," p. 4.

8. PROVIDENCE IN THE FALL OF A SPARROW:
Disney and the Denial of Death

1. Robert Kastenbaum, *The Psychology of Death* (New York: Springer, 1992), p. 139.

2. Sigmund Freud, "Thoughts for the Times on War and Death," in *Collected Works*, vol. 4 (London: Hogarth Press, 1953), pp. 304–305.

3. Herbert Spencer, *Collected Writings* (London: Routledge/Thoemmes Press, 1996), pp. 111–127.

4. Kastenbaum, *Psychology of Death*, p. viii.

5. Elisabeth Kübler-Ross, *On Death and Dying* (New York: Macmillan, 1969), p. 6.

6. Bettelheim, *Uses of Enchantment*, pp. 8–10.

7. Ernest Becker, *The Denial of Death* (New York: Free Press/Macmillan, 1973).

8. Watts, *Magic Kingdom*, p. 38.

9. Review of "The Skeleton Dance," *New York Daily Mirror*, 1929.

10. Richard Watts, "Thoughts on Cinema Optimism," *New York Herald-Tribune*, October 26, 1930.

11. Thomas, *Walt Disney*, p. 25.

12. Bettelheim, *Uses of Enchantment*, p. 8.

13. Becker, *Denial of Death*, p. ix.

14. Bettelheim, *Uses of Enchantment*, p. 8.

15. J. P. Telotte, *Dreams of Darkness: Fantasy and the Films of Val Lewton* (Urbana: University of Illinois Press, 1985), p. 28.

16. Bettelheim, *Uses of Enchantment*, pp. 7–8.

17. Woody Allen, *Love and Death* (United Artists, 1975).

18. Kathy Charmaz, *The Social Reality of Death: Death in Contemporary America* (Reading, Mass.: Addison Wesley, 1980), pp. 16–66.

19. Bettelheim, *Uses of Enchantment*, p. 18.

20. Ibid., p. 179.

21. Maltin, *Disney Films*, pp. 152–153.

22. Bettelheim, *Uses of Enchantment*, p. 8.

23. Charmaz, *Social Reality of Death*, p. 65.

24. Maltin, *Disney Films*, pp. 142–143.

25. Steven Spielberg, statement made in various TV and print interviews at the release of *E.T.*, his most Disney-like film; cited from interview with Leonard Maltin, 1978.

26. Samuel Johnson, *Collected Works* (London: W. Osborne, 1785), p. 132.

CONCLUSION. POPULAR ENTERTAINMENT AND PERSONAL ART: Why Should We Take Disney Seriously?

1. Douglas Bush, Introduction to "Alfred, Lord Tennyson," *Major British Writers II* (New York: Harcourt, Brace, and World, 1959), pp. 369–370.

2. T. S. Eliot, quoted in Bush, *Major British Writers*, p. 373.

3. Maltin, *Disney Films*, p. 89.

4. Ibid.

5. Ibid., p. 176.

6. Rudd, "Columbia: Notes on the Spring Rebellion," quoted in Haskins and Benson, *6os Reader*, p. 75.

7. John Lennon, quoted by Pattison, *Triumph of Vulgarity*, p. 145.

8. Walt Whitman, *Leaves of Grass* (Mattituck, N.Y.: Amereon House, 1855), p. 52.

9. Pattison, *Triumph of Vulgarity*, p. 173.

10. Bettelheim, *Uses of Enchantment*, p. 5.

11. Ibid.

12. Bush, Introduction to "Alfred, Lord Tennyson," *Major British Writers*, p. 373.

13. Pattison, *Triumph of Vulgarity*, p. 141.

14. E. M. Forster, *A Passage to India* (New York: Harcourt, Brace, and World, 1924), p. 149.

INDEX

Italicized page numbers indicate pages on which photographs appear. All films are listed with date.